SÜLEYMAN THE MAGNIFICENT
AND HIS AGE

Süleyman the Magnificent and His Age

The Ottoman Empire in the Early Modern World

Edited by Metin Kunt and Christine Woodhead

Longman
London and New York

Addison Wesley Longman Limited,
Edinburgh Gate
Harlow, Essex CM20 2JE, England
and Associated Companies throughout the world.

Published in the United States of America
by Addison Wesley Longman, New York.

First published 1995
Second impression 1997

ISBN 0 582 03828 6 CSD
ISBN 0 582 03827 8 PPR

British Library Cataloguing-in-Publication Data
A catalogue record for this book is
available from the British Library

Library of Congress Cataloging-in-Publication Data
Süleyman the Magnificent and his age : the Ottoman Empire in the early modern world / edited by Metin Kunt and Christine Woodhead.
     p.   cm.
    Includes bibliographical references and index.
    ISBN 0-582-03828-6 (CSD). -- ISBN (invalid) 0–582–03827–8 (PPR)
    1. Turkey--History--Süleyman I, 1520-1566. I. Kunt, İ. Metin, 1942- . II. Woodhead, Christine.
    DR506 S 1995
    956.1'015--dc20

                                               94–49636
                                                CIP

Set by 20B in 10/12pt Bembo
Produced by Longman Singapore Publishers (Pte) Ltd.
Printed in Singapore

Contents

LIST OF MAPS

Preface

The era of Süleyman the Magnificent has always been one of the principal research areas within Ottoman history. Once automatically labelled 'the golden age', it is now a period inevitably subject to reassessment. However, new lines of enquiry spread only slowly beyond the relatively small field of Ottoman studies, hedged in as it is by the linguistic thickets of the Ottoman and modern Turkish languages, and the dominant barrier of Otherness. One of the main purposes of this volume is to present to a wider non-specialist readership current work on certain aspects of the Ottoman sixteenth century and of how the Ottomans themselves conceived their world. There are few expert modern studies of individual Ottoman sultans, in Turkish or any other language, written essentially from the Ottoman point of view. Babinger's *Mehmed the Conqueror* (1952), though now somewhat dated, remains the best example. There is, as yet, nothing comparable on Süleyman. Essay collections such as the present volume, organised around specific themes, therefore have particular value in the absence of a major study.

The book comprises a major introductory chapter on the early development of the Ottoman state up to the time of Süleyman, followed by eight essays arranged in two groups. Part I, on the problems and policies of the age of Süleyman, examines both international and internal developments, with essays on Ottoman expansion in the Mediterranean and in the Indian Ocean, on the objectives and consequences of Ottoman rule in south-east Europe, and on the problems of social and political change during the sixteenth century. The issues are diverse, but the Part I introduction, as well as the last chapter of this section on internal problems, helps to provide an integrated picture. Part II addresses the ideology of Ottoman rule, in particular the concepts of the 'golden age' and the ideal king. The question is examined from different points of view – earlier Islamic concepts, Renaissance political thought, and Ottoman ideas prior to Süleyman's era – in order to provide a comparative perspective. Once again, the Part II introduction provides the context, and the last chapter pulls the various threads together.

In short, the book deals with both the reality of Ottoman power and with the ideology of Ottoman statecraft, separately but in essential relation to each other. We have tried to explain some aspects of how this multi-ethnic dynastic empire functioned, and what it meant to be the ruler of such an empire. Inevitably, there are significant and regrettable omissions. Most obviously, Ottoman military, diplomatic and trade relations with the various states of Europe and with Safavid Iran, are not included; cultural and intellectual history are also unrepresented. Problems of space, and of the unavailability of potential contributors during the period of the final preparation of the book have influenced its published form.

The immediate inspiration for the book was the British Museum's major exhibition 'Süleyman the Magnificent' held in the spring of 1988, in which a splendid array of art treasures loaned from the Topkapı Sarayı and other Turkish museums was displayed beside the British Museum's own collection. The majority of the essays in Part I originated as seminar papers in a series 'The Ottoman state and society in the 16th century', given at the Faculty of Oriental Studies, University of Cambridge, during the Lent term of 1988 and coinciding with the opening of the British Museum exhibition. Those in Part II were first presented at a one-day seminar, 'The "golden age" of Süleyman: myth and reality', held at the School of Oriental and African Studies, University of London, in March 1988.

Some essays remain virtually as originally written (Burke, Holt, Imber); others have been substantially revised or extended (Kunt, Özbaran, Dávid, Faroqhi, Woodhead); Ann Williams' essay was commissioned later. The differing styles of the nine contributors testify to the variety of scholarly traditions current in Ottoman historical studies and to the latter's truly international nature. We have attempted to ensure standardisation only in footnotes, references, and in the glosses provided for Ottoman terms. The bibliographical guide, though brief, suggests further material on aspects not covered in the book, and highlights recent major publications.

We have pleasure in acknowledging the help of several colleagues in the initial stages of this project. In Cambridge, encouragement and support was given by Gordon Johnson, Faculty of Oriental Studies, and Basim Musallam and Peter Avery, Centre for Middle Eastern Studies. Parallel events included an exhibition of Ottoman manuscripts at Cambridge University Library organised by Jill Butterworth, and a delightful display of 'Turquerie' at the Fitzwilliam Museum assembled by Robin Crighton. Grateful thanks are also due to the then Turkish Ambassador in London, H E Rahmi Gümrükçüoğlu, for his interest in, and financial support for, the Ottoman lecture series. In London, the Research Committee of the School of Oriental and African Studies provided a much-appreciated grant towards the costs of visiting speakers to the Süleyman 'golden age' seminar. The meeting was convened under the auspices of the Turkish Area Study Group, benefitting from the experience and encouragement of Margaret Bainbridge and the support of Tony Allan, then chairman of the Centre for Near and Middle Eastern Studies in the School.

To Andrew MacLennan of Longman we owe a tremendous debt of gratitude for his continued enthusiasm for this project and his belief that it would eventually appear in print. Appropriately perhaps, the book goes to press in the quincentennial year of Süleyman's birth in 1494.

Finally, but in domestic terms certainly not least, Laura Binkowski (in Cambridge) and Philip Williamson (in Durham) will be as relieved as we are to reach the end of this book. Both have seen it take shape from the early stages and have been equally sharp with editorial comments towards the end. We are particularly grateful that they, too, had faith.

December 1994

Metin Kunt
(Cambridge)

Christine Woodhead
(Durham)

Note on spelling and pronunciation of Turkish

Ottoman Turkish words are spelled here in conformity with modern Turkish spelling, and are italicised on each occurrence in the text.

A general guide is given below to the pronunciation of those consonants and vowels which either do not appear in the English alphabet, or which differ markedly from their English pronunciation.

c **j** as in **jam**
ç **ch** as in **church**
ğ has little sound of its own; usually lengthens the preceding vowel
s **s** as in **this** (not as in **these**)
ş **sh** as in **ship**

a (i) short **a** as in **apple**
  (ii) long **a** as in **father**
e **e** as in **red**
ı **i** in **cousin**
i **i** as in **pin**
o **o** as on **otter**
ö **eu** as in French **jeu**
u **u** as in **put**
ü **u** as in French **tu**

Vowels are usually pronounced short; long vowels (**a, i** or **u**) may be indicated by a circumflex.

A good introduction to Turkish grammar and pronunciation is G L Lewis, *Teach yourself Turkish* (2nd ed., 1989).

List of abbreviations

BA/BBA   Başbakanlık Arşivi (Prime Minister's Archives), Istanbul

BSOAS   Bulletin of the School of Oriental and African Studies, London

CNRS   Centre National de la Recherche Scientifique, Paris

EI²   Encyclopaedia of Islam, second edition, Leiden and Paris

İA   İslam Ansiklopedisi, Istanbul

TSA   Topkapı Palace Archives, Istanbul

Notes on contributors

Peter Burke: Reader in History, University of Cambridge and Fellow of Emmanuel College. He concentrates on the history of early modern Europe and is currently writing a book on the European Renaissance.

Géza Dávid: Department of Turkish Studies, ELTE University, Budapest. He has published on Ottoman administration in Hungary and on problems of interpreting data in Ottoman provincial survey registers. Current research: demographic history of Hungary in the sixteenth and seventeenth centuries.

Suraiya Faroqhi: Taught at Middle East Technical University in Ankara before moving to Munich in 1986 to take up the chair of Ottoman History. Books include *Towns and townsmen of Ottoman Anatolia: Trade, crafts, and food production in an urban setting, 1520–1650* (1984); has just completed a major work on material culture in Ottoman society.

P M Holt: Emeritus Professor of the History of the Near and Middle East, University of London; formerly Sudan Government Archivist. Research: the Mahdia, Mamluk and Ottoman Egypt. Books include: *The age of the Crusades: the Near East from the eleventh century to 1517* (1986), and a translation from the German of Peter Thorau's *The Lion of Egypt: Sultan Baybars I and the Near East in the thirteenth century* (1992).

Colin Imber: Lecturer in Turkish, Department of Middle Eastern Studies, University of Manchester, since 1970. Current research: sixteenth-century Ottoman law. Author of *The Ottoman empire*

1300–1481 (1990), and *Studies in Ottoman history and law* (forthcoming, Isis Press, Istanbul).

Metin Kunt: Newton Trust Lecturer, University of Cambridge; General Editor of the *Cambridge History of Turkey*, in preparation. Earlier work includes *The Sultan's Servants: the transformation of Ottoman provincial government, 1550–1650* (1983). Current research: social groups and networks, late eighteenth century.

Salih Özbaran: Since 1985, Professor of History Teaching at Dokuz Eylül University, Izmir, after teaching at Istanbul University and Ege University, Izmir. Main areas of interest are Ottoman southern expansion and the problems of history teaching. His most recent work *The Ottoman Response to European Expansion* is in press (Isis, Istanbul).

Ann Williams: Senior Lecturer in Mediterranean History and Director of the Centre for Mediterranean Studies at the University of Exeter. Research: Mediterranean urban history; the Knights of Malta in the early modern period. Forthcoming book *Servants of the sick: the convent of the order of St John, 1309–1631*.

Christine Woodhead: Honorary Lecturer, Centre for Middle Eastern & Islamic Studies, University of Durham. Research: the Ottoman central chancery system c. 1574–1630; sixteenth and seventeenth-century Ottoman historiography. Editor of *Ta'liki-zade's Şehname-i hümayun: a history of the Ottoman campaign into Hungary, 1593–94* (1983).

Introduction

METIN KUNT

State and sultan up to the age of Süleyman: frontier principality to world empire

Sultan Süleyman died on 7 September 1566 while on campaign: at seventy-two years of age, he had led his formidable army once again deep into central Europe, laying siege to Szigetvar in south-west Hungary. The frontier fortress, conquered just after the sultan's death, bolstered the Ottoman position in their confrontation with the rival Habsburg Empire. Although Ottoman lands reached their widest extent a century later, at Süleyman's death his vast empire was already perhaps the most formidable on earth, and certainly among the largest: the sultan ruled over territories stretching from Algiers to Azerbayjan, from Budapest to Baghdad and Basra, and from the Crimea to Qatif in the Persian Gulf and Mocha in Yemen. In the decade following Süleyman's death Ottoman statesmen were engaged in projects as diverse as cutting a canal between the Don and Volga rivers in the Ukraine, and sending a fleet to help petty sultans of Sumatra resist European encroachment. In the event, such far-flung projects failed to yield immediate results and were abandoned; yet the fact that they were contemplated and undertaken at all is a noteworthy indication of the extent of Ottoman global involvement. In the 1570s Ottoman fleets were active in the western Mediterranean, northern Black Sea and eastern Indian Ocean; Ottoman armies marched across the Caucasus to reach the Caspian Sea soon afterwards. The Black Sea in the north and the Red Sea in the south were Ottoman lakes; the empire controlled three-quarters of the Mediterranean shores. On land, territories in Europe included Hungary, all the countries in the Balkan peninsula, and the Crimea; in Asia Anatolia, the Fertile Crescent and Arabia; and in north Africa Egypt and the Maghrib up to Morocco.

Fundamental to an understanding of the nature of Süleyman's empire is the point that it did not constitute a coherent geographical and

3

cultural region. In this respect, Ottoman territories were unlike other great empires and regions of Asia – Iran, India, or China – let alone European national entities such as England or France. In such areas of historical continuity, states and dynasties came and went and there were movements of peoples through porous boundaries but the geographical entity itself remained recognisable even when political frontiers shifted and fluctuated. The Ottoman case is quite different. Though in Europe the empire was often referred to as 'Turkey', such a term itself – either as a political or a geographical entity – was totally unknown in the Ottoman Turkish language or in any of the many other languages spoken by its subjects within its borders; nor can one say without qualification that Ottoman territories constituted a land of 'Turkey' or even a 'Turkish empire' in any immediately meaningful sense.

The closest historical equivalent was the empire the Ottomans supplanted – Byzantium. The Ottoman realm of the sixteenth and seventeenth centuries was very similar in extent to the Eastern Roman or Byzantine empire of a millennium earlier, if slightly smaller in the west and somewhat larger in the north, south and east. Like the Byzantines, Muslim Ottomans too called themselves 'Rumi' – Roman – at least in the so-called core areas of the empire, in the Balkans and in Anatolia. As for the empire, the Ottoman term for it was *devlet-i âl-i Osman*, 'the domains and rule of the House of Osman': it is this terminology – here abbreviated to Ottoman – that truly reflects historical reality and not the 'Turkey' or 'Turkish' of outsiders to the west.[1] Whereas Byzantium referred to the capital that ruled over its empire, the Ottoman Empire was the rule of a single dynasty. Dynasties were replaced in Byzantium while the state lived on; in the Ottoman case the dynasty *was* the state throughout its 622-year career.

The eponymous founder of the state and dynasty, Osman Bey, lived around 1300 in north-west Anatolia. He was a minor march lord between Byzantium, by then much reduced, and the crumbling Seljuk state. Byzantine rulers had recently returned to their capital, having rescued it in 1261 from errant 'Crusader' hands; thereafter they were more preoccupied with their entanglement with various European powers, Crusaders, merchant-princes, and mercenaries, rather than with their eastern, Muslim rivals in Anatolia. In any case, the Seljuks had declined greatly since their heyday in the mid-thirteenth century.

The rise of the Ottoman state in the course of the fourteenth

---

1 Özbaran notes that the Portuguese referred to the Ottomans as 'Rume'; alone among Europeans to do so, the Portuguese must have picked up this name in the Indian Ocean, from the southern and eastern neighbours of the Ottomans. See below, p. 62.

century from Osman Bey's obscure and insignificant band of frontiers-men to the status of a world power in the time of its tenth ruler, Süleyman, has long been an intriguing question for historical scholar-ship. Who were these Ottomans and how did they achieve such a 'miraculous' rise? These questions were posed with a degree of pressing contemporary relevance early in the twentieth century amidst the politi-cal events surrounding the dissolution and final collapse of the empire: *who* the Ottomans had been and *how* they governed their empire, it seemed to some, would determine whether the empire should be allowed to continue and, if so, in what form, with what ethnic constitu-ents. 'Expel the Asiatic Turks from Europe!' was a political slogan heard throughout six centuries of Ottoman rule, but uttered with even greater conviction and urgency by nineteenth-century Europeans and finally shouted as a battle cry in the Balkan Wars of 1912–13.[2] Ottoman Turks may have arrived in south-eastern Europe hundreds of years earlier but they did not belong there; these 'uncouth barbarians', ignorant of the principles of civilised politics, had not so much governed the various peoples of the Balkans as suppressed and oppressed them with brute force. Now they had lost that power, it was time for them to go back where they had come from, wherever that was. Such notions may sound grotesque to later generations, for we now realise that even technologically-advanced totalitarian regimes cannot maintain them-selves in power simply by force; the idea that any empire could have ruled for more than a generation or two without at least a semblance of good government and justice is insupportable. Yet even now there are some who hold these convictions, or at least use them to suppress Turks or even other Muslims in former Ottoman territories in the Balkans.

For Ottoman-Turkish intellectuals, too, it was important to consider where they had started in an attempt to understand how they had arrived at their predicament at the turn of the twentieth century.[3] The beginnings of the Ottoman state seemed to them a truly heroic age: how else could one explain the spectacular rise of an empire from a very tiny kernel? In their eyes, the first Ottomans were virtuous, gallant, wise, yet modest and moderate; that innocent nobility of spirit was surely the secret of their success, or so it seemed to the last adherents of the Ottoman ideal.

More than seventy years after the demise of the empire we are in a

---

2 In this context Norman Angell, *Peace theories and the Balkan war* (London 1912) is very instructive.

3 For example, Namık Kemal's pamphlet, *Devr-i Istila* (Istanbul 1866), and in his *Osmanlı Tarihi* (Istanbul 1908), the chapter on the 'emergence of the Ottomans'; and Seyyid Mustafa Nuri Paşa, *Netaic ül-Vukuat* (Istanbul 1909).

much better position to understand its origins. Historical scholarship is rarely – if ever – totally dispassionate, and Ottoman historiography is perhaps still one of the more disputed areas of research; but we have shed much of the sense of political urgency so acutely felt early in the century. Even after its collapse in the aftermath of the First World War the empire continued to evoke negative sentiments, especially in its successor states, not least in republican Turkey. In terms of historical research, however, a generation of scholars led by Paul Wittek and Fuat Köprülü laid down strong foundations for the study of Ottoman origins.[4] Wittek's main conclusion that the life-force for the empire came from religious zeal, the *gazi* spirit of holy war, has been plausibly challenged in recent years, but the old masters' analysis is still valid that Ottoman origins can be understood only in a wider context, with reference both to Byzantium and to the Islamic world of West Asia.[5]

OTTOMAN ORIGINS AND EARLY DEVELOPMENT

The early Ottomans, followers of Osman Bey, were among many similar groupings that emerged in the frontier zone between the two weakened states in Anatolia. Toward the end of the thirteenth century Byzantium still held the coastal plains along the Aegean in the west and the Marmara and Black Seas in the north-west, while the Anatolian Seljuks struggled to hold the Anatolian plateau. Defeated by a Mongol contingent in 1243 while trying to defend their prosperous domains, the Seljuks were no longer in a position to threaten Byzantium. They had escaped the fate of many a state in Asia and eastern Europe who had faced the Mongol onslaught; at least they still maintained a semi-independent existence while acknowledging Mongol Ilkhanid suzerainty. From the 1260s Seljukid lands were divided diagonally across Anatolia into two zones, with the north-eastern half more tightly controlled by the Ilkhanid seat in Tabriz, and the south-western half around the capital Konya relatively free of Mongol pressure. Even there, Seljuk dynastic power, deliberately weakened by the Mongol sultans in

---

4 Paul Wittek, *The rise of the Ottoman empire* (London 1938); M Fuad Köprülü, *The origins of the Ottoman empire*, tr. and ed. Gary Leiser, Albany 1992 (from the 1935 French original and the expanded Turkish version of 1959).

5 The debate was reopened by Rudi P Lindner, *Nomads and Ottomans in medieval Anatolia* (Bloomington 1983).

Azerbayjan, was no longer in a position to control let alone govern march lords on the Byzantine borders.[6]

With the weakening of political authority from Konya or Constantinople, the frontiersmen gained greater independence of action and expanded their territories at the expense of both states. The leaders of the frontiersmen were of various backgrounds: some had been Seljuk officials posted to guard the frontier who in time broke free of the state's authority, some emerged as chiefs of Türkmen tribal groupings encouraged by Konya to move from central Anatolia on to the Byzantine frontier. Seljuk officers or Türkmen chiefs provided leadership to the settled people of such areas – peasants and townsmen, Greek and Turkish – who, forgotten by their distant and powerless capitals, needed protection in the increasingly uncertain conditions of the frontier. In the last decades of the thirteenth century, a new frontier political authority significant enough to be termed a principality emerged in Caria, the distant south-western corner of Anatolia, under Emir Menteşe.[7] Other emirates followed to the north, along the Aegean coast: Aydın, Saruhan, Karası.[8] Absorbing the local sea-faring Byzantine population and carrying frontier raids to the sea, the Aegean emirates were the first to flourish; meanwhile in the north-west, facing the coastal plain around Marmara, Osman Bey led a lesser group of followers. He was sufficiently successful, however, for other local Türkmen chieftains and even some renegade Byzantine lords to come under his leadership. In the early years of the fourteenth century he defeated a Byzantine army sent to suppress him and thus emerged as an emir in his own right. Although he had taken over from his father, Ertuğrul Bey, as chief of his band some years earlier, this first victory is traditionally regarded as the beginning of his state, inasmuch as from then on many more frontiersmen came to join his banner.[9]

Early Ottoman chronology is hazy because Osman Bey's frontier state was still too insignificant to have a written history. Authentic contemporary documents to illuminate this heroic age are extremely rare. Oral traditions from these early days were written down only later in the century, while substantial chronicles came even later. Nevertheless, these chronicles of the fifteenth century are far from worthless.

6 The standard account of the Anatolian Seljuk state and its relations with Byzantium is Claude Cahen, *Pre-Ottoman Turkey* (London 1968); revised version, *La turquie pré-ottomane*, (Istanbul-Paris 1988).

7 Paul Wittek, *Das Fürstentum Mentesche* (Istanbul 1934).

8 Halil İnalcık, 'The rise of the Turcoman maritime principalities in Anatolia', *Byzantinische Forschungen*, 9 (1985), 179–217.

9 Halil İnalcık, 'Osman Gazi's siege of Nicea and the battle of Bapheus', Elizabeth Zachariadou (ed.), *The Ottoman Emirate (1300–1389)* (Rethymnon 1993), 77–100.

Byzantine histories and accounts of Muslim travellers to these outposts of the Islamic world also help in a reconstruction of early Ottoman developments. We now know, for example, that while Osman Bey, like other western Anatolian emirs, acknowledged the supreme power of the Ilkhanids who held sway from their centre in Azerbayjan over an area stretching from eastern Iran to central Anatolia, he nevertheless issued coins in his own name in his petty emirate, an act signifying independence.[10] At the time of his death in 1324 Osman Bey's followers had increased in strength to the extent that they were about to capture Byzantine Bursa, their first sizeable city.

In the first decade or so of the rule of Osman's son and successor expansion continued toward the north, skirting the eastern shores of the Marmara Sea. Orhan Bey captured Nicea and Nicomedia, respectively Iznik and Izmit in Turkish, and halted only about a day's march east of Constantinople itself. In the 1330s Orhan Bey was among half a dozen or so of west Anatolian emirs each controlling a territory of a few thousand square miles, with towns and markets as well as peasant and semi-nomadic populations.[11] Each was capable of fielding tens of thousands of fighters or, in the case of those on the Aegean coast, putting dozens of ships to sea for naval raids and skirmishes with Latins and Byzantines. Once most of the Byzantine territories in Anatolia had been occupied, the most successful of these emirates were those who could carry the *gaza* to the sea, otherwise they had no room for expansion on land. But when in 1344 the Knights Hospitaller, settled in Rhodes since leaving Palestine, joined with other European seamen and the Byzantine navy to defeat Aydın, the most powerful of the Türkmen maritime principalities, *gaza* at sea effectively ceased.[12] At that point the Ottomans as well as all the other emirates, having run out of a frontier for expansion, could have stagnated. They were now in danger of losing the original frontier impetus that had carried them to independent political existence. Among all these emirates the Ottomans were the only ones who succeeded in opening new frontiers, an achievement that eventually carried them to greatness as a world empire.

The new frontier for expansion was across the Dardanelles strait, in Thrace, Macedonia, and eventually in the whole Balkan peninsula.

---

10 Ibrahim Artuk, 'Osmanlı beyliğinin kurucusu Osman Gazi'ye ait sikke', in O Okyar and H İnalcık (eds), *Social and economic history of Turkey* (Ankara 1980), 27–33.

11 Osman Turan, 'Anatolia in the period of the Seljuks and the beyliks', *The Cambridge History of Islam* (Cambridge 1970), 231–62.

12 Elizabeth Zachariadou, *Trade and Crusade: Venetian Crete and the emirates of Menteshe and Aydin (1300–1415)* (Venice 1983); A Luttrell, 'The Hospitallers of Rhodes confront the Turks: 1306–1421', in P Gallagher (ed.), *Christians, Jews and other worlds* (Lanham 1988).

Between Bursa and the strait, however, was the neighbouring Karası emirate; only after Orhan Bey had invaded its territory and incorporated its officers and people into his own domains was he able to carry the frontier struggle to south-east Europe. Increasing territory and power at the expense of Muslim neighbours in Anatolia in order to expand in Christian Europe: this is the recurrent theme of Ottoman history in its formative period. Absorption of the Anatolian emirates took various forms. In the 1340s Orhan Bey seems to have taken advantage of a struggle for the *bey*'s seat among Karası princes. After crossing the Dardanelles in the 1350s and gaining sole access to the trade and plunder of south-east Europe, the Ottomans became the richest and most powerful of the emirates. They were then in a position to coerce Anatolian neighbours into submission or even to conquer them if they put up a resistance.[13]

THE FRONTIER IN EUROPE: *GAZİ* IDEOLOGY

Once Orhan Bey's troops had established themselves on the Gelibolu (Gallipoli) peninsula on the European side of the Dardanelles, they used this as a base for raids into Thrace. Orhan Bey died soon after this momentous crossing, but under his son Murad Bey expansion continued. One line of frontier raiders moved east, toward the outskirts of Constantinople itself. The main body of Ottoman troops pushed north toward Adrianople and west along the northern shores of the Aegean. After the conquest of these Byzantine territories, Ottoman forces soon came into contact with Bulgaria and Serbia across the Balkan mountains. By then both these kingdoms, especially Serbia which had only recently been mighty under Stephan Dushan, had broken apart into fragments and so offered only sporadic resistance. After thirty years of rule Murad Bey was assassinated after the battle of Kosovo in 1389, when his troops decisively defeated Serbia.[14] By then Bulgaria had been incorporated into Ottoman domains which now stretched from the Danube across Macedonia to the Albanian highlands, an area coming to be known as 'Rumeli' or 'Roman lands' in Ottoman parlance.[15]

Conquest in south-east Europe made the Ottoman state the most

---

13 Zachariadou, 'The emirate of Karasi and that of the Ottomans: two rival states' and Feridun Emecen, 'Ottoman policy of conquest of the Turcoman principalities of western Anatolia', in Zachariadou, *The Ottoman emirate*, 225–36 and 35–40.

14 Stephen Reinert, 'From Niş to Kosovo Polje: Reflections on Murad I's final years', in Zachariadou, *The Ottoman emirate*, 169–211.

15 H İnalcık, 'Ottoman methods of conquest', *Studia Islamica* 2 (1954), 103–29.

powerful in the area; it also assisted considerable expansion in Anatolia. Ottoman historical tradition describes the incorporation of Muslim lands as a peaceful process, in some cases as voluntary submission. According to these accounts, Murad Bey bought land from a neighbouring emirate, Hamid; another emir, Germiyan, gave land as dowry when his daughter married Murad Bey's son, Bayezid Bey; the same emir bequeathed his remaining territory because he had no son to succeed him. Even if we were to accept these accounts of peaceful absorption as the literal truth, why Murad Bey was able to purchase land, why Ottoman princesses never took land away as dowry, and why an old neighbour would make a bequest of his land to the Ottomans and not to anybody else (indeed, why such a bequest at all) remain unanswered. Presumably Murad Bey had become the rich and powerful neighbour to impoverished backwater emirs, who accepted that he had made independent existence unsustainable.[16]

If the source of Ottoman wealth and strength vis-à-vis their less fortunate Türkmen neighbours was frontier raids and expansion in Europe, the secret of Ottoman success on the marches of Europe was, in turn, the flow of manpower from Anatolia. Over the previous centuries there had been a steady movement of Turkish population from Inner to West Asia, most recently at a faster pace under pressure of Mongol expansion.[17] This influx of Turkic, mainly Oğuz, tribesmen into Anatolia may have subsided in the fourteenth century; however, from about the middle of the century, as the other emirates were forced to give up the frontier struggle and turned to settled and therefore relatively static living, coming under the Ottoman banner remained the only way open to the dangerous but lucrative life of the frontier for newcomers and adventurous brave youth alike. As population in inner areas stabilised, and after the south-east European marches were opened, the rush to swell the ranks of Ottoman frontiersmen continued and quickened.

Looking at the effects of the frontier struggle on the life of the Byzantine people on the defensive, Elizabeth Zachariadou recently pointed out an unexpected reason for the growth of Ottoman population. On the basis of Byzantine sources she established that some Byzantine peasants, unable to bear the constant dangers of a poorly defended frontier zone, preferred to move, not further away from the reach of the raiders but in fact toward the Ottoman domains. Once

16 In addition to Emecen, above, see M Ç Varlık, *Germiyanoğulları Tarihi* (Ankara 1974), and Colin Imber, *The Ottoman Empire, 1300–1481* (Istanbul 1990), 26–8.
17 Faruk Sümer, *Oğuzlar*, 2nd edn (Ankara 1972).

they came under Ottoman protection they were free from harassment; they changed their masters and thereby were able to pursue their lives in peace and security, even if they had to pay an extra capitation tax to their new Muslim overlords.[18]

Consideration should also be given to the effects of the mid-fourteenth century Black Death on the demography of Anatolia and the Balkan peninsula. In later Ottoman sources we find no mention of the plague which devastated so much of the Mediterranean and Europe, though event-book 'calendars' have scattered references for various years.[19] Constantinople and other Byzantine territories suffered, as did parts of Islamic West Asia such as Syria and Egypt, but not, it seems, the *gazi* Türkmen emirates. It may be that the Turkic and Mongolian population of Anatolia and parts of Iran were relatively immune to the plague strain, which seems to have had its origin in the great Eurasian steppe, carried by Genoese ships from Crimea through Constantinople to the Mediterranean and beyond to northern Europe. If it is true that the plague had less of an impact on the Oğuz of Anatolia than on Greeks and other peoples of the Balkans, this would have been another factor in the swift success of Murad Bey's troops in the Balkans.[20]

Expansion in Anatolia and that in south-east Europe thus reinforced each other. Success on the frontier assured a steady supply of Anatolian Turks to join the Ottoman command; the riches gained in raids into Bulgaria, Macedonia, and Serbia allowed Murad Bey, now a ruler rather than a simple chieftain, a dominant position against his Turkish neighbours. Given these two wings, it was necessary to pursue policy on two fronts. As a consequence much of the frontier struggle was left in the hands of march lords such as Evrenos Bey, earlier in his long career a Karası commander; the descendants of Mihal Bey, one of Osman Bey's earliest Byzantine supporters; and others who established distinguished families on the frontier. Such lords were immensely wealthy and powerful, each more mighty than the Balkan princelings they faced. Sources indicate that Murad Bey had to treat his captains with due consideration for their powerful status.[21] One wonders if Evrenos Bey, for example, was ever tempted to defy Ottoman authority and establish himself as an independent ruler, perhaps in a coalition

18 E Zachariadou, 'Notes sur la population de l'Asie Mineure turque au XIVe siècle', *Byzantinische Forschungen* 12 (1987).
19 Osman Turan (ed.), *Tarihî Takvimler* (Ankara 1954).
20 William McNeill, *Plagues and Peoples* (New York 1976); Michael Dols, *The Black Death in the Middle East* (Princeton 1977), contains few references to Anatolia, mainly as refuge from Syria.
21 I Beldiceanu-Steinherr, *Recherches sur les actes des règnes des Sultans Osman, Orhan et Murad I* (Munich 1967).

with other march lords, to form a frontier state in Rumeli; such an act would have been similar to the emergence of west Anatolian frontier emirates a century earlier.

A hypothetically possible breakaway never happened. Again, population movement seems the best explanation for Murad Bey's success in keeping his two-winged state together. Whereas in the late thirteenth century incoming Oğuz tribesmen could join the frontier at any number of marches, in the late fourteenth century the Gelibolu crossing from Anatolia to Thrace was a bridgehead easily controlled. Any brave fighter with ambitions for the life of the frontier had first to become an 'Ottoman' before he could seek his fortune across the Dardanelles. Not only did Murad Bey have control over the supply of fresh manpower to the Balkan marches, he also decided to share in the wealth of the frontiersmen by instituting a one-fifth tax for the ruler's household, collected at the Gelibolu crossing, on any goods and slaves brought from the Rumeli raids for sale in Anatolia. The march lords needed Murad Bey as an overlord; without the Anatolian hinterland, both as the market for frontier booty and as the source of potential *gazi*s, the frontier enterprise would have stagnated and withered.

In addition to the strategic advantage of Gelibolu, another dimension of internal cohesion was that the Ottoman *bey*s raised the frontier struggle to the level of ideology. Fighters on the marches were not simple raiders, *akıncı* as the straightforward Turkish term goes, but were engaged in *gaza*. A *gazi* was not a mere raider or plunderer but a fighter for the glory of Islam. All west Anatolian Türkmen emirates had once been *gazi* polities, but by capturing Gelibolu, the key to Thrace, Orhan Bey had eclipsed all other *gazi*s; controlling the only route left for *gaza* activity, Murad Bey's Ottomans promoted themselves as the only true *gazi*s. By the end of the fourteenth century writers singing the praises of the House of Osman emphasised this above all else as the basis of the Ottoman claim to rule in the Balkans and in Anatolia. *Gaza* was the greatest virtue; Ottomans the most virtuous of *gazi*s. The march lords of the Balkans too were honoured by the title, as Gazi Evrenos Bey, Gazi Turahan and so on, but the members of the House of Osman were the greatest *gazi*s; even when they claimed grander titles such as 'sultan', the title of *gazi* was retained and given prominence.

This powerful ideology served not only to bind the march lords to the House of Osman but was useful in dealing with Anatolian emirates. In Ottoman eyes, these had lost their mandate to rule when they ceased to be *gazi*s, even if the reason was that they no longer had a frontier to fight on. When Murad's successor Bayezid the Thunderbolt – so named from his sudden, swift and unexpected military campaigns – invaded west Anatolian emirates by force, leaving aside any pretence of peaceable acquisition, his justification was that the dormant potential of these emirates would best be brought to harness to bolster his power as the conqueror of the infidels. The strongest of these emirates, Karaman, successfully resisted Ottoman occupation for almost another century; each time the Ottomans attempted to vanquish the Karaman they did so with the accusation that their neighbours time and again took advantage of Ottoman preoccupation in Europe to stir up trouble in their rear. If *gaza* was virtuous, hindering it was evil; the House of Karaman came to personify this perfidy, an image which lingered long after the last Karamanid pretender was decisively defeated. So powerful was the impact of this fourteenth-century ideology and so enduring the special appeal of the title that, centuries later, long after the closing of the frontier and the reversal of Ottoman fortunes against their European rivals, after other ideological platforms had been introduced and developed, the term *gazi* was revived at the very end of the empire's long career as an honorific for Abdülhamid II when his armies defeated Greece in 1897. By act of the fledgling Ankara parliament, the title was also bestowed on Mustafa Kemal Paşa when Anatolian troops repulsed the Greek invasion in 1922.

FROM *GAZİ* EMIRATE TO SULTANATE

In the 1390s Bayezid the Thunderbolt swept into southern and eastern Anatolia to conquer most other Türkmen emirates, captured Salonica, the last important Byzantine city in the northern Aegean, pursued the frontier further into European territories, laid siege to Constantinople itself, building a castle on the Asian shore of the Bosphorus to maintain pressure on Byzantium, and decisively defeated a Crusader army on the Danubean front, so putting to rest European designs to dislodge him from the Balkans. All this was achieved in the space of a dozen years as Ottoman sultan.

Bayezid's swift and spectacular career came to a sudden end, however, because he found himself forced to challenge a much grander world-conqueror, Tamerlane. Timur the Lame had in mind an Asia-wide empire, a revival of Ghengis Khan's great realm. Western Anatolia played little part in his overall design – still less did the Balkans – but he could not allow an upstart frontier princeling such as Bayezid to remain unbowed. To teach him a lesson and to make sure that Ottoman territories did not remain in the hands of a single ruler, Timur marched into Anatolia in 1402, defeating and capturing Bayezid himself. As the sultan died in the humiliation of captivity, Timur not only restored the Anatolian emirs recently defeated by Bayezid, but allowed various Ottoman princes to emerge as independent *bey*s themselves. Less than a decade later, however, Bayezid's domains had been reunited by Mehmed I who emerged victorious over his brothers and proceeded to recapture the western Anatolian emirates. The severe blow suffered at Timur's hands proved, in the end, not decisive at all.[22]

This remarkable resilience of the Ottoman state, and its recuperative powers need to be considered. That the two wings of the Ottoman realm were mutually dependent must have been well understood by Rumeli march lords as well as by Anatolian townsmen. Furthermore, over the previous century Ottoman *bey*s had developed a central 'state' apparatus with many servitors whose interests were tied to the revived rule of the House of Osman. As the two geographical regions of Anatolia and Rumeli needed each other, so did the burgeoning Ottoman centre and its periphery, the sultan's courtiers and the march lords.

In its early organisation the Ottoman polity resembled other Türkmen emirates with some Asian-Islamic notions and institutions of government reinforced with the adoption of local, Byzantine administrative usages. By the end of the fourteenth century, however, the Ottoman state was not only much larger than its Muslim neighbours and therefore had relatively better articulated and more complex institutions, it had also started to add its own improvements and flourishes to customary organisation. The most important feature of government was the ruler's household; the Ottoman household was much grander than in neighbouring emirates; recruitment to it gave rise to an Ottoman peculiarity. We shall consider Ottoman social and political organisation in greater detail further on, but at this point it would be useful to trace the emergence of the ruler's household as the main instrument of 'central' government.

Recently Halil İnalcık suggested that, at the very inception of the state, Osman Bey had gathered around him a small, tight-knit band of followers loyal to him personally, similar to the chieftain's *comitatus* in a Germanic tribe.[23] Inner Asian tradition had the term *nöker* for such loyal men of the chief. From this nucleus, as the state expanded and the power of the ruler was enhanced, a fully-fledged sultanic household

22 P Wittek, 'De la défaite d'Ankara à la prise de Constantinople', *Revue des Études Islamiques* 12 (1938) should be read in conjunction with C Imber, 'Paul Wittek's "De la défaite . . ." ', *Osmanlı Araştırmaları* 5 (1986).

23 H İnalcık, 'The question of the emergence of the Ottoman state', *International Journal of Turkish Studies* 2 (1981–2), 71–9.

was organised as in all other Islamic polities. The main feature of an Islamic ruler's palace was that the household troops were composed of foreign servitors (*mamluks*) of the ruler, who had been captured in battle against infidels. Many pagan Turks had served as *mamluks* of Islamic caliphs or princes before their own large-scale Islamisation. *Mamluks* had to come from outside the ruler's realm, otherwise such a master–client relationship implying personal bondage to the ruler would have been legally impossible to force upon his subjects, whether Muslim or non-Muslim. According to Ottoman historical tradition even Osman Bey, though of modest means, had a few such slave lieutenants in addition to Turkish or Greek volunteers serving as his personal *nökers*.

By the reign of Bayezid I, now sultan and not simply a *bey* among many other *beys*, the royal household numbered perhaps a thousand troops, some cavalry and some infantry. The formidable *yeniçeri* household infantry, the janissary of European tradition, gained renown for its fighting prowess. For the Ottoman household, however, the six regiments of the cavalry constituted the senior, more prestigious branch. The names of some of these regiments may indicate their origins: two were known as the *gureba*, literally 'strangers', implying that they were the pick of the young men flocking from elsewhere to join the Ottoman banner. Two other regiments were termed the *ulufeciyan*, wage-earners, implying that they were hardened mercenaries. The two senior regiments were known as the *sipahi*, literally cavalry, and *silahdar*, expert weaponsmen. We have full records for the household troops from later centuries but by then whatever original differentiation there might have been had disappeared; all six regiments were staffed from among the numbers of the palace pages of the inner service when their education and training were completed and they passed out to the outer service. Almost all the palace pages were of slave origin; most were recruited through the specifically Ottoman system known as the *devşirme*. The one-fifth share of the human booty from the frontiers taken by Murad Bey's officers at the Gelibolu crossing, which had earlier formed the most important source for the *bey*'s household, still continued to provide candidates for *yeniçeri* ranks; there were also other sources for household slaves, but the *devşirme* recruits though smaller in numbers, nevertheless formed the most important single group.

Devşirme is a term used both for this peculiar system of recruitment and for the youngsters so recruited. What makes the *devşirme* levy unique in the Islamic practice of household-building is that they were forcibly recruited from among non-Muslim subjects from *within* the realm. The *devşirme* process afforded a much greater element of scrutiny in selecting suitable candidates for the palace than the somewhat haphazard capture of slaves in raids or battle. This advantage in itself may have been a consideration, but it is possible that the *devşirme* custom came about in the strange conditions of the frontier zone, where a carefully demarcated boundary would have been an anomaly. In a zone where it was difficult to tell what was within and what without, and to distinguish friend from foe, subject from legitimate enemy, residents of recently invaded but not fully-integrated lands may have been considered fair game for capture or forcible recruitment, as the case may be. When it was fully established the *devşirme* process was a royal prerogative; the recruits were taken only by the sultan's own officers for his own palace system. No other *bey* or potentate could collect *devşirme* for his own lesser household. Recently, however, it has been suggested that it may have been the old march lord Evrenos Bey himself who started the practice of recruiting *devşirme* levies.[24] This plausible suggestion would fit well with what we surmise about manpower needs on the European frontiers. Be that as it may, the Ottoman rulers must have quickly become aware of the method's potential, for soon afterwards they came to monopolise the privilege of *devşirme* recruitment.

In Balkan nationalist historiography the *devşirme* is frequently seen as another method of forced conversion to Islam. In Bulgaria during the 1980s the argument was put forward that since many contemporary Bulgarian Muslims were the descendants of those who had been forced to convert, it would be legitimate to force them to give up their centuries-old Muslim identity, so that they could now be proper citizens of a homogenised Bulgaria. Such religious-nationalist considerations of course had no place in Ottoman socio-political thinking. Although non-Muslims did pay an extra poll tax and anybody who decided to convert to Islam was encouraged with presents and promise of a new life to welcome him into the Islamic *umma* (society/community) at a time when he had lost his place in his original community, there was no policy of large-scale forced conversion. The *devşirme* was in reality so limited in numbers that it is impossible to think of it as an aspect of a policy of conversion. During the two centuries or so that the *devşirme* was applied it may have been viewed as oppression by most non-Muslim subjects of the Ottoman realm; we should note, however, that some, at least, also saw *devşirme* as a boon, a guarantee of privileged life in the sultan's service in contrast to a peasant's lot at home.

Household-building, first by forming a band of *nökers* and then by accepting wandering volunteers into service, in time through the ruler's

---

24 Vassilis Demetriades, 'Some thoughts on the origins of the devşirme', in Zachariadou, *The Ottoman emirate*, 23–34.

one-fifth share of human booty and later through *devşirme* levies ensured the increasing strength of the ruler's position within his domains, especially vis-à-vis his formidable march lords. Maintaining such a large and expensive household would only be possible with the revenues of a sizeable territory. As for the sultan's servitors, by the time of Bayezid I they had come to enjoy access to considerable political power upon leaving service in the royal household; they, too, found it in their own interests to try to reconstitute the Ottoman realm after the dispersal suffered at Timur's hands. These officers needed a powerful master as much as the sultan needed loyal servitors. In the end Balkan march lords and Anatolian merchants, central authority personified by the sultan and his servitors, and the older powerful families all contributed to the remarkable Ottoman resurrection after 1402.

Social features, too, helped foster cohesion in areas recently brought under Ottoman rule. Anatolian Türkmen emirates were very similar in character. Each had a comparable mixture of Turkish and local Greek folk, as well as equivalent attitudes and institutions. Turkish was the dominant language although Greek continued to be widely spoken. The polities were Muslim, but in their own fashion, quite different from that of the older, long-established Islamic centres such as Cairo, Baghdad, Damascus, or even Konya, the former capital of the now-defunct Seljuks. In the frontierlands syncretic practices abounded, and there was a sense that while Islam was the most perfect of the mono-theist traditions of West Asia, essentially it was not much different from Judaism and Christianity. Continuity with the older religions rather than superiority over them was emphasised.

Social and religious networks provided connections between various parts of the realm which had only recently been under separate rulers. In towns, merchants and artisans formed themselves into *ahi* organis-ations for social and economic solidarity, locally and across political boundaries. Not merely guilds for different trades, *ahi* brotherhoods served to unite the business community with ceremonial, ethics, and social benevolence. In addition to controlling the marketplace, they provided hospitality for travellers – scholars such as the famous Ibn Battuta as well as traders from neighbouring emirates and from distant lands.[25] The relative economic prosperity of fourteenth-century Anato-lia, despite political turmoil and disintegration, owes much to the effectiveness of the *ahi* network. Ottoman historical tradition relates that Murad Bey, the third ruler of the House of Osman, ceremonially

25 H A R Gibb, *Travels of Ibn Battuta*, vol. 2 (Cambridge 1962): on *ahi*s, 418, Orhan Bey, 451.

joined the *ahi* brotherhood, no doubt to ensure the support of Anatolian merchants and townsmen for Ottoman rule in Anatolia and in the Balkans.

Religious brotherhoods, *sufi tarikats*, provided a different but equally effective bond. Sufism – Islamic mysticism – was almost as old as Islam itself. First seen in the centres of Islam, sufism also flourished in its Central Asian borderlands. Shamanist Turks, when they embraced Islam, adapted their pagan ceremonies with drumbeat and chanted praise to a new form of mystic worship of Allah. Orthodox teachings of the *ulema* scholars were reinforced, sometimes even replaced, by the ecstatic poetry of *sufi* sheyhs (teachers: *şeyhs*) read and sung in communal rituals. The tradition of the Central Asian mystic poet Ahmed Yesevi took root among the highland Türkmen while in the cosmopolitan urban culture of Konya Mevlana Celaleddin Rumi's sophisticated, intellectual yet equally ecstatic exposition of divine love was embodied in the Mevlevi brotherhood. Both in urban and in rural settings, the *sufi* brotherhoods, with their tolerant, non-dogmatic and exuberant brand of Islam, facilitated conversion of non-Muslims or at least coexistence in close proximity and with a degree of mutual respect, providing a focus for social as well as religious gatherings. Recognising their import-ant functions, the Ottomans encouraged the spread of Anatolian sufism in the Balkans by giving land grants to brotherhoods. On balance, Muslims appeared not as arrogant conquerors but often as tolerant and, at times, benign neighbours. Gradually, a typically Ottoman Muslim society developed in the Balkan towns where new converts and Turks immigrating from Anatolia came together in dervish convents and merchant lodges.

Because of social linkages already in existence, Ottoman take-over of Anatolian emirates did not occasion noticeable resentment. Expan-sion in the Balkans, too, does not seem to have been traumatic. For the peasantry, the imposition of the *cizye* capitation tax may have been offset by the lessening of feudal obligations of earlier regimes. For townsmen there was greater prosperity through increased trade, stimu-lated by growing connections with Anatolia, under the protective umbrella of Ottoman rule. In many details, accustomed features of daily routines continued as Ottoman rule adopted and by and large main-tained earlier regulations. Non-Muslim religious communities were also allowed to maintain their own institutions, their leaders even being allocated revenues. It appears that common folk, Turkish, Greek and Slav, accepted Ottoman rule as readily as the ruling elite tried to reconstitute it after 1402.

MEHMED II AND THE CONQUEST OF
CONSTANTINOPLE

During the first half of the fifteenth century, having recovered from Timur's blow, the Ottoman sultans had nevertheless to tread carefully, wary of possible new threats from the east and forced, on occasion, to fight defensive battles against renewed European crusades on the Serbian and Danubian fronts. Internally, too, the sultans were still primarily first among (almost) equals, arbiters who had to keep a keen balance among various powerholders in the realm. However, when the twenty-one-year-old Mehmed II succeeded to the throne in 1451, he had a clear vision of the conquest of Constantinople as the first step in establishing himself as the ruler of a formidable empire. The city was a pale shadow of its earlier grandeur; its population had shrunk as its resources had dwindled. Yet it was still *the* city, as the Greeks referred to it colloquially, *the* imperial capital; its continued existence as practically a city-state meant that the two territorial wings of the Ottoman realm remained separated.

The course of the conquest itself is noteworthy: it began in 1452 with the construction in record time of a mighty fortress on the European shore of the Bosphorus, across from the much more modest one built a half-century earlier by Bayezid I. The northern sea approach to the old imperial capital was thus effectively cut. Ottoman territory, both to the east and to the west of the city, was only a day's march away. Ottoman naval capacity was greatly expanded in an attempt to control the approach from the Mediterranean via the Marmara Sea. The greatest siege cannon the world had then seen were cast under the supervision of a Hungarian master. All the resources of the Ottoman realm were mobilised for the attack in the spring of 1453; the siege lasted a month and the prize was won on 29 May. As in the case of all conquests of cities and fortresses which had refused to surrender, the fallen city was pillaged for three days, but the sultan spent the rest of his thirty-year reign rebuilding and repopulating his new capital to raise it once again to its earlier glory and majesty.

Bursa and then Edirne (Adrianople) had been earlier seats of Ottoman rulers. Sultan Mehmed, now known as 'Fatih' (the Conqueror) kept palaces in the older capitals which continued as imperial cities, but there was now no question but that *the* city was *the* capital. The Greek colloquial name of the city was adopted into everyday Turkish as Istanbul; in official usage, on documents and on coins, Kustantiniyye remained the name to the end of the Ottoman empire itself. Two imperial palaces were built in quick succession; the second, Topkapı, remained the sultan's principal residence and the centre of power until the construction of the European-style Dolmabahçe palace elsewhere in the capital in the mid-nineteenth century. A grand imperial mosque, flanked by eight colleges, was built where the decaying Greek patriarchate building once stood. The grand bazaar with inns for long-distance merchants, stores for the goods of the world brought to this once again prosperous city, dozens of streets and alleys, and thousands of shops became the commercial centre of the empire. All vezirs and pashas contributed their own building projects with mosques, colleges, schools, bath-houses, and public fountains. Muslim and non-Muslim populations were transferred from the provinces: Greeks from Trebizond, Turks from Karaman, Jews from the Balkans, Armenians from Anatolia.[26] Efforts to enlarge and embellish this priceless jewel continued for the next century. Süleyman himself commissioned a mosque complex even grander than the Conqueror's. The mid-sixteenth-century population of the city has been estimated at half a million; it certainly was among the largest, grandest, most prosperous of the world's capitals. Its fame continued well into the nineteenth century: Napoleon Bonaparte is said to have considered it a natural world-capital, and his contemporary the utopian socialist Charles Fourier agreed with him.[27]

Kustantiniyye-Istanbul was at the junction of Asia and Europe as well as of the Black Sea and the Mediterranean. All roads in south-east Europe and many in West Asia led to this 'New Rome', while the riches of the Mediterranean and the products of the Eurasian steppe were brought by sea routes. Mehmed II took the epithet 'the sultan of two lands and the great khan of two seas' to reflect the strategic importance of his great conquest and his pride in holding this prize. During the rest of his thirty-year reign he eliminated any remaining Byzantine successors in Trebizond and in Greece; he used his new navy to turn the Black Sea into an Ottoman lake, dislodging from its shores long-established Genoese colonies, and to push Venice back from the Aegean Sea; he marched his armies north of the Danube into Wallachia and Moldavia and west into Bosnia. But for all this territorial expansion, the fame of his first conquest, *the* conquest, was never eclipsed.

Fatih Sultan Mehmed is also regarded as the sultan who established the Ottoman imperial tradition, complete with elaborate court procedure, significant additions to the Ottoman legal corpus, complete subordination of other powerful lords of the realm, and expansion of

26 H İnalcık, 'Istanbul', EI² (Leiden and Paris, in progress).
27 Vernon J Puryear, *Napoleon and the Dardanelles* (Berkeley and Los Angeles 1951), 191.

sultanic power to the civilian-religious sphere through the take-over of pious foundations (*vakıf*). His power was in part due to the enhanced numbers and prestige of the imperial household which now supplied most of the highest ranking administrative–military officials of the empire. In addition, the ideological and ceremonial aspects of the sultan's power were based on earlier Islamic-West Asian and Byzantine imperial traditions. Old-fashioned European comments that the crude early Ottomans learned everything they knew of statecraft from Byzantium was refuted many years ago by Fuad Köprülü who argued that whatever traces of Byzantine influence might be detected had already been borrowed by the Seljukids of Rum or by even earlier Islamic polities, and so came down to the Ottomans in an Islamic-West Asian guise. On the other hand it is quite clear that Ottoman provincial regulations on administration and taxation very often incorporated existing custom, whether in former Byzantine, Bulgarian, or Serbian lands in the west, or in areas in Anatolia captured from other emirates or larger states, such as the realm of Hasan the Tall, the shah of the Akkoyunlu Türkmen. Affinities have also been detected between specific Byzantine provincial military groupings and similar troops in Ottoman as well as other Türkmen emirates of western Anatolia.[28] Furthermore, we now realise that the question is not just a one-sided Byzantine-on-Ottoman influence; during the century and a half of coexistence Byzantium had itself adopted certain Ottoman features of administration.[29] Mutual borrowing should not be surprising. As reflected in his titles, Mehmed the Conqueror regarded himself as a sultan in the Islamic tradition and a great khan in the Inner Asian mould as well as a 'kaisar', caesar, of the Romans or the Rumi, Byzantine and Turkish. In ruling his empire, Sultan Mehmed Khan, the Kaisar of Rum, increasingly used as his instruments members of his own household, mostly of *devşirme* origin; scions of older families of the Ottoman establishment, whether at the centre or on the frontiers, succumbed to his power without seriously challenging it.

TOWARDS SÜLEYMAN'S WORLD EMPIRE

Sultan Süleyman, born in 1494, ascended the Ottoman throne in 1520, as a young ruler of an already vast empire in the age of the Habsburg

28 K Zhukov, 'Les levées de troupes de *yaya* et de *müsellem*', *VII. CIEPO Sempozyumu* (Ankara 1994), 493–500.
29 N Oikonomides, 'Ottoman influences on late Byzantine fiscal practice', *Südost-Forschungen* 45 (1986), 1–24.

Emperor Charles V, Martin Luther's Protestant movement, and the Safavi Shah Ismail in Iran. Since the death of his great-grandfather Mehmed II in 1481, his patrimony on the western and northern fronts had been consolidated, but the main expansion had come in the east and the south. At the turn of the sixteenth century the Safavi sufi brotherhood of Azerbayjan had taken the final step in its politicisation, and their dynasty of sheyhs (*şeyhs*) had become shahs, supplanting the Akkoyunlu empire in eastern Anatolia and western Iran.[30] The Safavi empire was not, however, of a particular territory any more than the Ottoman state itself was; it had as much appeal to the Oğuz Türkmen of Ottoman Anatolia as it did to their ethnic brethren in the Akkoyunlu domains. This millenarian movement of the charismatic Shah Ismail threatened to push the Ottomans into Europe, and to form a vast new Turko-Iranian empire stretching from the Aegean Sea to Central Asia. Süleyman's grandfather Bayezid II defended his domains by suppressing Safavi sympathisers among his subjects, often removing them forcibly from their ancestral Anatolian pastures to resettle them across the Aegean in the Morea and elsewhere in Rumeli. When Süleyman's father, Selim I (the 'Grim' as he was commonly known in Europe, although 'intrepid' or 'resolute' might better translate his Turkish epithet 'Yavuz') dethroned his father and fought off his brothers in 1512, his main justification was that his aging father had been too lenient toward the Safavis and had underestimated the gravity of the danger to the very foundation of the Ottoman state. As soon as Selim had eliminated all internal challenge to his rule, he moved his great army east toward Safavi heartlands. In 1514, at Çaldıran near Lake Van, close to the present-day boundary between Turkey and Iran, he not only defeated the seemingly invincible Safavi army but by doing so also shattered Shah Ismail's charisma. Although this victory led to some Ottoman conquest in eastern Anatolia, Çaldıran was essentially a defensive battle. Yavuz Selim's musket-bearing *yeniçeris* and field artillery won the day with firepower over the superb Safavi cavalry, but Ottoman occupation of the Safavi capital Tabriz was brief, and Selim's army soon retreated from Azerbayjan. The main achievement was that from then on the threat of Safavi subversion in Anatolia ceased to be an immediate and urgent danger.

In a sudden, surprising move Selim next turned south and marched

---

30 John Woods, *Aqquyunlu: Clan, Confederation, Empire* (Minneapolis and Chicago 1976); Adel Allouche, *The origins and development of the Ottoman-Safavid conflict 1500–1555*) (Berlin 1983); J-L. Bacqué–Grammont, 'Les Ottomans et les Safavides dans la premiere moitié du XVIe siècle', *La Shi'a nell'impero Ottomano* Accademia Nazionale dei Lincei, (Rome 1993).

his armies against the Mamluk sultanate of Syria and Egypt. In earlier centuries this once mighty state had withstood the Mongol Ilkhanids and Timur's invasion; just a generation earlier they had fought Bayezid II to a standstill in Cilicia, south of the Taurus mountains. In the intervening decades, however, they had been shaken by some of the events that heralded the early modern age: Mamluk prosperity did not depend only on the agricultural yield of Syria and Egypt; most of the cash that flowed into the state's coffers came from taxes on the great Asian trade in spices and other valuable goods that came up the Red Sea to Cairo and Alexandria or across the Syrian desert to Aleppo on its way to the Mediterranean and Europe. When the Portuguese, rounding Africa, reached the Indian sources of this trade they attempted a blockade of the narrow entrance to the Red Sea from the Indian Ocean; soon the supply of spices reaching the markets of Cairo and Aleppo dwindled to a trickle. Unlike the Ottomans the Mamluk state had never developed a serious naval capacity, nor did the proud Mamluk horsemen have any desire to take up firearms.[31] Caught with inadequate and unsuitable means of warfare they depended on help from their Mediterranean trading partners, the Venetians, and their erstwhile rivals, the Ottomans, to be able to repulse the Portuguese navy.

Yavuz Sultan Selim's successful campaign resulted in the complete conquest of the Mamluk lands in 1516–17. This unexpected Ottoman thrust south can be seen in the context of the religious and ideological struggles occasioned by the Safavi movement. In his own domains Shah Ismail had adopted a policy of forced conversion to Shi'*ism* to effect a harmonious bonding of his Türkmen and Iranian subjects. Selim I responded, according to this view, by conquering the Mamluks to establish himself as the defender of the holy cities, Mecca and Medina, and therefore as the most important Sunni ruler in the Islamic world.[32] There is no doubt that in the early sixteenth century religious ideology was extremely important politically in Islamic West Asia as it was in Christian Europe during the Reformation. Nevertheless, when we consider that the Ottomans swiftly built a naval base at Suez and immediately challenged the Portuguese in the Indian Ocean the importance of the Asian spice trade in Ottoman strategic thinking becomes evident. Indeed, Ottoman naval presence in the Black Sea, the Mediter-

31 D Ayalon, *Gunpowder and firearms in the Mamluk kingdom* (London 1956).
32 H A R Gibb, 'Lütfi Pasha on the Ottoman caliphate', *Oriens* 15 (1962), 287–95.

ranean, and now in the Indian Ocean was one of the most important developments at the beginning of Süleyman's reign.[33]

Through Selim's conquests in eastern Anatolia and in Arab lands, the population balance of the Ottoman empire had changed significantly within the space of a few years from Muslims and non-Muslims in roughly equal proportions to a decisive majority of Muslims. Islamic ideological issues and the subdued but persistent threat of Safavi subversion continued during Süleyman's reign, even after victorious Ottoman campaigns which gained little in the Safavi heartland in Azerbayjan but bound Iraq (Mosul and Baghdad at first and later Basra as well) to Ottoman domains. Campaigns and conquests at the other extreme of Süleyman's empire, toward central Europe and in the Mediterranean, occupied the sultan to an even larger extent. His father had neglected the European front while he concentrated on ideological and strategic challenges in West Asia. Süleyman's first campaigns were against two targets which had eluded Mehmed the Conqueror, Rhodes and Belgrade, one the lock in the southern Aegean and the other the key to Hungary. Once the Belgrade stronghold was captured the Hungarian army had to take to the field to face the Ottoman might. Crushed at Mohacs in 1526 the Hungarian kingdom was incorporated in stages over the next three decades. From then on Austrian armies hesitated to accept Ottoman challenges for field battles; warfare on this front was reduced to the siege of individual strongholds, as in Süleyman's last campaign.

The sultan's navy was equally successful in the Mediterranean. The descendants of the western Anatolian sea *gazis*, the naval frontiersmen, had at the turn of the century roamed the length of the inland sea to Iberian shores. The greatest of these, Barbaros Hayreddin Paşa, was invited to Istanbul to become the sultan's grand admiral; the province of the Aegean Islands, including districts of mainland Anatolia and Greece as well, was created as a *beylerbeyilik* for him. In 1538 he repaid the sultan's trust by defeating a united Christian navy with an imperial Habsburg core and fleets from several allies. By the end of Süleyman's reign north Africa, except Tunis, had become Ottoman territory. Only Malta resisted the Ottoman onslaught in the fierce siege of 1565 and continued to block Ottoman ambitions further west; the failure at

---

33 Andrew C Hess, 'The evolution of the Ottoman seaborne empire in the age of oceanic discoveries, 1453–1525', *The American Historical Review* 75 (1970), 1892–1919; Palmira Brummett, 'Kemal Reis and Ottoman gunpowder diplomacy', in S Deringil and S Kuneralp (eds), *Studies in Ottoman Diplomatic History* V (Istanbul 1990), 1–15.

Malta, in fact, may have spurred the aging sultan to his last campaign the following year, against Szigetvar.

THE OTTOMAN STATE AS A DYNASTIC EMPIRE

Sultan Süleyman ruled over an empire where Turkish, or the courtly variant of it known as 'Ottoman', was the main language, and the ideology and rhetoric of Islam played a central role. The promotion of the office of the *şeyhülislam* during Süleyman's reign to become one of the most respected and highest ranking state dignitaries attests to this 'Islamisation' of the polity.[34] Ottomans argued that the sultan could now be considered the caliph of all Muslims, as the greatest Sunni ruler, though the title was not adopted officially until much later and in very different circumstances, when a pan-Islamist policy was developed in the late nineteenth century. Yet the ruling elite was made up of recent Muslims, many only first generation. Many ethnic groups were represented in the establishment; they were fused to form a class with a new identity. They were now all Ottomans, not in an ethnic but a political-cultural sense. They shared an outlook, a political and literary culture, and loyalty to the sultan. There were Ottomans of Greek, Bulgarian, Serbian, Armenian, Jewish origin; Germans, Italians, Frenchmen, Russians, Poles, some captured in battle but some volunteers, became Ottoman officials. Whatever their origins might have been all took pride in their new identity. There were also ethnic Turks in this ruling elite but as officers few of them hoped to reach the highest ranks.

The sultan ruled through the imperial council which met at Topkapı Palace. Although the imperial palace was the seat of power, members of the *divan* council were not household officials, but 'state' officers in their own right. As the absolute instrument of the sultan, the *divan* included members representing all branches of government: vezirs who had risen from the military-administrative *ümera* career serving as district governors (*sancakbeyi*) and governors-general of provinces (*beylerbeyi*); two high state judges, *kadiaskers*, one each for the Rumeli and Anatolian territories, promoted from the *ulema* ranks of the provincial magistrates, *kadıs*; and the *nişancı*, expert on sultanic *kanun* law and so responsible for edicts, *fermans*, and other documents issued in the ruler's name bearing the imperial signet, *tuğra*.

Both the vezirs and the *kadiaskers* served in the provinces before

34 R C Repp, *Mufti of Istanbul* (Oxford 1986).

promotion to the imperial council at the centre. The *ümera*, governors as well as commanders, represented the will of the sultan in provincial government while the *ulema* magistrates cooperated with them in administration, also applying in their courts Islamic law, *şeriat*, to Muslims and sultanic *kanun* to all subjects. *Kanun*, theoretically subordinate to principles of *şeriat*, nevertheless covered not only administrative matters but made inroads into commercial and criminal law as well; in that sense the *kadi*s were not independent Islamic judges at all but officials of the state, obeying the ruler's commands and upholding his law.

The *kadi*s derived their income by collecting fees from cases they heard and certificates they issued. The *ümera*, on the other hand, were assigned livings, *dirlik* in Ottoman usage. The lowest provincial *sipahi* cavalryman was assigned annual *timar* revenues, in cash and in kind, from a particular village or villages sufficient to meet his needs while serving on campaigns. Commanders of towns received market revenues as well as specified shares in agricultural production in their *zeamet dirlik* area. *Sancakbeyi*s as district governors and *beylerbeyi*s as governors of provinces had *hass* livings many times greater than the *sipahi timar*s; having a larger proportion of urban revenues, their income in cash was greater than in kind. Other revenues, including mines and forests, not assigned in *dirlik*s to officers and *sipahi*s, scattered throughout the empire but concentrated especially in the largest, commercially most developed towns and yielding significant cash income, were reserved for the sultan's imperial revenues, the *havass-ı hümayun*. In size, the imperial reserves are difficult to estimate in proportion to total revenues generated in the realm, but it is clear that the sultan's *hass* was greater by many times than the revenues assigned to even the highest vezir.[35]

With the exception of the lowest-level *timar*s, sufficient only for the holder, *dirlik*s were required to supply other troops in addition to the recipient himself. For each multiple of the basic *timar* revenue the *dirlik* holder was responsible for an additional armed man, a *cebeli* trooper. A town commander, with a sizeable *zeamet*, might be required to maintain a personal retinue of a dozen or more *cebeli*s; *sancakbeyi*s and *beylerbeyi*s might have personal followers in the hundreds; sumptuous vezir households could reach a thousand or more troops. The *dirlik* system encouraged, in fact required, households; in one sense, all *dirlik* holders and their household men together formed the 'Ottoman state'. The imperial household itself had grown considerably during Süleyman's reign, reaching 30,000 or so, including the six cavalry

35 I M Kunt, *The Sultan's Servants* (New York 1983).

regiments, musket-bearing *yeniçeri* infantry, artillerymen, armourers, and various companies of palace guards. The size of the sultan's household was commensurate with the large revenues included in the *havass-ı hümayun*, but the imperial household was also distinguished with the privilege of *devşirme* levies and the use of firearms, muskets and artillery.

The three-part division of the army among the imperial household, *dirlik* holders and their retinues, and the *akıncı* frontiersmen, was reflected in naval organisation as well. The imperial fleet, maintained out of the sultan's *havass* revenues and based in Istanbul, was joined by ships furnished and captained by *beys* of the districts of the Aegean islands and the Aegean littoral, under the command of the governor-general with his seat at Gelibolu, and supported by the privateers or corsairs as the sea *gazis*. There was the distinction that whereas the household troops expected to be commanded by their master the sultan himself, the grand admiral commanded the imperial fleet as well as the provincial navy in the name of the sultan.[36]

The Ottoman state, then, was organised with the sultan at its apex and commander-administrators carrying out his will. Many of these, certainly the highest ranking, were products of the imperial household, from various ethnic backgrounds. The *ulema*, mostly from Muslim families, were equally servants of the sultan though they were freeborn and not bound to the ruler in a master-client relationship. The empire was not confined to any geographical region, nor was its administration in the hands of a particular ethnic group.

This was an inclusive polity and society, in its ruling elite as well as in its relations with its subjects. The tolerant traditions of its formative age were maintained even as central authority grew. Although for centuries Europeans expected non-Muslim Ottoman subjects to rise up against their supposed oppressors, such resistance never materialised.[37] Until the age of nationalism in the nineteenth century, the Ottoman empire remained the legitimate government not merely of Turks, nor even of Muslims, but of all its subjects. The sultan's power reached his lowliest subjects through his officials, *ümera* and *ulema*, providing prosperity through protection and justice across the realm. If the *şeriat* was for the Muslims, the sultan's *kanun* was for all his subjects; all could appeal to the sultan's justice through *kadı* courts or even to the imperial council. The main legitimation of the ruler in Ottoman political thinking was justice; in retrospect Süleyman's age was regarded as a golden

36 Colin Imber, 'The navy of Süleyman the Magnificent', *Archivum Ottomanicum* 6 (1980).

37 Kenneth Setton, *Western Hostility to Islam and Prophecies of Turkish Doom* (Philadelphia 1992).

age precisely because dynastic law was further developed and always upheld. The sultan himself was accorded the highest respect in his epithet, not 'Magnificent' as he was called in Europe but '*Kanuni*', the law-abiding, the law-giver. Within the domains of the House of Osman imperial justice reigned supreme through *kanun-ı Osmani* or 'Ottoman law'.

The virtues of a dynastic empire were that there was no favoured ethnic group, nor was there ethnic oppression. Islam provided the dominant ideology, yet non-Muslim subjects, though inferior in status, were allowed unhindered communal expression and protection under imperial law and justice. The main problem of the dynastic empire, especially during Süleyman's reign, remained the question of succession: as in all polities tracing their idea of rule to inner Asian origins, there was no established principle of succession. The idea was that there should be no set way to the seat of power: let the claimants, all members of the ruling house, pursue their claims as best they can and may the best man win. Thus would the polity, whether the empire of the Seljuks or the great Mongol khanate or the empire of the House of Osman, be assured of the most capable ruler. This was a recipe for instability or even civil war, yet an indolent or an idiot prince who might have seniority would be avoided. On some occasions in the Ottoman past rival princes had mustered as much political and military support as they could; the rivals and their supporters took to the field and eyed each other from their camps; overnight, the camp of the seemingly weaker claimant dissolved, and the successful leader emerged not by force of arms but by political acumen in gathering support in preparation for battle. On many other occasions, however, there was civil war. The clash between the sons of Mehmed II was especially serious in its consequences. When he lost the struggle Prince Cem made his way to Europe where he was held as a royal hostage by popes and kings. While he lived in France and Italy Ottoman western policy was in paralysis for fear that he might be freed to return to renew the fight.

While the prize of success was the throne, the price of failure was life itself. Few losers besides Cem survived defeat. The successful prince, when he became sultan, killed all rivals and their male offspring, for they were members of the dynasty and therefore potential rivals. This killing was sanctioned not just by custom but by the code of Mehmed II which argued that stable rule could be thereby re-established once the succession struggle was resolved.

When a sultan lived to old age, his adult sons might even grow impatient and precipitate an accession struggle. This had happened in 1511–12, when Süleyman's father Selim I first dethroned his father

Bayezid II and then fought his brothers. As a young prince of seventeen Süleyman had aided his father's cause; he knew the rules full well. Later, during his reign of forty-six years he was forced to intervene and to suppress the political ambitions of his sons. In 1553 he had his eldest son, Prince Mustafa, strangled. A few years later the two remaining princes started a political confrontation which soon turned to military conflict. The sultan could not remain an impartial observer, so he lent his own household troops to Prince Selim to assure his victory. Thus when Süleyman died eight years later, there was no crisis, for the succession had already been settled.[38]

Power may not have corrupted Süleyman, but its awesome weight certainly made him a very lonely and frail old man in the last few years of his long life. Perhaps it was an attempt to reassert his dignity as a man as well as his majesty as a ruler that took him to his final battle at Szigetvar.

---

38 A D Alderson, *The structure of the Ottoman dynasty* (Oxford 1956) is the standard guide to the dynasty in English, although Gültekin Oransay, *Osmanoğulları* (Ankara 1968) is more accurate and detailed. For the role of the *harem* in the politics of succession see Leslie P. Peirce, *The Imperial Harem* (Oxford 1993).

PART I

Sixteenth-century Ottoman policies and problems

METIN KUNT

Introduction

In the introductory chapter a view was expounded of Ottoman state and society based on 'livings' (*dirliks*) allocated at all levels from the sultan down to the simple provincial cavalrymen, requiring the holders to maintain their own households, and pay the daily wages and expenses of household officers and retinues. A *dirlik*-holder, however small his living, was an independent official; a household officer, however high his rank, served his own master. The emphasis that livings and households were twin aspects of the military–administrative *ümera* organisation, and that even the ruler's royal reserves should properly be seen in this context, differs somewhat from other analyses of Ottoman state structure. The second significant point is that *ümera* administration was supported by *ulema* magistrates (*kadıs*) who applied not only the Muslim *şeriat* but also state regulations and sultanic law, with a common conception of the supremacy of justice and the rule of law.

As a consequence of *dirlik* allocation there were different sorts of revenue collectors in provincial administration. A district governor, for instance, was the commander of the troops throughout the whole of his *sancak*, but he directly administered only those sections of his district, towns and villages, whose revenues had been included in his own *hass* income. If the district happened to have within it taxes allocated to the *hass* of the provincial governor, *beylerbeyi*, or to a vezir of the imperial council, or to the ruler's *havass-ı hümayun*, the revenue collection-cum-administration of these was in the hands of the agents, usually household officers, of the *beylerbeyi* or the vezir or the sultan. The *sancakbeyi*'s authority did not extend to such agents who acted free from local interference. What regularised the administrative activities of all these various officials was the check and control of the provincial *kadı* magistrates.

Suraiya Faroqhi refers to the issue of categorising this Ottoman system of revenue collection in universal terms. Was it a feudal arrangement? Can it be considered under the Marxist rubric of 'the Asiatic Mode of Production'? As the debate continues, proponents of these two schools agree that historians should no longer be content to view the Ottoman case as *sui generis*, that our historiography should be sharpened and enriched by reference to social theory and by means of a comparative look at other imperial systems. One can only agree, but also note that the debate involves refinements and further definitions of the models no less than the discernment of Ottoman features.

As in feudalism, the Ottoman *dirlik*-household system developed in the context of inadequate supplies of precious metals, and of relatively meagre means of transportation for rural levies in kind to reach markets. Revenues were allocated at the source and became the responsibility of the holder to collect and consume in lieu of pay. As opposed to feudalism, however, what was allocated was not land as such but the right to collect revenues, rural as well as urban. Nor were the *dirlik*-grants hereditary: the descendants of *dirlik*-office holders could expect to have their own appointments eventually but not to inherit what their fathers held. In the active career of an official, too, there were occasions – demotion and promotion as well as other reasons – when the *dirlik* assignment was changed, augmented, or cancelled. Higher *dirlik*-grants were specific not to persons but to office, though balanced by considerations of rank and seniority. Looking at things from the 'bottom up', the peasants were not the serfs of a *dirlik*-holder but owned their plots of arable land. On the other hand, they did have some servile obligations, a few relics of earlier, non-Ottoman feudal regimes and, more seriously, suffered limitations on their freedom of movement. It is also important to note that especially in larger *dirliks*, commercial revenues in cash made up a significant portion of *hass* revenues. Ottoman sultans and their highest officials therefore had a direct interest in the free flow of trade and were sensitive to issues with a bearing on long-distance commerce. Flourishing trade was important not just for the overall prosperity of the realm but directly for the wealth and therefore the power of the sultan and the ruling elite.

This model comes closest to full historical reality in the 'classical age' of the empire in the fifteenth and sixteenth centuries and in the 'core provinces' – very roughly the Anatolian and Balkan areas held before the large-scale conquests of Selim I. Again as Suraiya Faroqhi mentions, the complete 'Ottomanisation' of territories went through certain stages. A period of suzerainty was followed by conquest in earnest, at which time Ottoman officials and scribes arrived with their regulations and their registers to take stock of the population and resources of the area. Once revenues were estimated, taking into consideration local custom and production, they were allocated in *dirliks*. Then *kadı* magistrates arrived, together with the newly-appointed *dirlik*-holders: thus began Ottoman administration. But this process of Ottomanisation was not inevitable; certain areas difficult to conquer because of terrain or distance were brought into the Ottoman sphere as vassals and remained as such for many generations or even for centuries. Géza Dávid provides examples of this two-tier arrangement in Ottoman Europe. Elsewhere, the Crimea was left in the hands of the Tartar khans; Kurdish chiefs in the mountainous border zone between the Ottomans and the Safavids were also recognised in nuanced degrees of autonomy. The aim of full conquest remained but, at least in these cases, in abeyance. The Ottoman ideal was to establish central authority without local intermediaries, but in practice Ottoman statesmen were pragmatic.

Sixteenth-century conditions led to certain other arrangements, somewhere in between the two types of full Ottomanisation and vassalage, as we shall soon discuss. The reasons for such new administrative measures had partly to do with the administration of far-flung territories and partly with naval commitments in a much broader compass. The articles by Ann Williams and Salih Özbaran both attest to the heightened significance of the high seas in Ottoman strategic perceptions. Ottoman struggle in the Mediterranean first against Venice and later, in epic proportions, against the Spanish Habsburgs, continued throughout the century. After the failure to capture Malta in Süleyman's last years, even with the disastrous rout at Lepanto in 1571, the Ottoman navy renewed the fight to conquer Cyprus; in 1574 Spain could not prevent the definitive Ottoman conquest of Tunis. Ottoman encouragement to English and Dutch merchants and envoys was a consequence of the struggle against Spain. At the same time, Ottoman fleets were active in the Indian Ocean to counterbalance the Portuguese presence and to insure the flow of South Asian goods through Ottoman-controlled West Asia, and also as part of their newly-assumed leadership of Sunni Islam. We have already seen the conquest of Egypt in this context. The quickest communication between the capital and Cairo was through the Mediterranean; the conquest of Rhodes – Süleyman's first act as sultan – removed the Hospitaller menace to this route as well as allowing the naval struggle to be carried in earnest to the western Mediterranean.

The *dirlik*-household model also applied in districts assigned to the navy. Such districts, whether Aegean islands or mainland *sancak*s surrounding the Aegean, were required to provide a number of galleys in proportion to the revenues of the district. The sultan also paid for a central, household, navy out of his *hass* revenues. Yet as naval commitments were carried beyond the Mediterranean and expenditures increased to much higher levels, new methods of funding emerged, most significantly the *saliyane* system Özbaran discusses. The provincial and district governors in areas where this method came into practice did not collect their own revenues but were paid an annual amount out of taxes raised in that locality by other agents. Neither were there any other provincial *dirlik*-holders in these areas: other officers and troops were also paid in cash, soldiers receiving daily wages just as if they were household retinues. Cash levies not allocated to these officers were at the disposal of the central government to be spent on the spot for naval bases or for fitting of fleets. Any surplus cash would be sent annually to Istanbul, to the sultan's treasury. *Saliyane* literally means 'annual'; *dirliks*, too, were always given in annual figures, but here the difference is the direct cash payment rather than *dirlik*-style revenue collection in cash and in kind.

The *saliyane* system applied in areas at some remove from the heartlands where a handful of high-ranking Ottoman officials administered through locally recruited agents. This could only be possible in areas such as Egypt or Yemen with a relatively high cash yield in revenues, mainly because of significant long-distance trade. The *saliyane* provinces were not vassal areas with local chiefs; they were areas of direct Ottoman rule but without the *dirliks*. This is almost a contradiction in terms, yet the *saliyane* method is an example of the resilience and pragmatism of Ottoman administration. It also happened in some cases that when an area was first conquered there might not be sufficient revenues to support the Ottoman officials appointed there: the warfare before the conquest might have left the area in some disarray so that the peasantry might be allowed tax exemptions for a number of years, or frontier conditions after the conquest might require expenditure on defensive measures. (Géza Dávid mentions the example of the *beylerbeyi* of Budin who, at first, received his income from interior districts.) Or, in frontier provinces such as Budin or Yemen, the expense of maintaining fortresses or naval bases could not always be met out of local levies; in such situations the sultan could divert *hass* revenues from neighbouring provinces, for example from Cairo to Yemen, or send funds directly from Istanbul, until such time that local resources might suffice. Ottoman administration was prudent and patient as well as pragmatic.

The changes sketched above had implications which need to be brought out. The availability of larger amounts of cash, both from the

restored Asian trade and from the increased exports in the Mediterranean, allowed the sultan to increase his own household as well as to
pay for fortresses and naval bases on the empire's frontiers. Some
imperial household detchments were stationed in important provincial
centres – those with significant imperial *havass* revenues, and at frontier
fortresses. Moreover, there were other frontier troops in *saliyane* provinces paid in cash. Under these circumstances the classic definition of
'household' was somewhat blurred. Tax farmers and other collectors,
agents of the ruler and of the vezirs at the capital, became more
prominent in provincial affairs.

All these changes required adjustments, sometimes painful. At first
these developments allowed greater central power and greater manifestations of imperial glory, certainly in Süleyman's lifetime. With the
emergence of *saliyane* provinces and the assignment of *yeniçeri*s to provincial duties, household accounts, both in revenues and in expenditures,
became so varied and complex that a financial bureaucracy emerged
from the royal household into an increasingly distinct government
department. Leaving such matters of administration in the hands of his
vezirs and the *defterdar* – hitherto merely the household financial secretary, now elevated to 'state' treasurer – the sultan developed a more
distant, more imperial posture and image as he grew into old age. He
had transcended the relatively restricted role of the master of his household, and even that of the 'warrior-king', as discussed by Christine
Woodhead. Yet in the decades after the magnificence of the Süleymanic
age had passed, it is essentially the same developments that were seen
with their negative consequences, whether in revenue collection from
the subjects or in the career prospects of officials. Toward the end of the
century, when cash outlays had increased faster than did cash supplies,
Ottoman financial administrators resorted to debasing the silver coinage,
which brought immediate and violent reaction from the recipients, the
sultan's household troops resident in the capital. So painful was
the transformation that there were also serious provincial disturbances
– limited, however, to the Turkish population of Anatolia in the main
– as the sixteenth century, and in 1591 the first Muslim *hicri* millenium,
drew to a close.

Suraiya Faroqhi rightly points out the futility of dating Ottoman
'decline' from this time. In recent years students of Ottoman history
have learned better than to discuss a 'decline' which supposedly began
during the reigns of Süleyman's 'ineffectual' successors and then continued for centuries. Süleyman's sons and grandsons, as sultans, merely
continued in the same detached imperial tradition that was first
fashioned during Süleyman's long reign. As for broader institutional

and social fluctuations and dislocations, these are properly to be seen as features of a transition which eventually reached a new equilibrium in the seventeenth century. The 'time of troubles' may have seemed of millenial significance to Ottomans themselves; we should see its features rather as aspects of the Ottoman effort to confront the challenges of a changing and widening world, beyond their frontiers and experience.

ANN WILLIAMS

Mediterranean conflict

Ottoman interest in the Mediterranean and their increasing involvement as a sea power was a direct result of the conquest of Constantinople in 1453 and of their inheritance of the Byzantine maritime frontier, an ill-defined line which drew them more deeply into the politics of the middle sea. The eastern Mediterranean on their doorstep had already been fragmented by the Fourth Crusade of 1204 into a complex network of small powers watched over by the trading cities of Venice and Genoa. This instability increased in the late fifteenth century when the ambitions of Spain, France and the Holy Roman Empire in the Italian peninsula were reflected in wider Mediterranean activities. Over and above this, the papacy kept a spiritual brief, bringing out the banners of crusade when it seemed that the Ottoman advance was becoming too threatening, or when the pressures of the divided Christian church demanded it.

In 1453 Venice's empire and its strategic links stretched from the lagoons to the major colony of Crete and the trading settlements in Pera (Istanbul) and Alexandria. In Greece itself they had the valuable settlement of Negroponte and fortresses in the south, Lepanto at the entrance to the Gulf of Patras, Modon, Koron, Nauplia and Monemvasia. They held the island of Naxos for rent, first to the Byzantines and then to the Ottomans, and maintained forts on smaller islands such as Tinos.

The Venetian government kept its possessions under tight control, demanding detailed reports from its colonial governors and sending out commissions to regulate their activities. Genoa had a more informal empire.[1] The Banco di San Giorgio, rather than the Genoese government, administered the investment of trade. Many of its eastern pos-

---

1 G L Scammel, *The world encompassed* (London 1981) 86–224, summarises the Venetian and Genoese trading activity and settlement in the Mediterranean.

sessions, like Chios and Lesbos, were in the hands of independent Genoese families who frequently acted without reference to the mother city. Cyprus, where they had an important base, was ruled by the Lusignan dynasty until 1473, when the line died out and, by the terms of a previous marriage contract, the island then reverted to Venice.[2]

The island of Rhodes, originally part of the Byzantine empire, was occupied by the Order of St John, the Knights Hospitaller, from 1309.[3] Founded in Syria as a military religious order during the period of the early crusades, after the fall of Acre in 1291 they had moved first to Cyprus, and then to the group of islands at Rhodes with a mainland fortress at Bodrum. They became a small but efficient sea force, a thorn in the flesh of the Turkish emirates along the mainland coast. They held Izmir for over forty years in the fourteenth century.

Although Mehmed II wanted to encourage trade between the Italian cities and the Ottomans after he took Constantinople, the high-handedness of Venice in Salonica led to a prolonged period of war between 1463 and 1479.[4] After losing control over the valuable Negroponte in 1470, Venice felt the first twinges of an anxiety that was to determine her policy throughout the following century. The problems of maintaining an adequate defence for her Mediterranean empire vied with her need to defend herself against encroachments on her possessions on the Italian mainland. Mehmed ended his reign with an abortive siege of the island of Rhodes in 1481, intended to combat the irritating naval harassment by the Order of St John, and to justify Ottoman acquisition of the Anatolian emirates by being seen to fight their traditional enemy. He also sent a force to the southern Italian city of Otranto in 1480–81. This has often been seen as the wayward action of a ruler in his declining years, but in fact it showed an appreciation of the ambitions of Naples to take up historic claims to the throne of Byzantium.[5] Though previously unwilling to help the Greek emperors in the last years of their struggle with the Turks,

2 Sir George Hill, *A History of Cyprus* (Cambridge 1948), III, 657–764.
3 A T Luttrell, 'The Hospitallers at Rhodes 1306–1421', in H W Hazard (ed.), *A history of the crusades: III, The fourteenth and fifteenth centuries* (Madison, Wisconsin 1975), 278–313.
4 H İnalcık, 'An outline of Ottoman-Venetian relations', in H.-G. Beck *et al* (eds), *Venezia, centro di mediazione tra oriente e occidente (secoli XV-XVI): aspetti e problemi* (Florence 1977), II, 83–90.
5 Palmeria Brummett, *Ottoman seapower and Levantine diplomacy in the age of discovery* (Albany, New York 1994), 51–6. This book, published after this article was written, suggests a very strong Ottoman Mediterranean policy in the three reigns before Süleyman. Its bibliography, together with that in John H Pryor's *Geography, technology and war: studies in the maritime history of the Mediterranean 649–1571* (Cambrige 1988), provide supplementary reading; see below p. 43 n.12, 48.

western rulers now showed interest in the possibilities of winning back the eastern Mediterranean for Christianity.

Bayezid II was less concerned than his predecessor with Mediterranean expansion. Financially, some respite was needed from the wars of conquest: diplomatically, the existence in the west of the Ottoman pretender Cem urged caution and consolidation. But by the end of Bayezid's reign, the desire to gain imperial and religious legitimacy in the face of Safavid claims in Persia renewed Mamluk strength in Egypt and the ambitions of the Portuguese in the Indian Ocean, all of which threatened hostile combinations of alliances and forced the Ottomans into extensive shipbuilding and commercial activity in the eastern Mediterranean. Also in the latter part of Bayezid's reign did the need to teach Venice another lesson lead to renewed warfare between the two powers, from 1499–1502. The area of conflict, the Adriatic, was significant. Venice had traditionally regarded the Adriatic as a Venetian lake; towns on both shores were drawn into the Serenissima's orbit, and the Venetian fortifications of Corfu guarded the entrance to the sea. The south-western part of the Morea also boasted Venetian forts which protected the city's fleets on the next stages of their voyages to the eastern Mediterranean. Under the lax authority of the last Byzantine rulers, the fortified ports were welcomed as protecting the area from pirates, but when the Ottomans inherited Byzantine claims and took on the Greek frontiers of the empire, they were conscious of the pressure of potentially hostile elements within the boundaries they claimed.

During the course of the war of 1499–1502 Venice lost Lepanto, the last mainland outpost on the Isthmus, and the port which protected the Gulf of Patras, and also the strongholds of Modon, Koron and Navarino in the Morea. The ease with which the Ottomans took these places pointed to their technical superiority in this stage of the naval conflict between east and west. Guilmartin has shown how the combination of fleet backed by strong fortress was to be the pattern of naval warfare in the sixteenth century;[6] the thin walls of Modon and Koron were no match for Ottoman gunfire. The treaty of 1503 led to a general peace for seven years.[7] Venice could not be punished too severely, as her assistance in the redistribution of goods from the eastern

---

6 J F Guilmartin, Jnr., 'Ideology and conflict: the wars of the Ottoman empire 1453–1606', in R I Rotberg and T K Rabb (eds), *The origin and prevention of major wars* (Cambridge 1989), 149–75.

7 J von Hammer-Purgstall, *Histoire de l'empire Ottoman* (trs J J Hellert, Paris 1836), IV, 174–7.

Mediterranean was too valuable to lose – a point indicated clearly by the embassy of Taghribirdi from Mamluk Egypt to Venice in 1506.[8]

After 1512 Selim I returned to the more aggressive policies of Mehmed II. His prestigious victory over the Egyptian Mamluks in 1517 allowed the Ottomans to assume guardianship of the Muslim holy places of Mecca and Medina, and brought them into contact with the Portuguese, whom they kept at bay initially by a victory off Jidda. Control over Egypt also emphasised the need for good sea communications between Alexandria and Istanbul. The tribute cargoes from Egypt have been likened to the treasure fleets coming from the New World to Spain: the Ottomans needed to ensure that this route would not be harried.

Nevertheless, Venice could not be excluded from the new Ottoman territories. In 1520, within a month of Süleyman's accession, a *ferman* to the Republic confirmed trading privileges.[9] As both Ottomans and Venetians were apprehensive about Portuguese expansion in the Indian Ocean, there was a common purpose in making arrangements for the best exploitation of the traditional trade route via Alexandria. Less fortunate were the Knights of St John in Rhodes. Their aggressive attacks on the coast and on shipping could not be tolerated. Süleyman made it one of his first tasks to besiege the island which Mehmed II had failed to take.[10] Although the Knights' fortifications were known to be formidable, the position of Rhodes was not so distant from Istanbul that a long siege could not be contemplated, especially as the likelihood of relief from the west was remote. The Ottoman fleet reached Rhodes in June 1522 and took up an attacking position; in December the sultan wrote to the besieged grand master, Philippe de l'Isle Adam, offering him an honourable evacuation. The Knights had little choice, and the community left the island with their movable possessions, accompanied by some three hundred Greek Catholics who followed them on their travels around Europe.[11] Süleyman acquired a valuable fortress needing very little repair which was of great service in protecting the Egyptian treasure fleets.

L'Isle Adam reported in person to Pope Hadrian VI, who urged a

---

8 J Wansbrough, 'A Mamluk ambassador to Venice in 913/1507', *BSOAS* xxvi (1963), 503–30.

9 K M Setton, *The Papacy and the Levant 1204–1571* (Philadelphia 1984), III: *The sixteenth century to the reign of Julius III*, 183–4.

10 E Rossi, *Assedio e conquista di Rodi nel 1522, secondo le relazioni edite ed inedite dei Turchi* (Rome 1927), publishes descriptions of the siege, but does not clarify Süleyman's motives for the conquest.

11 They went to Crete, Sicily and Viterbo, where they were too close to the papacy for comfort; see below p. 44.

three or four years' truce on the rulers of Europe so that a counter-expedition could be planned. His proposal did not meet with immediate approval. Two formidable rulers faced one another on the European stage: Francis I, who had succeeded to the French throne in 1515, and Charles V, who had become king of Spain in 1516, and Holy Roman Emperor in 1519. The scene of their rivalry was Italy, where the papacy and Venice were drawn inevitably into the conflict. Francis had inherited the Angevin claim to Naples through Charles VIII of France,[12] whose brother Louis XII had had claims by marriage to Milan. Charles V, too, had claims on Naples since Aragonese rulers had succeeded the Angevins.[13] In particular, Alfonso of Aragon, king of Naples 1422–58, had had strong interests in the eastern Mediterranean, and in the chaotic half-century after his death Naples became prey to internal rivalries which had encouraged the Ottoman gesture at Otranto in 1480. Charles, who was developing ideas of crusade, saw control of Naples as essential.[14]

Francis and Charles were not prepared to make peace at the pope's bidding. In 1524 Charles attacked Marseille, a city which was not then part of the French kingdom but from where a Spanish garrison would obviously threaten Francis. The latter foiled this attempt, marched towards Milan, and in January 1525 joined the pact made by the papacy and Venice against Charles.[15] A month later, however, the imperial army defeated and captured Francis near Pavia. The pope, hoping that the imprisonment of the French king would stop the bickering among the Christian powers, again attempted to revive the idea of crusade.

The Venetians, meanwhile, had moved over quickly to ally with Charles V and were not anxious to provoke the Ottomans. In June 1524 Süleyman had written to the doge that the Republic must share his anxiety about piracy in the Adriatic; he knew that the pirates were

---

12 This claim went back to 1259 when Manfred of Sicily married Helen, the daughter of Michael II of Empiros, who gave a number of towns, including Valona and Durazzo on the Adriatic coast, as dowry. Michael himself claimed the throne of Constantinople in rivalry with the emperor of Nicaea. Manfred inherited the ambition which, in turn, the Angevin rulers of Sicily appropriated.

13 T Pedio, *Napoli e Spagna nella prima meta del cinquecento* (Bari 1971), 52–71; A Ryder, *The kingdom of Naples under Alfonso the Magnanimous: the making of a modern state* (Oxford 1976), 17–26.

14 M H Hantsch, 'Le problème de la lutte contre l'invasion turque dans l'idée politique générale de Charles-Quint', in *Charles-Quint et son temps* (CNRS, Paris 1959), 51–60.

15 Setton, *Papacy and the Levant*, III, 216; 'Les campagnes narales franco-ottomanes en Méditerranée au XVIᵉ siècle', in Irad Malkin (ed.), *La France et la Mediterranée vingt-sept siècles d'interdépendence* (Leiden 1990), 311–34.

Ottoman subjects, and would send five ships under Bustan Reis to deal with them. Whether with cooperation or not, the Venetians were unhappy about the armed presence of the Ottomans in the Adriatic, and were proved right in their fears. The port of Valona, which had had a chequered career under Angevins and Venetians (among other claimants), had finally come under the control of Sinan Paşa in 1518.[16] It then became the base for the preparation of Ottoman naval campaigns in the 1530s, for an attack on Corfu in 1537, and for another before Lepanto in 1570. Venice was therefore hedging her bets by allying with the emperor on the one hand, and by trying not to get drawn into the Holy League on the other.

Since the papacy had traditionally considered that it had the right to approve the rulers of Naples and Sicily, Clement VII withdrew his support of the imperial claim to Naples after Pavia, and proposed to give it to a French prince as heir to the Angevin cause. Charles responded by marching on Rome and sacking the city in 1527, sending on his general, Lautrec, to invade Naples. The French then tried to invest Naples by sea but, worn out and reduced in numbers by plague, they withdrew. By the treaty of Cambrai in 1529, Francis gave up his claim to Naples. Once joined as part of the Aragonese kingdom, Naples and Sicily again became united as part of Charles V's Mediterranean empire.

This drew the Spanish presence in the central Mediterranean and North Africa even closer to the Ottomans. After the expulsion of the Moors from Granada in 1492, Spain had captured Melilla in 1497, Peñon de Velez in 1508, Oran a year later, and in 1510 Algiers and Tripoli. The form of *presidio* that the Spaniards set up was a garrison isolated from the hostile hinterland in which it was set, and demanding a firm link with Spain by sea. It was not an easy arrangement, but it flourished for some years in the unstable political climate of the Maghrib. After the Knights of St John had left Rhodes, Charles V spent eight years trying to persuade them to take on the islands of Malta and Gozo, then nominally under the control of Sicily, but prey to attack by pirates. The larger island had a magnificent harbour which he felt would be better in the hands of Christians than Muslims. Eventually in 1530, the Knights, who would have preferred a more fertile territory – part of Sicily, a base in the Morea, or a reconquered Rhodes – accepted the gift of the Maltese island together with the obligation to defend Tripoli, in exchange for a falcon.[17]

16 W Miller, *Essays on the Latin Orient* (Cambridge 1921), 429–44, Valona.
17 Archives of the Order of Malta, Arch. 59 Lettere di Castiglia, Portogallo ed Aragona (1522–1704): Letters 14–19, 23.

Meanwhile, as this formidable concentration of Spanish power was growing in the middle Mediterranean, the Ottomans were getting drawn more closely into the politics of the Maghrib. The conquest of Egypt gave them influence, as protectors of the holy places of Islam, over Muslim communities in North Africa. In the early part of the sixteenth century three dynasties were predominant in the Maghrib: the Hafsids in Tunis, the Zayanids in Tlemcen, and the Wattasids in Fez. The governments of these sultans were firmly based in the cities with support from merchant groups, who feared that the nomadic local tribes of the hinterland, who had never been brought under control, would disrupt their livelihood. A pretext for Ottoman involvement came from Muslims in Spain who had first appealed in 1487 to both the Ottomans and the Mamluks for help, a plea that was to become more insistent after 1492.[18]

The corsair Kemal Reis was employed by the Ottomans to investigate the Spanish coast and to make links with Muslim leaders in the North African cities. Based in Bougie and Jerba, he spent some years raiding the coasts of Sicily and southern Italy. By the accession of Selim I in 1512, two other corsairs, the Barbarossa brothers, had already gained a reputation for their piratical activities. Supported originally by the Ottoman prince, Selim's brother, Korkud, they feared retribution when their patron failed to win the sultanate, and retreated to the protection of Muhammad V in Tunis, where they were given shelter in the port of La Goletta.

Oruç and Hayreddin Barbarossa came originally from Mytilene,[19] one of the Greek islands which served as a source of naval manpower for both Muslim and Christian fleets. They were well placed to provide a link between the rulers of North Africa and the Ottomans. Within two years they had approached Selim through the offices of Piri Reis, the geographer, himself the nephew of a corsair. Selim appreciated their role and granted them not only honours and gifts but also, of more immediate practical value, two Ottoman war galleys.

With these ships, the Barbarossas returned to the western Mediterranean to assist the Hispano-Muslims, and to attack Spanish cities in North Africa.[20] While their first attempt to take Bougie failed, in 1516 they agreed to help the Muslim ruler of Algiers remove the Spanish

---

18 A Hess, *The forgotten frontier: a history of the sixteenth century Ibero-African frontier* (Chicago 1978), 46.
19 R Le Tourneau, 'Aru*dj*', *EI²*, I, 677–8; A Galotta, 'Khayr al-Din Barbarossa', *EI²*, IV, 1157–8. The best account of Hayreddin is Enver Ziya Karal, 'Barbaros Hayreddin Paşa', *İA*, 2, 311–15.
20 Hess, *Forgotten frontier*, 60.

garrison at Peñon de Argel, a small island at the entrance to the harbour, possession of which enabled the Spaniards to demand dues from the Muslims. Oruç was not immediately successful in this enterprise either, but it gave him the opportunity to question the commitment of the ruler of Algiers to the holy war, and subsequently to make himself master of the city. A year later, in 1517, Oruç moved against Tlemcen, where merchants and religious leaders welcomed help against the Spaniards. Here too he took the opportunity to overthrow the incumbent Zayanid sultan, and to make himself ruler. It was at this stage that Selim, now conqueror of Egypt, saw the value of a sympathetic ruler to balance the independent sultans of Tunis and Fez, and to act as a goad to the Spanish. These events coincided with the renewed interest that Charles V, as king of Spain, took in his fortress cities of North Africa.

The first Spanish initiative against Algiers and Tlemcen in 1518 defeated and killed the corsair leader, leaving his brother Hayreddin to approach Selim for more help and to put himself under the protection of the Ottoman sultan. 'Sometime, thereafter, between 1517 and 1520, the Ottoman commander performed in Algeria those symbolic acts that announce the arrival of a new Muslim dynasty; the name of the Turkish sultan was read in the Friday prayer and placed upon the coinage'.[21] Hayreddin's problems were not over, however, and he spent the 1520s – when Süleyman was engaged in Belgrade (1521) and with the Mohaç campaign in Hungary (1526) and Charles was preoccupied with the revolt of the Comuneros (1520–21) – in consolidating his hold over Algiers, using the continuing stream of Hispano-Muslims to buttress his authority and to take on Berber tribes in the Kabyle. Eventually, in May 1529, he also succeeded in pushing the Spaniards off the island of Peñon de Argel.

At the beginning of the 1530s, the now experienced Hayreddin made the first encounter with an opponent worthy of his attention. As Holy Roman Emperor, Charles V was deeply concerned with the spread of Protestantism in his German lands, and with the threat from the Ottomans, both on his Balkan frontiers and in the Mediterranean. To take care of his sea frontier, he employed the Genoese admiral Andrea Doria. In 1530 Doria's attack on Chercel was repelled by Hayreddin, and although the Spaniards responded with a victory near Oran the following year, there was a temporary stalemate in the Maghrib. Charles V, worried by Ottoman advances in the Balkans, then moved his naval war back to the Morea. He proposed an attack on Koron in 1532, a decision which was welcomed enthusiastically by the

21 Hess, *Forgotten frontier*, 67.

Knights of St John who hoped to be able to give up their rocky stronghold of Malta. Charles also hoped that the union of Western and Orthodox Christians could be revived.[22] The Christians regained a temporary foothold in the Morea, but Süleyman's quick reaction early in 1534 was to send for Hayreddin Barbarossa and appoint him *kapudan paşa* (grand admiral) of the Ottoman fleet. The appointment was a vote of confidence in the corsair, and evidence of the sultan's commitment to his Mediterranean frontier. The same year, Hayreddin forced the Spaniards to leave Koron, and then returned to Tunis to overthrow the Hafsids.[23] This established him within a worrying distance of Sicily.

Pope Clement VII died in September 1534, to be replaced by the aged Farnese Pope Paul III, a man with whom Charles V felt more sympathy than with his predecessor. As Charles moved towards rapport with the papacy, Francis I looked for an alliance with the Ottomans, and in February 1535 sent the French Hospitaller Jean de la Fôret to Istanbul to suggest a joint land and sea attack on Sicily and Sardinia.[24] Süleyman was not prepared to provoke Charles so openly at this stage, but these negotiations paved the way for that year's commercial treaty with France which secured trading rights for French merchants in the Ottoman empire, and an anchorage for the Ottoman fleet in the Bay of Lions.

Charles' response to the conquest of Tunis was to send a fleet of 400 ships and 26,000 men into North Africa to restore the Hafsid ruler Mulay Hasan. After dislodging Hayreddin, the Spanish virtually destroyed Tunis; the city given back to the Hafsids on a tributary basis was a weak centre for the restoration of their power. The Spaniards themselves reinforced La Goletta but Charles had no intention of expanding the Spanish *presidio* system by moving into the hinterland. The next six years saw no more Christian attacks in North Africa, although Hayreddin's ships continued to raid Sicilian and southern Italian ports, in particular making a symbolic attack on Otranto in July 1537.[25]

Venice was well aware of Ottoman naval preparations at Valona, and by the end of 1536 had increased her fleet of galleys from twenty-seven to sixty, putting in reinforcements at Candia, Corfu and Zante, as well as nearer home in Dubrovnik and Venice herself.[26] At the same time, the doge was both fending off invitations by the sultan to commit

---

22 For many of the Greek Orthodox communities, Ottoman rule was preferable to that of western Christians.
23 W Miller, *Latins in the Levant* (London 1908), 505–7.
24 Setton, *Papacy and the Levant*, III, 392.
25 G Coniglio, *Il viceregno di Napoli e la lotta tra Spagnoli e Turchi nel Mediterraneo* (Naples 1987), 6–7.
26 Setton, *Papacy and the Levant*, III, 401–28.

the Republic openly to the Franco-Ottoman alliance, and also trying not to commit her to a Holy League which the pope was urging against the Ottomans. In the summer of 1537 a large Ottoman fleet of 320 ships, among them 170 galleys, arrived in Valona, and although they did not sail to the western Mediterranean they ravaged Corfu on their way back to Istanbul in September. The doge now agreed, in February 1538, to a defensive and offensive league against the Ottomans with the papacy and Charles V. He was to contribute just under a third of the cost, the pope one sixth, and the emperor the rest. The ambitious nature of the enterprise was shown in the arrangements made for the division of the spoils. Charles was to have Istanbul – boldly restating the old claims of Naples; Venice would again control Koron and hold Valona and Castelnuovo at the mouth of the Cattaro; the Hospitallers would be restored to Rhodes. Naval preparations were put under way, and the Venetian and papal ships made the rendezvous at Corfu in the early summer; Doria did not arrive until September.[27]

Hayreddin, meanwhile, had been joined by contingents from North Africa, and had sailed round the Morea to the west coast of Greece and the Gulf of Prevesa, where the guns of the fortress and the batteries at the entrance to the harbour gave him great protection. In spite of his superior numbers, Doria was unable to take the fort and, deciding to withdraw, was chased by Hayreddin and had his ships badly mauled.[28] The retreating fleet eventually took Castelnuovo, but only to lose it to Hayreddin the following year. By this, the initiative in the Adriatic returned to the Ottomans, and Venice lost completely the taste for a Holy League. The treaty the Republic made with the sultan in October 1540 promised an indemnity of 300,000 ducats, and surrender of her Morean fortresses of Nauplia and Monemvasia.[29]

In the same year 1540 peace was also made between France and Spain, with the French king renouncing his claim to Milan. Charles gave the city to his son Philip. This opened the way for Charles to concentrate on the Maghrib, and in the spring of 1541 he sent a large force to Algiers. The siege was frustrated by extreme weather conditions which ruined the Spanish powder and finally broke up the fleet.[30] Andrea Doria withdrew, having lost 140 ships in the storm, and a further ten

27 J Guilmartin, Jnr., *Gunpowder and galleys: changing technology and Mediterranean warfare at sea in the sixteenth century* (Cambridge 1974), 43–5, suggests that Doria was attempting to make a deal with the Ottomans to protect Genoese-held Chios.
28 Guilmartin, *Gunpowder and galleys*, 42–56.
29 Miller, *Essays*, 373. Venice now held only the Ionian dependencies of Parga and Butrinto, and Cyprus, Crete, Tinos, and six Ionian islands.
30 Hess, *Forgotten frontier*, 74.

in the retreat; Charles' reputation suffered a serious blow in both west and east. Francis renewed war against the emperor in 1542, and a year later Hayreddin attacked Nice and boldly wintered in Toulon, supplied by French provisions.[31] On his way back to Istanbul in May 1544 he attacked the Italian islands and the south-west coast of Naples.

Charles was in no position to put out a new fleet immediately and, desiring also a respite from land warfare, he made peace with Francis in September 1544. The papacy meanwhile was trying to prevent Venice from trading with the eastern Mediterranean, in return for tithes to help maintain her fleet. This prohibition was impossible to accept. The Republic had the double anxiety of trying to please the papacy to obtain money, and trying not to offend the Ottomans by negotiating with their enemies, particularly problematic as the new grand vezir Rüstem Paşa was regarded as more difficult to please than his predecessor.[32] Charles V, already contemplating abdication, sent an ambassador to Istanbul to negotiate a truce in the Balkans, hoping to extend the peace to the Maghrib if this could be achieved without betraying the Hafsid sultan in Tunis.

In July Hayreddin Barbarossa died and was succeeded as *kapudan paşa* by Mehmed Sokullu, not a corsair but an Istanbul-trained career administrator. His appointment signalled that the North African province would be drawn more closely into the Ottoman empire. The five years' peace Charles and Süleyman signed in 1548 included a ceasefire in the Maghrib but failed to prevent the Ottomans from consolidating their position there, with moves against the Saadian dynasty in Morocco. The latter had since the 1510s been trying to build an inland state based on Taroudant. Their *cihad* in the south conflicted with the growing influence of the Ottomans, and their attempt to take Tlemcen in 1550 drew the Ottomans further west to fend off their attack. A year later Ottoman naval forces took Tripoli from the Knights of St John, who had held it with great difficulty from their base in Malta. The city was taken by Turgut Paşa, who succeeded Hayreddin in the legends of the west.[33] Charles tried to persuade the Knights to take on instead the poorly-defended al-Mahdiyya, but they wisely refused to stretch their limited manpower resources any further. This city had to be abandoned in 1554, with the result that a further stretch of Tunisian coast passed into Ottoman hands. Under Salih Paşa, governor

---

31 Setton, *Papacy and the Levant*, III, 472.
32 Setton, *Papacy and the Levant*, III, 475, no. 100, quotes the Venetian letter and list of presents sent to Rüstem Paşa.
33 İ H Uzunçarşılı, *Osmanlı tarihi II: Istanbul'un fethinden Kanunî Sultan Süleyman'in ölümüne kadar* (Ankara 1983), 384–90.

of Algiers from 1552, the Ottomans also moved inland against the Saadians, occupied Fez and installed a puppet ruler.

The situation in western Europe continued to change. Following Francis I's death in March 1547 his successor Henry II was able to renew the peace treaty with the emperor without interference from the Ottomans, since the latter were preoccupied with war on their eastern frontier against Safavid Iran. Papal policy both in Italy and in the Mediterranean veered with each new pontiff; Paul IV, elected in 1555, again played the dangerous game of setting Valois against Habsburg. Philip, king of Naples, duke of Milan, and heir to Charles V was betrothed to Mary Tudor in July 1554. France was thus surrounded and isolated diplomatically. The pope therefore proposed to form a league against the empire, promising Naples and Milan to France, and Sicily to Venice. For Philip, about to assume the responsibilities of the whole empire on the abdication of Charles V, the situation was a difficult one; his immediate solution upon succeeding Charles in 1556 was to arrange a five-year truce with the French at Cambrai. Although the Venetians were quick to inform Süleyman of Philip's difficulties, there seemed little likelihood of immediate Ottoman expeditions to the west due to a recent major earthquake in Istanbul.[34]

Paul IV nevertheless continued to prepare for a war with the emperor. Just before Charles' abdication, the duke of Alva anticipated an attack by himself marching from Naples towards Rome. Both the pope and Philip attempted to win Venice to their side, but the Republic, as always, tried to keep out of the quarrel, sending an embassy to Rüstem Paşa to assure Süleyman that she wanted nothing more than peace. She tried to act as honest broker between the papacy and the Spanish king, but was battered on all sides by Philip's request to allow troops through her territory, and by Paul's surprising threat that if she did not supply ships to him he would ally with the Ottomans and persuade them to raid the Adriatic coast. In March 1557 Cardinal Carafa wrote to Süleyman to try and persuade him to send an armada against Naples and Sicily, rather than to continue a fruitless war in Hungary. The chaos in Italy suited the sultan, however, and he was well able to leave the contestants to their own problems, especially as France was persuaded to back the truce with Philip and send a force to Naples. The French defeat at St Quentin and Alva's march on Rome forced the pope to make peace in September 1557, an event highlighted by the massive flooding of the Tiber.

At the end of the same month Henry II's ambassador returned to

---

34 Setton, *Papacy and the Levant, I: The sixteenth century from Julius III to Pius V,* 647.

Istanbul to ask Süleyman to send troops and a fleet to Valona, and from there to Naples. He asked also for a loan of two million ducats. Süleyman did not respond to either request, appearing more interested in Hungary and his own internal problems. Nevertheless, in April 1558, the Ottoman fleet sailed through the Dardanelles, making its way slowly towards the west. By June it was off Zante, to the alarm of the Venetians, but then moved more quickly round into the Bay of Naples, sacking Sorrento. It then proceeded to the western Mediterranean and put in at Minorca, rather than meeting up with the French fleet at Corsica as proposed. On its return journey the Ottoman fleet stopped at Genoa where it was well received. The French were dismayed at the lack of support from their supposed ally, especially as they had broken their truce with Spain in the expectation of Ottoman help.

The uncertainty of the Ottoman alliance and France's need for peace with Philip II induced her to conclude the treaty of Cateau Cambrésis in April 1559. Marriage alliances drew the parties into family ties, and Spain kept her hold on the kingdom of Naples and the duchy of Milan. Genoa took over French ports and fortresses on Corsica and the two states were drawn together more closely in trade agreements. In the same year both Pope Paul IV and Henry II died, the latter leaving his weak son Francis II in the hands of the Guise faction. Although the turmoil surrounding the election of Pius IV in December 1559 and the punishment of the previous pope's faction diverted for a time the attention of Rome from external affairs, Pius was determined that his pontificate would be known both for its work of reform and also for its resistance to the Ottoman advance. He took particular interest in new appointments to Latin sees in the eastern Mediterranean, urging the bishops to be resident in their dioceses, and showed practical concern for a proposed Christian attack on the island of Jerba.

Philip II remained concerned by the loss of Tripoli, now under the control of Turgut Reis. He had support from the Knights' new grand master, Jean de la Vallette, whom the Order of St John had elected in 1557. La Vallete was to prove one of the ablest rulers the Knights Hospitaller had produced, and a man who fully appreciated the dangers of a hostile force so close to Malta and Sicily. A fleet assembled by Philip under the duke of Medina Celi sailed from Messina to Malta to join the Knights' squadron in December 1559, much later than the summer rendezvous that had been planned. It was further delayed by bad weather, and eventually sailed to Jerba in March. The island was taken successfully, apparently with the agreement of the local sheikh.[35]

35 Setton, *Papacy and the Levant*, III, 760.

The fortress was rebuilt to provide a base for Christian sorties against Turgut Reis in Tripoli. Piali Paşa had meanwhile left Istanbul with a fleet to assist the corsair. Medina Celi was not prepared for a direct engagement and in May 1560 the Ottoman fleet caught the Christian ships trying to leave, and took a number of prisoners. The garrison of about 5000 on Jerba was left without an adequate water supply, but even so managed to hold out for eighty-two days, until it was finally overcome on 31 July. On his return Piali Paşa ostentatiously raided and burnt Augusta and then, passing Corfu, went on to Prevesa to display his prisoners and to emphasise Christian helplessness.

Süleyman was relieved at this latest success in the Mediterranean, preoccupied as he was with internal problems of revolt. In the west Pius IV wished to reconvene the Church Council at Trent to complete the programme of reform begun more than a decade earlier. During the long debates that followed, the question of a Christian expedition against the Ottomans arose from time to time. The 'orator' of the Order of St John, Martin de Rojas Portalrubio, who was vice-chancellor of the Knights, spoke in 1563 of Malta's vulnerability and the need for positive financial support against the Ottomans and their North African allies. However, no practical help was forthcoming, and it was fortunate that in the three years from 1561 to 1564 the Ottoman fleet made no move against the west. An eight-year truce between the sultan and the emperor arranged in November 1562 nevertheless did not prevent the corsairs of Turgut Reis continuing to raid the coasts of Italy and the islands.

This period of peace came to an end in March 1565, with news of the preparation of an armada in Istanbul. Venice made ready to defend Cyprus, Crete and Corfu, but instructed her captain general not to come into conflict with the Ottomans if he could possibly avoid it. The Republic had been harried by the Uskoks in the Adriatic and by Maghribi pirates in Zante and Corfu, and her resources of money and manpower were stretched to the limit. However, grand master la Vallette was already convinced that the Ottoman fleet was destined for Malta, a move of which Süleyman had indeed appreciated the logic. The island was a manageable voyage from Istanbul, while the fleet could call upon the additional support of Turgut Reis in Tripoli. In Ottoman hands the great harbour would be a constant threat to Sicily and Naples, and together with the strongholds in the Maghrib would control the seaways of the middle Mediterranean.[36]

The Hospitallers were not well prepared for a major attack. They

---

36 Guilmartin, *Gunpowder and galleys*, 176–93, on the reasons for the choice of Malta and the course of the siege.

had settled at Birgu on the western side of the main harbour, leaving the barren high ground of Mount Sciberras defended by a fortress, Fort St Elmo, at the tip of the promontory. The combined Ottoman and corsair force landed in May 1565 in Marsamuscetto harbour on the other side of Mount Sciberras. Ottoman strength has been estimated at some 36,000 fighting men, while the defenders had a mere 2500, of whom only 500 were Knights, 400 more Spanish, and the rest ill-equipped Maltese and merchant residents; Don Garcia de Toledo, Viceroy of Sicily, promised help by sea. Fort St Elmo held out under siege until 18 June, its acquisition costing the Ottomans the life of Turgut Reis. The long siege of Fort St Angelo and Birgu lasted until 8 September, when Don Garcia's relief fleet eventually arrived. The Knights saw their delay as perfidious, but in retrospect it appears to have been the right tactical move.[37]

The failure to take Malta could be regarded as a dismal end to Süleyman's Mediterranean expeditions, but there is little evidence that either he or his successor saw it in this light. It was a setback, but one which might be reversed at a later date. *Gazi* attacks against the Christians, particularly on the Mediterranean frontier, relied on a continual change of target which would not allow them to settle and consolidate their resources.[38] In 1566 the Ottomans decided to take Chios, where Genoese factions had created an unstable situation very near to the coast of Ottoman Anatolia, and in this they were successful. Piali Paşa next moved slowly via Navarino and Modon, where he took on supplies, to the Adriatic. He landed a force on the coast between Valona and Corfu, but was attacked by the local inhabitants; the fleet then sailed further north to Fiume and Trieste. Venice's usual anxiety about her position was, however, allayed by Selim II's confirmation of the 1540 peace treaty.[39]

The west regarded the raising of the siege of Malta as a much more dramatic turning point. Subsequent years saw the creation of a Holy League and the formation of a fleet under the command of Don John of Austria, which led to the naval victory off Lepanto in 1571. Both the relief of Malta and the success at Lepanto were greeted with public rejoicing and the ringing of church bells in the west. Nevertheless the Ottomans once again made little fuss and recovered quickly from the loss of their fleet in 1571.[40] The peace agreed between the Ottomans

37 Guilmartin, *Gunpowder and galleys*, 191–3.
38 See note 6.
39 P P Argenti, *Chius Vincta* (Cambridge 1941), 69–70.
40 A C Hess, 'The battle of Lepanto and its place in Mediterranean history', *Past and Present* 57 (1972), 53–73.

and Spain in 1580 marked a cessation of open warfare between these two powers, but did little, as always, to stop the 'limited warfare' of the privateers, both Muslim and Christian, which continued to be a characteristic of the Mediterranean. The disunity of the Christians throughout the sixteenth century, and their intermittent attempts to stage crusades or holy leagues, left them vulnerable to criticism when their enterprises failed. The Ottoman sultan was not dependent upon allies and his *gazi* attacks could be accounted victories when they succeeded, and ignored when they did not.

SALIH ÖZBARAN
Ottoman naval policy in the south

I

When Albuquerque entered the Red Sea in 1513 he reported the fact to
his king in the following words: 'At the rumour of our coming, the [native]
ships all vanished and even the birds ceased to skim over the water, so
overcast was the Red Sea by our coming and so deserted'.

The imagery of this passage is fully in keeping with the heroic style of
the *Lusiadas* and the Portuguese historians, but it is questionable in how far
it reflected reality; certainly it was not applicable to the situation in the
Indian Ocean.[1]

And when the Ottoman sea-captain Selman reported in 1525 to the
grand vezir İbrahim Paşa in Cairo, he described Ottoman power in
the Red Sea with these words:

> Each ship resembles a dragon with open mouth. It is impossible for anyone
> to appreciate the power of these arms and ships unless he actually sees
> them. Nor is it possible to describe them . . . when our ships are ready,
> and, God willing, move against [the Portuguese], their total destruction will
> be inevitable.[2]

This passage is also questionable: it was certainly not applicable to the
Ottoman situation in the Indian Ocean.

Although historians agree that the Portuguese made a deep
impression upon the Orient, particularly upon leading circles in the

---

1 M A P Meilink-Roelofsz, *Asian trade and European influence in the Indonesian archipelago
  between 1500 and about 1630* (The Hague 1962), 116.
2 Salih Özbaran, 'A Turkish report on the Red Sea and the Portuguese in the Indian
  Ocean (1525)', *Arabian Studies* IV (1978), 83–4.

Muslim world, and that the Ottomans made their presence felt on the shores of Yemen, Basra and Lahsa, we still lack the knowledge necessary to evaluate properly the accounts of the opposing sides. The British Orientalist Denison Ross first drew attention to the problem some seventy years ago, remarking 'how much care and labour will be required before the imperfect and often conflicting accounts of the Franks and the Muslims can be weighed in the balance and reduced to something like historical fidelity'.[3] Since then a number of studies have improved knowledge of Ottoman expansion in the southern seas, of their naval and land organisation along the coasts of Arabia and eastern Africa, and of commercial activities between the Levant and the Indian Ocean. However, this is still far from satisfactory when compared with current knowledge of other aspects of Ottoman history, and of most European history.

What has kept Ottoman activities in the southern lands and seas in obscurity? Silence in Ottoman historiography of the sixteenth century, disinterest among native historians of Iran, Arabia and the African countries in the world about them, and until recently, delay or neglect in using the rich archival material surviving – particularly Portuguese and Ottoman – can no doubt be counted among the factors which have prevented a better understanding of Ottoman southern policy.

Within the last three decades, many historians of the western world – including Braudel, Lane, Magalhaes Godinho, Meilink-Roelofsz, Boxer and Steensgaard[4] – have been interested in Eastern trade, and have shown that trade routes through the Middle East regained their importance in the middle decades of the sixteenth century, after the Portuguese appearance in the Indian Ocean and their blockade of the entrance to the Red Sea and the Persian Gulf in the first quarter of the century. All these historians, though unable to use original sources in Middle Eastern languages, have attempted to counter their inevitably eurocentric view of the subject by looking principally at the

---

3 Denison Ross, 'The Portuguese in India and Arabia between 1517–1538', *Journal of the Royal Asiatic Society* 1922, 18.

4 Fernand Braudel, *The Mediterranean and the Mediterranean world in the age of Philip II* (tr. S Reynolds), v. I (London 1972), 543–70; F C Lane, 'The Mediterranean spice trade: further evidence of its revival in the sixteenth century', in B Pullan (ed.), *Crisis and change in the Venetian economy in the 16th and 17th centuries*, (London 1968), 47–58; Vitorino Magalhaes Godinho, *Os Descobrimentos e a Economia Mundial*, v. I (Lisbon 1965), 111–72; Meilink-Roelofsz, *Asian trade*; and 'The structure of trade in Asia in the sixteenth and seventeenth centuries', in *Mare Luso-Indicum* v. IV (Paris 1980), 1–43; C R Boxer, 'A note on Portuguese reactions to the revival of the Red Sea spice trade and the rise of Acheh, 1540–1600', *Journal of Southeast Asian History* X/3 (1969), 415–28; Niels Steensgaard, *Carracks, caravans and companies: the structural crisis in European–Asian trade in the early 17th century* (Odense 1973).

records of the Levant trading companies and of the minority communities, and have made certain pioneering and theoretical contributions to its study.

Complementing this is the work of Middle East historians – such as İnalcık, Hess, Blackburn and Mandaville[5] – who have attempted to place Ottoman southern policy in a world perspective, and have demonstrated the need for historians of the early modern era to take into consideration the Ottoman view. Lewis, also, placed early emphasis upon the importance of the study of the Ottoman archives for the history of those Arab lands from which the Ottoman authorities had directed their activities into the Indian Ocean.[6]

The contributions of three further, particularly noteworthy, scholars should also be mentioned here, since their work on local sources, both archival and narrative, has made it possible to place the study of the Ottoman past in southern parts of the Middle East within a considerably broader historiographical tradition. The French scholar Aubin, a formidable linguist, demonstrated in various works, but particularly in his *Mare Luso-Indicum*, the range of Portuguese and Persian material relating to the history of the sixteenth-century Indian Ocean.[7] Sergeant's valuable translation from Arabic into English of certain Hadrami chronicles gives wider access to contemporary Arabian views of Ottoman activities in that area.[8] In an appreciative critique of Sergeant's work, Orhonlu pointed out that it showed that 'Turkish administrators in Yemen were much more active in their attempts to establish Ottoman rule on the coastlands of Arabia than Ottoman authorities state'.[9] Orhonlu considered his own work on the Ottoman campaign of 1559 against

5 Halil İnalcık, 'The Ottoman economic mind and aspects of the Ottoman economy', in M A Cook (ed.), *Studies in the economic history of the Middle East* (London 1970), 207–18, and other writings; Andrew Hess, 'The evolution of the Ottoman seaborne empire in the age of the oceanic discoveries, 1453–1525', *American Historical Review* LXXV/7 (Dec. 1970), 1892–1919; also his 'The Ottoman conquest of Egypt (1517) and the beginning of the sixteenth-century world war', *International Journal of Middle East Studies* 4 (1973), 55–76; J Richard Blackburn, 'Arabic and Turkish source materials for the early history of Ottoman Yemen, 945/1538–976/1568', in *Sources for the history of Arabia* pt 2 (Riyad 1979), 197–209; also his 'The collapse of Ottoman authority in Yemen, 968/1560–976/1568', *Die Welt des Islams* XIX/1–4, 119–76; Jon S Mandaville, 'The Ottoman province of al-Hasa in the sixteenth and seventeenth centuries', *Journal of the American Oriental Society* 90/3 (1970), 488 ff.

6 Bernard Lewis, 'The Ottoman archives as a source for the history of the Arab lands', *Journal of the Royal Asiatic Society* 1951, 149.

7 See, e.g., Jean Aubin, 'Quelques remarques sur l'étude de l'Océan Indien au XVIe siècle', *Agrupamento de Estados de Cartografia Antiga* LXXV (Coimbra 1972), 3–13.

8 R B Sergeant, *The Portuguese off the South Arabian coast: Hadrami chronicles*, Oxford 1963.

9 Cengiz Orhonlu, *Tarih Dergisi* XIV/19 (Istanbul 1964), 168–71, review of R B Sergeant, *The Portuguese off the South Arabian coast* (Oxford 1963).

Bahrain to have been severely hampered by the lack of information in these Ottoman narrative sources, the works of major historians such as Celalzade, Peçevi, and Mustafa Ali.[10] He was later the first to make extensive use of Ottoman archival sources, in his study of the Ottoman province of Habeş (Abyssinia).[11]

Profiting from the work of all these historians, it is now possible to give a general, revised picture of the Ottoman presence in the south and south east. However, it must not be forgotten that the great majority of the most authentic sources for this aspect of sixteenth-century Ottoman history – the mass of Portuguese and Ottoman archives – still remain largely untapped.[12] It is therefore not yet possible to establish in any detail the political, military and socio-economic achievement of the Ottomans on such a wide frontier. What follows can only be a preliminary assessment.

II

> ... when the first man from Da Gama's crew reached Calicut he was accosted by two Spanish-speaking Tunisians. They asked him: 'What the devil has brought you here?', to which he replied: 'We have come to seek Christians and spices'[13] – *Vimos buscar cristãos e especiaria.*

Indeed, the Portuguese imperial adventure – *o advento do imperialismo da pimenta*[14] – was achieved with astonishing speed. Their aim, particularly after 1510, when Albuquerque became governor of the Portuguese East, was to close the mouth of the Red Sea, and to seize Hormuz in order to control the entrance to the Persian Gulf. This policy badly affected the economies of the Levant and of some European states. There was no naval power in the Indian Ocean at that time to challenge the European visitors. Mamluk forces were insufficient to repulse the Lusitanians from the area, even though their presence dealt a sudden and severe blow to Egyptian trade. When in 1513 three *naus* (large ships) carried nearly 500,000 kg of spices to Lisbon via the Atlantic,

10 C Orhonlu, '1559 Bahreyn seferine ait bir rapor', *Tarih Dergisi* XVII/22 (1967), 1. For a similar complaint sixty years earlier about Ottoman chronicles on the 1559 campaign, see the Ottoman historian Saffet, 'Bahreyn'de bir vak'a', *Tarih-i Osmani Encümeni Mecmuası* III (Istanbul 1328/1910), 1139.

11 C Orhonlu, *Osmanlı imparatorluğunun güney siyaseti: Habeş eyaleti* (Istanbul 1974).

12 On the Portuguese archives for this topic see esp. Georg Schurhammer, *Die Zeitgenössischen Quellen zur Geschichte Portugiesisch-Asiens* (Rome 1962 (reprint)).

13 C R Boxer, *The Portuguese seaborne empire, 1415–1825* (London 1969), 37.

14 Godinho, *Os Descobrimentos* I, 487.

and in 1517 a further six *naus* took more than 2,000,000 kg, the Egyptian economy was in crisis.[15] By the time the Ottomans succeeded the Mamluks there was already established in the Indian Ocean 'a political sea power with an economic goal supported by a commercial organization'.[16]

What then had brought the Ottomans to the shores of the Ocean? Did Ottoman policy-makers have a master plan, particularly from the economic point of view, towards the south? Can we acknowledge the positive views of İnalcık and Orhonlu that the Istanbul government was aware of political and commercial developments in that wider world?[17] Or should we accept the negative opinion of Akdağ, and Cook's notion that in this respect the Ottomans lacked imagination?[18]

Behind the political and military factors of struggle with the Safavids and Mamluks over eastern and south-eastern Anatolia, there were no doubt considerations of the commercial activities and economic links between Anatolia and her neighbours. From a geographical point of view, Ottoman Anatolia held an excellent position between the eastern Mediterranean and Iran, Iraq and Syria; through it passed caravan routes linking these various areas. Egypt, meanwhile, occupied a very important position between Africa, Asia and Europe for the exchange of commercial items. Its manufactured products such as cotton, cloth and sugar, and also cereals, had markets in various countries.[19] Conversely, material necessary for the Mamluk navy had to come from Anatolia. Timber, iron and pitch were brought first to Alexandria, then taken to Cairo and Suez. Despite the severe rivalry between them before 1517, the Ottomans helped their southern neighbours by providing guns, iron and timber; and Rumi (Anatolian) volunteers were used by the Mamluks on the Portuguese front.[20] After their conquest of Egypt in 1517 the Ottomans assumed the additional responsibility of guardianship of the holy places of Islam in the Hijaz, and found

15 Godinho, *Os Descobrimentos* II, 103; Ibn Iyas, *Journal d'un bourgeois du Caire* (tr. G Wiet, Paris 1955), v. I, 391.
16 Meilink-Roelofsz, *Asian trade*, 119.
17 İnalcık, 'Ottoman economic mind', 212; Orhonlu, *Habeş eyaleti*, 5–6.
18 Mustafa Akdağ, *Türkiye'nin iktisadî ve ictimaî tarihi*, v. II (Ankara 1971), 159; on the Ottomans 'lacking imagination', Michael Cook, paper at conference on 'The age of Süleyman the Magnificent', (Princeton 1987).
19 C H Becker, 'Mısır', *İA* 8, 232 ff.
20 Halil İnalcık, 'Capital formation in the Ottoman empire', *Journal of Economic History* XXIX (1969), 109–10.

themselves appealed to for help against the Portuguese by various Muslim rulers around the Indian Ocean.[21]

In expanding its influence southwards, the Istanbul government had the advantage of powerful guns and firearms. In his 1525 report, Selman Reis, an Ottoman admiral who had previously served in the Mamluk navy and defended successfully the port of Jidda against a potentially disastrous Portuguese attack, emphasised the potential for Ottoman naval success in that area. There were stationed at Jidda eighteen ships and 106 large guns of various types ready to serve 'to capture and hold all the fortresses and ports in India, which were under Portuguese domination'. Selman was not, however, content with his government's policy:

> One cannot escape from painful feelings when one sees these [ships] and arms lying idly at Jidda . . . if they [i.e. the Portuguese] hear that these ships are not operational and lack crews they will inevitably come with a big armada for, apart from these ships, there is nothing to deter these accursed Portuguese.[22]

Economic factors must also be considered. Selman himself, in addition to his military capabilities, appears to have been well aware of commercial movements of grand scale, and it is probable that this aspect of his report also influenced the development of Ottoman southern policy. Despite the effective Portuguese blockade of the Red Sea, a certain – though limited – amount of revenue still came from trading activities, as indicated in an Ottoman account dated 1527–28/933–34.[23] Had they been more active in the Indian Ocean, the Ottomans would undoubtedly have gained greater commercial income. Portuguese and Hadrami sources are full of references about harm caused there by the Portuguese to merchant shipping. A report in the Hadrami *Tarih al-Shihr* that a Portuguese ship arrived at the port of Shihr and challenged an Ottoman vessel containing a cargo of madder in 1528;[24] or Gaspar Correia's story that Portuguese and Muslims became involved in a fight over a large ship carrying pepper to the Red Sea from India in 1529[25]

---

21 For further discussion of the Ottoman political-religious image in the southern ocean, see e.g. L Ribeiro, 'Em torno do primeiro cerco de Diu', *Studia* 13–14 (Lisbon 1964), 102–3; M Y Mughul, *Kanunî devri Osmanlıların Hint Okyanusu politikası ve Osmanlı–Hint Müslümanları münasebetleri, 1517–1538* (Istanbul 1974), 122 ff.; A Reid, 'Sixteenth-century Turkish influence in western Indonesia', *Journal of Southeast Asian History* X/3 (Dec. 1969), 395–44.
22 Özbaran, 'Turkish report', 83.
23 Ö L Barkan, 'H. 933–934 (M. 1527–1528) malî yılına ait bir bütçe', *İktisat Fakültesi Mecmuası* XV/1–4 (Istanbul 1953), 291.
24 Sergeant, *Hadrami chronicles*, 54.
25 G Correia, *Lendas da India* (Lisbon 1858–61), v. III, 302.

– are only two examples of numerous hostile encounters. To be safe on this frontier and to continue expansion to the south, the Ottoman government spent about two million *akçes* building new ships at Suez in 1530.[26] The following year, Pero Caraldo, the Portuguese ambassador in Venice, reported the information that '40 small galleys, 10 big galleys, 20 large and small vessels were being prepared [at Suez]. . . . As soon as the fleet became ready, Süleyman Pasha [the governor of Egypt] would set sail to look for the armada of the King'.[27]

At the end of the year 1531, the Ottoman galleys were almost ready to challenge the Portuguese in the Indian Ocean, to defend Muslim merchants and to help those Muslim states which needed Ottoman assistance. The news reaching Lisbon from India[28] and also from Venice the following year[29] suggested that the Ottomans were determined to push as far as India. This intention could not, however, be put into practice. Considering events on the Mediterranean and Safavid frontiers to be more urgent and important, the Ottoman government ordered these guns and munitions to be transferred from Suez to the Mediterranean, and Süleyman Paşa, governor of Egypt, to join the sultan on his way to Iran.[30] Despite long preparation, the Ottoman naval campaign to the Indian Ocean was thus delayed.

This campaign did, however, take place in 1538, with what proved to be the most powerful fleet the Ottomans ever mustered in the Indian Ocean. Süleyman Paşa, with seventy-two ships under his command, first took Aden and then appeared in Indian waters off Diu. Although this posed a clear threat to the influence of the *Estado da India*, in the event there was no full-scale naval war between the Portuguese oceanic fleet and the Ottoman Mediterranean-type galleys. It is generally held that the Diu campaign had no result to Ottoman credit. This is, however, to overlook the fact that it was during and in consequence of this naval expedition that the Ottoman province of Yemen was established, which later came to play a major role in the development of Ottoman southern policy.[31] A further outcome was that Ottoman technology, particularly that concerning firearms, spread further to

26 Başbakanlık Arşivi, Istanbul [BA]: Kamil Kepeci, Bahriye 5638.
27 Arquivo Nacional da Torre do Tombo, Lisbon: Gaveta 20, Maço 7, Documento 15.
28 L Ribeiro, 'Preâmbulos do primeiro cerco de Diu', *Studia* 10 (1962), 161–3.
29 Archivo General de Simencas, Estados, 1309–34.
30 See A Allouche, *The origins and development of the Ottoman–Safavid conflict (906–962/ 1500–1555)* (Berlin 1983), 104 ff; Şerafettin Turan, 'Süleyman Paşa (Hadım)', *IA* 11, 194.
31 Salih Özbaran, 'Osmanlı imparatorluğu ve Hindistan yolu', *Tarih Dergisi* XXXI (1978), 98–104.

Muslim states around the Indian Ocean.[32] In the 1530s, Ottoman firearms experts seem to have travelled even as far as Atjeh, a Muslim state in Sumatra, where warfare between Atjeh and the Bataks turned in favour of the former only after 'there came to the Tyrant (Ala'addin) 300 Turks, whom he had long expected from the Strait of Mecqua [i.e. the Red Sea], and for them he had sent four vessels laden with pepper'.[33]

The Diu campaign undoubtedly inspired fear in the Portuguese bases, leaving the impression that the Ottomans could come at any time to take their share of the economic revenues of the Ocean, as evidenced by the king of Portugal's instructions to his commanders in the *Estado da India*. The existence of the Suez arsenal and shipyard was always a danger to the Portuguese naval points; a fleet under the command of Dom Estavão da Gama attempted to burn the Ottoman galleys at Suez in 1541, but without success.[34]

Having proved themselves masters of the Red Sea, the Ottomans attempted various ventures in east Africa. Help sent in 1542 to Ahmed ibn Ibrahim, a Muslim leader in conflict with the king of Abyssinia, was particularly significant because of the Ottoman supply of guns and arquebuses.[35] Further evidence of the Ottoman impact appears in a letter of João de Sepulveda from Mozambique, dated 10 August 1542, to the king of Portugal:

> In the past year I wrote telling Your Highness how, on the coast of Malindi, things were going in regard to your service, after the stir caused by the foist of the Rumes [i.e. the Ottomans] that came there and also because there was a strong belief that there was coming that year a great fleet of them to take these fortresses and punish all our friends. . . . At the end of August I arrived in Malindi where the coming of the Rumes was regarded as very certain because they had strongly affirmed it.[36]

However, economic considerations sometimes directed the Ottomans and the Portuguese to make agreements on the southern frontier. The Ottomans wanted the trade routes open and wished to receive pepper and spices from India and the Far East. The Portuguese needed grain from the north. It is known through documents preserved at the Torro

32 See esp. Halil İnalcık, 'The socio-political effects of the diffusion of fire-arms in the Middle East', in V J Parry and M E Yapp (eds), *War, technology and society in the Middle East* (London 1975), 202 ff.
33 See Reid, 'Sixteenth-century Turkish influence in western Indonesia', 401.
34 E Sanceau, 'Uma narrativa de expedição Portugusa de 1541 ao Mar Roxo', *Studia* 9 (1962), 209.
35 Orhonlu, *Habeş eyaleti*, 26–7; Özbaran, 'Hindistan yolu', 103–4.
36 *Documentos sobre os Portugueses em Moçambique e na Africa Central, 1497–1840*, III (1540–1560), Lisbon 1971, 130, 132.

de Tombo in Lisbon, and also from the activities of Duarte Catanho, the Portuguese agent, that in the years after 1538, the two empires exchanged accredited envoys.[37] Although Ottoman demands for safe-conduct for Muslim merchants in the Indian Ocean, and for the Shihr-Aden-Zeila line to mark the frontier between the two rival navies, could not be met in practice by the Portuguese, the middle decades of the sixteenth century did witness the revival of the spice trade through the Levant.

Meanwhile, the Ottomans were making their presence felt upon another route to the Ocean. In 1546, Ayas Paşa, governor of Baghdad, wrote to the Arab ruler of Jezayir in the Shatt al-Arab that he had been ordered by Süleyman 'to go against Basra, to take it, from there to Hormuz and India, and to fight against the Portuguese'.[38] He did indeed take Basra, and established there a new *beylerbeyilik* (province).[39] In the following year, the new Ottoman governor of Basra sent an envoy to the Portuguese *capitão* of Hormuz, requesting the opening of the sea route through the Persian Gulf.[40] In 1548, the Ottomans retook Aden (lost only the previous year) and two years later they occupied the important port of Katif on the west Arabian coast opposite Bahrain. Ottoman influence was thus greatly extended on a wide frontier around the Indian Ocean.[41] In the middle of the sixteenth century it seemed that they were close to mastering the southern seas and lands.

After Diu in 1538, the second and in the event the last major Ottoman campaign in the Indian Ocean occurred in 1552. This time the target was Hormuz, one of the most important places from which the Portuguese controlled maritime traffic to and from the Gulf. This time Piri Bey, a highly-regarded Ottoman admiral and geographer, author of the *Kitab-i bahriye (The book of the seas)*, left Suez with thirty galleys and galleons, taking 850 soldiers on board. He first sacked the city of Muscat and then besieged Hormuz. According to Alvaro de Noronha, the Portuguese governor of Hormuz, the Ottoman attack failed only because 'they were extremely short of munitions, gunpowder and other war materials, a great quantity of which they had lost in a

---

37 See Özbaran, 'Hindistan yolu', and references therein from Arquivo Nacional da Torre do Tombo, Lisbon.
38 Arquivo Nacional da Torre do Tombo, Lisbon: Colecção de São Lourenço IV, fols. 140b–41b.
39 Salih Özbaran, 'XVI yüzyılda Basra körfezi sahillerinde Osmanlılar', *Tarih Dergisi* 25 (1971), 53 ff.
40 Salih Özbaran, 'The Ottoman Turks and the Portuguese in the Persian Gulf, 1534–1581', *Journal of Asian History* 6/1 (1972), 54.
41 Özbaran, 'Hindistan yolu', 120 ff.

galleon which had sunk while passing the strait'.[42] With no allowance made for differences in climate, sea, or style of combat, Piri Bey was held responsible for this failure and later executed. In 1554 his successor, Seydi Ali, another competent Mediterranean seaman, also failed in his mission to the Indian Ocean – this time to bring back Piri Bey's fleet from the Gulf to Suez. The Ottoman Mediterranean-type galleys, equipped with big guns of various types and more suited to coastal warfare, were unable to prevail in open seas in the Indian Ocean, and were either taken by the swifter sailing vessels of the Portuguese, or were wrecked at sea.[43]

III

Although Braudel refers to 'the war between Turkey and Portugal (1560–1563)',[44] the southern seas, unlike the Mediterranean, did not witness further large-scale Ottoman campaigns after 1554. However, this does not mean that naval activities in that area came to an end altogether. The Ottomans did succeed in establishing a land empire on the Arabian and east African shores, which necessarily required a naval presence. The Mamluk port and arsenal at Suez, which the Ottomans inherited with the conquest of Egypt in 1517, played a crucial role in Ottoman southern expansion. Although regular information on the Suez arsenal is lacking, sporadic data may throw some light on the situation.[45]

Selman Reis was the first Ottoman naval commander at Suez, with the title *Mısr kapudanı*, admiral of Egypt. His report of 1525 provides first-hand information on the composition of ships and guns of the Suez fleet stationed at Jidda in that year:

ships (all of the Mediterranean type)
   6 bastards (*baştarde*)
   8 galleys (*kadırga*)
   3 galliots (*kalyate*)
   1 caique (*kayık*)

---

42 Salih Özbaran, 'Two letters of Dom Alvaro de Noronha from Hormuz: Turkish activities along the coast of Arabia', *Tarih Enstitüsü Dergisi* IX (Istanbul 1978), 245.
43 Cengiz Orhonlu, 'Seydi Ali Reis', *Tarih Enstitüsü Dergisi* I (1970), 39–56; Şerafettin Turan, 'Seydi Ali Reis', İA 10, 528–29; Seydi Ali Reis, *Miratü'l-memalik* (Istanbul 1313/1895), 13, for a description of the 1554 battle. On the significance of the different types of vessel, see C M Cipolla, *Guns and sails in the early phase of European expansion, 1400–1700* (London 1965), 102–3.
44 Braudel, *Mediterranean* II, 549.
45 C Orhonlu, 'Hint kaptanlığı ve Piri Reis', *Belleten* XXXIV/134 (1970), 235.

armaments
  7 basilisks (*badaluşka*) for bombarding fortresses
  13 *yantopu*
  57 *zarbozan*
  29 *şayka*
  95 iron guns
  97 falconets
  400 *quintars* of gun powder
  530 copper basilisk cannon balls
  900 copper falconet cannon balls

Naval supplies, such as pitch, sail–cloth, and oars, are also indicated.[46] In addition, there are listed fifty caulkers, twenty carpenters, two ironsmiths, and two sawyers representing the shipbuilding crafts. This constitutes a higher figure for caulkers or carpenters than those given for the principal Ottoman arsenals at Gallipoli in 1518, or Galata (Istanbul) in 1530.[47] The list further includes twenty artillerymen, and 1000 sailors recruited from Anatolia. Selman estimated that in eight years 1,200,000 Egyptian *sultanis* had been spent on the Suez arsenal, while an Ottoman account book for 1530–31/937 gives an official figure of some two million *akçe* assigned for shipbuilding at Suez.[48]

Selman's account of the Ottoman Red Sea fleet may be compared with that of Pero Caraldo, reporting information received in 1531:

> according to a man who had been at Suez and who came here [Venice] from Alexandria, 40 small galleys, 10 big galleys, 20 big (*não*) and 10 small (*fusta*) vessels were being prepared at Suez... 3000 men were working continuously for this purpose. The sultan (*o turquo*) gave orders that sail-cloths, ropes, guns and munitions of war should be sent to Suez. Camels carried all the timber to Suez. In addition 3000 janissaries, oarsmen and others were transferred there... the commander of the fleet would be Hadim Suleyman Pasha (*o governador do Cairo*).[49]

Another Venetian report suggests that Venetian gunners, rowers, carpenters, caulkers and officers were to assist in fitting out the Ottoman fleet.[50]

Though with over seventy ships, the Ottoman Red Sea fleet seemed

46 Özbaran, 'Turkish report', 92.
47 Salih Özbaran, 'Galata tersanesinde gemi yapımcıları, 1529–1530', *Güney-Doğu Avrupa Araştırmaları Dergisi* 8–9 (Istanbul 1980), 97–102.
48 Özbaran, 'Turkish report', 83; BA. Bahriye 5638. The Egyptian *sultani*, Venetian ducat and the Portuguese *cruzado* were of nearly the same value in the sixteenth century.
49 Arquivo Nacional da Torre do Tombo, Lisbon: Gaveta 20, Maço 7, Documento 15.
50 'A particular relation of the expedition of Solyman Pasha from Suez to India against the Portuguese at Diu written by a Venetian officer who was pressed into the Turkish service on that occasion', in Robert Kerr (ed.), *A General History and Collection of Voyages and Travels*, VI (Edinburgh 1824), 257 ff.

large and numerous, its construction, composition and sea-going policy may explain the difficulties it encountered. What was lacking above all was 'a determined policy to train and increase [the small nucleus of competent sailors]'.[51]

Apart from the Suez fleet there was a small squadron based at Mocha, for use in the defence of Aden and Bab al-Mandab, and for the purposes of piracy. From the mid-sixteenth century this naval unit was under the command of the admiral of Mocha. An account for the Ottoman province of Yemen states that in 1561 there were 141 men at Mocha, including sea captains (rüesa), marines (azeban) and riggers (aletçiyan). In the same account the governor (mirliva) Sefer Bey is also entitled kapudan-ı derya-yı Hind, i.e. admiral of the Indian Ocean.[52] This office is particularly interesting from the point of view that its concern was not only within the limits of the Red Sea. Through this naval organisation, the Ottomans claimed the right to interfere in the affairs of the southern ocean, and a chance to share in its rich revenues.

In the Persian Gulf, however, the Ottomans were never able to maintain a large fleet. They did build ships in Basra, materials for which came from some distance. Timber, for example, was brought from the mountains around Maraş in southern Anatolia.[53] The officer in charge of the Basra fleet was known as Lahsa kapudanı, i.e. the captain of vessels stationed on the shores of eastern Arabia (modern al-Ahsa). The function of ships in the latter area was never more than keeping watch on the Portuguese, and sometimes only on local Arab activities.[54] Ottoman administrative control in the Shatt al-Arab region was always beset with difficulties, and required a permanent naval presence to control the marsh Arabs.[55]

IV

Ottoman archival records, in particular the mühimme registers of orders sent from the central government to the governors of Egypt, Yemen, Basra, Lahsa (from 1555) and Habeş, show how the commercial, military and administrative life of this long frontier was regulated. Other

51 S Soucek, paper given at conference on 'The age of Süleyman the Magnificent', Princeton 1987.
52 Topkapı Sarayı Arşivi, Istanbul [TSA]: D. 314.
53 Özbaran, 'Basra körfezi', 60; C Orhonlu-M Işıksal, 'Osmanlı devrinde nehir nakliyatı hakkında araştırmalar: Dicle ve Fırat nehirlerinde nakliyat', Tarih Dergisi XIII/17 (1963), 79.
54 Özbaran, 'Ottoman Turks and the Portuguese', 69.
55 Özbaran, 'Basra körfezi', 63.

useful detail is found in the *rüus* registers (of appointments, honours, etc), and the *maliye* or financial registers of income and expenditure, and of salaries and wages. Although in İnalcık's view, military considerations usually dominated the lengthy process of *beylerbeyilik* formation,[56] in this case economic trends were equally if not more important, and it is with this aspect that the remainder of this survey will deal, with particular reference to the province of Yemen.

In Yemen, as in Egypt, Habeş, Basra and Lahsa, the need to raise money in cash made it inappropriate administratively to introduce the archetypal *timar* system in use in the core areas of Rumeli and Anatolia. The widespread use of tax-farming and the difficulties of control this presented for the central government may to a certain extent explain the uneven nature of Ottoman expansion southwards.[57]

A number of annual accounts surviving from the sixteenth century illustrate some of the principles of Ottoman fiscal organisation in Yemen. Revenues came from the collection, largely by tax farmers, of land tax (*harac-ı arazi*), commodity taxes and dues (*mukataat*), taxes on trade and commerce through ports (*iskeleha*), and other miscellaneous sources. The bulk of the revenue came from the four main sub-provinces (*sancaks*) of Zabid, Taizz, Sana and Sade. In 1561–62/969, 5,795,080 *para*s were collected from Zabid and its dependencies, 4,657,665 of which represented the land tax, and 1,137,415 of which came from the other tax farms. The combined total of port taxes throughout the province – for Mocha, Aden, Salif, Kameran, Jazan, Hüdeyde and Shihr – was 4,273,806 *para*s. Table 1 below shows the proportion of revenue which came from the port taxes in typical years in the middle and at the end of the century.

Table 1. Revenues of the province of Yemen (in para)[58]

year	land tax & tax farms	port taxes	other	total
969 (1561–2)	20,681,358 (65.5%)	4,273,806 (13.5%)	6,775,787 (21%)	31,730,951
1008 (1599–1600)	8,829,288 (54%)	4,845,951 (29%)	2,749,815 (17%)	16,425,054

56 Halil İnalcık, *The Ottoman empire: the classical age, 1300–1600*, trs N Itzkowitz and C H Imber (London 1973), 105.

57 Salih Özbaran, 'Ottoman administration in Arabia in the sixteenth century', *International Journal of Turkish Studies* 3/1 (1984/5), 93–9.

58 TSA, D.314. Halil Sahillioğlu, 'Yemen'in 1599–1600 yılı bütçesi' in *Yusuf Hikmet Bayur'a armağan* (Ankara 1985), 302–10.

Although relatively small in percentage (c. 13.5 per cent) in the 1560s, the significance to the Ottomans of the revenue from port taxes clearly grew throughout the second half of the century, particularly in view of the fall in revenue from other sources within the province. Evidence of the growing importance of Red Sea trade is corroborated by the increase in shipments of pepper reaching Venice from Alexandria (and therefore through the Ottoman-dominated Red Sea) between the years 1560 and 1564: a yearly average of 1,310,454 lbs, in contrast to the c. 1,150,999 lbs per annum which had reached Venice before the Portuguese interference in the early years of the sixteenth century.[59] Portuguese sources are also full of references to the revival of Red Sea trade. Antão de Noronha, then viceroy of Goa, wrote to the Portuguese crown in 1566 that 20,000 or 25,000 *quintals* of pepper were reaching the Red Sea annually in Atjehnese and other Muslim ships, whereas the Portuguese Indiamen were only carrying 10,000 or 12,000 *quintals* around the Cape of Good Hope to Lisbon.[60] This cannot be explained simply by the fact that the Portuguese had changed their policy. It was also the result of improved Ottoman organisation along the Red Sea route.

Revenues were used by the governor for direct payment of all military and administrative expenses within the province. Most had to be spent on the salaries of military/administrative officials (*beys*) and on soldiers' wages. Yemen was thus one of the *saliyaneli* provinces, i.e. 'a province with salaries and wages', as opposed to provinces with *timars*.[61]

Table 2. Expenditure of the province of Yemen (in para)[62]

year	governor's salary	commanders' salaries	wages of govt. officials & soldiers	other	total
969 (1561–2)	1,667,925 (6%)	2,166,639 (8%)	18,479,035 (69%)	4,424,410 (17%)	26,738,009
1008 (1599–1600)	294,390 (c.1%)	2,744,071 (12%)	15,639,609 (68%)	4,337,422 (19%)	23,015,492

In 1561–2/969 expenditure on military and government salaries took up c. 70 per cent of the total revenue of the province. The revenue

59 Lane, 'Mediterranean spice trade', 47.
60 Boxer, 'Note on Portuguese reactions', 419, n.18.
61 Salih Özbaran, 'Some notes on the *salyane* system in the Ottoman empire as organised in Arabia in the sixteenth century', *Osmanlı Araştırmaları* VI (Istanbul 1986), 39–45.
62 TSA, D.314.

remaining after these and other expenses had been met was then remitted to Istanbul as *irsaliye* (lit. 'that which is sent'). This represented the benefit of the province, in financial terms, to the central government. The Yemen accounts for 1561–62/969 show that 2,028,000 *para*s were sent to Istanbul as *irsaliye* in that year.[63] This amounted to 6.4 per cent of total revenue collected. Although in 1595/1004, 110,000 out of a total revenue of 668,479 gold coins (*sikke-i hasene*) was apparently remitted to the capital (16.5 per cent),[64] this was probably an anomaly. By the end of the century it had become normal for the Ottomans to have deficit budgets in Yemen, since the north-west European trading companies had by then struck a decisive blow at Levant trade. One example is the account for 1599–1600/1008, where expenditure on salaries and wages alone, at 18,678,070 *para*s, exceeded by some two million *para*s the total revenue, chiefly as a result of the major decline in collections of land-tax and tax farms. No sum was therefore sent as *irsaliye* that year.[65] Archive documents show that in such cases money to cover the deficit would be transferred from the Egyptian treasury.

With the trend at the end of the century towards regular deficits, the attractions of maintaining a strong Ottoman presence in Yemen must obviously have paled in simple financial terms. In addition, a state of almost permanent conflict with local Zeydi tribes in Yemen made it essential for the Ottomans to maintain a large military force there. By 1635, however, this continual drain on resources, for comparatively little other return, resulted in the Ottoman decision to abandon the province.

The expansion of Ottoman rule to the south as far as Yemen, Habeş, Basra and Lahsa, parallels to some degree the similar territorial expansion to the west, north and east during at least the first half of the sixteenth century. Against the Portuguese, and particularly among the Muslim countries around the Indian Ocean, the Ottomans were able to appear a true imperial power. The attempt by Mustafa Paşa, governor of Lahsa, to take Bahrain in 1559, the exchange of imperial envoys in the years 1562–64, the raids of Ali Bey on Muscat in 1581 and his subsequent attempts to drive out the Portuguese from the coast of Mozambique in 1585 and 1589 – all these made the Ottoman presence felt in the Indian Ocean. Nevertheless, they failed to make as much profit as they had expected out of this expansion. They could not move the Portuguese from the region; neither could they prevent

63 TSA, D.314, fol. 12a.
64 BA, Maliyeden müdevver 7092, 5.
65 See Sahillioğlu, 'Yemen'in 1599–1600 yılı bütçesi', 287–319.

the coming of Dutch and English companies at the end of the sixteenth century to give a new commercial and political colouring to the Indian Ocean.

GÉZA DÁVID

Administration in Ottoman Europe

By 1520 the governmental and administrative system of the Ottomans had already undergone a number of significant developments in the transformation from a semi-nomadic emirate[1] to a strongly centralised military empire with a remarkably efficient redistributive machinery. Various traditions were amalgamated in Ottoman political theory and practice, the most important heritage being undoubtedly the Islamic (within this the Ilkhanid-Seljukid), while several Byzantine institutions were also taken over.[*]

In Süleyman's reign most of Anatolia, certain Arab, and the European provinces were organised within a more or less uniform 'classical' administrative structure,[2] based upon the prebendal *timar* system, one of the prime constituents of Ottoman military organisation. However, the territorial extent of the empire had now reached such a point and encompassed so many different peoples, religions and cultures, that local variations had perforce to be accommodated alongside this standard system. It was also practical to allow the existence of two more kinds of local government, one in south-eastern Anatolia, the other in Egypt, in a part of Arabia and in Abyssinia – systems which remain outside the scope of this survey.

Within the classical Ottoman *timar* system, the *sancakbeyi* was entrusted with the general administration of a larger region, the *sancak*

---

1 The nomadic background of the early Ottoman state was emphasised by Rudi Paul Lindner, *Nomads and Ottomans in medieval Anatolia* (Bloomington, Indiana 1983).

* An Alexander von Humboldt scholarship held in Munich (1990) allowed the opportunity to work on the revised version of this article.

2 Outlined in Halil İnalcık, *The Ottoman empire: the classical age 1300–1600* (London 1973), 104–10. More detailed is the survey by İ Metin Kunt, *The sultan's servants: the transformation of Ottoman provincial government, 1550–1660* (New York 1983), 9–29.

or *liva*, comprising a variable number of *timar*s and *zeamet*s. Although his authority as a military official did not place the *sancakbeyi* in contact with the whole population of his district,[3] he also had a parallel role as a state official with responsibilities affecting all subjects in his *sancak*. It was his duty, among other things, to maintain public order and to enforce capital or other serious punishments.

Alongside the *sancak* revenues distributed to *timar* holders, were several local taxes and duties reserved for the sultan. These were collected by local treasuries at *vilayet* level.[4] The directors of these offices were the provincial *defterdar*s who exercised general control over cash income and expenditure and to whom two department chiefs were subordinated, one dealing with the registration of holdings of higher sums, the other with ordinary *timar*s. The detailed lists and accounts prepared by these officials enable us now to investigate the economic condition of each region.

The representatives of legal administration were the *kadı*s, of whom there could be one or more in a *sancak* depending on its extent. Their role was rather complex and ranged over a variety of matters, including jurisdiction, establishing fixed market prices, dealing with Muslim pious foundations, maintenance of public buildings and roads, provisioning of towns, and supervising various registers and accounts. Occasionally they were also charged with ostensibly military duties such as the levying of auxiliary troops.[5] A *kadı*'s authority extended theoretically over the entire populace of his *kadılık*.

Few concrete descriptions can be found about the spheres of activity in practice of Ottoman provincial officials; even the general descriptions given above have to be deduced mostly from indirect evidence. The patrimonial character of the Ottoman state constitutes the main reason why the duties of the bureaucratic layer were nowhere officially laid down in a written form.[6] As long as these were left unspecified every unfulfilled order or an allegedly missing personal quality could serve as a reason for dismissal or even for capital punishment. To a certain extent

3 Kunt, *Sultan's servants*, 15, 23.
4 Cornell Fleischer, *Bureaucrat and intellectual in the Ottoman empire: the historian Mustafa Ali (1541–1600)* (Princeton 1986), 221, no.14: 'provincial treasuries were first established in the middle of the sixteenth century'. But see Nicoară Beldiceanu, *Le timar dans l'état ottoman (début XIVe-début XVIe siècle)* (Wiesbaden 1980), 44–5, for provincial treasuries in Karaman and Thessaloniki already existing in the late 15th century.
5 Robert Mantran (ed.), *Histoire de l'empire ottoman* (Paris 1989), 209.
6 The very few *kanunname* sections relating to *beylerbeyi*s and *sancakbeyi*s concern their sons' rights to inherit part of their *hasse*s: M Tayyib Gökbilgin, 'Kanûnî Sultan Süleyman'in timar ve zeamet tevcihi ile ilgili fermanları', *Tarih dergisi* XVII (1967), 42–3.

it is still curious that the sultans' decrees were very often addressed in parallel to the *beylerbeyi*s and the *kadı*s without indicating how their collaboration in solving the matter in question was conceived by the central government. Only a thorough analysis of, for instance, all the *ferman*s of Süleyman, preserved mostly in abbreviated versions in the *mühimme* and *ahkam-i maliye defterleri* and in the *kadı sicilleri* (records of the *kadı*s' courts) could give some clue as to the main fields where either the *kadı* or the *beylerbeyi/sancakbeyi* was normally instructed to act.

Due to this lack of definite knowledge about the practical functioning and daily routine of the individual officials in Ottoman Europe,[7] administration will be dealt with here in the broader sense of the term. Our main concern will be to portray those characteristics that were peculiar to the European lands, and to make comparisons between Ottoman Hungary and the Balkans, regional differences which remain mostly untouched by previous research.[8] Further, since archival material from Süleyman's time is not always ample enough to illuminate some of the issues concerned, documents from the later sixteenth century will occasionally be used in relation to issues in the latter part of Süleyman's reign.

THE BALKANS

The process of Ottoman conquest of the Balkans lasted for approximately 125 years, from their first outpost in Europe, the small town of Tzympe (1352), to the occupation of most of Albania in 1478/79 and the final subjugation of Herzegovina in 1483. During this early phase, several of the rapidly established administrative units were named after their previous owners;[9] they were partly ruled by prominent families also of non-Turkish origin (e.g. the Mihaloğulları), coming mostly from Anatolia. These ruling clans were in time replaced by the usual representatives of the central government, and by 1520 the territories south of the Danube had become part of the standard Ottoman administrative system. The whole of the Balkans, including Greece, originally

---

7 On the activity of Turkish law-courts and *kadı*s generally, see Uriel Heyd, *Studies in old Ottoman criminal law*, ed. V L Ménage (Oxford 1973), 208–311.

8 For an exception, see Klára Hegyi, 'La province hongroise dans l'empire ottoman', *Acta historica* 33 (1987), 209–15. A general description of the Balkans is offered in Bistra A Cvetkova, *Les institutions ottomanes en Europe* (Wiesbaden 1978).

9 Examples in Halil İnalcık, 'Stefan Duşan'dan Osmanlı imparatorluğuna: XV asırda Rumeli'de hlristiyan sipahiler ve menşeleri', in *Fuad Köprülü armağanı* (Istanbul 1953), 215, 225; and his *Fatih devri üzerinde tetkikler ve vesikalar* I (Ankara 1954), 159.

comprised a single *beylerbeyilik*, that of Rumeli.[10] In 1534 certain islands and coastal regions, including the *sancak* of Gelibolu (Gallipoli), the original seat of the commander of the navy, were removed to create a new province for Hayreddin Paşa, newly appointed Ottoman grand admiral, and henceforth remained separate.[11] A few areas were added to the province of Rumeli after 1534, but a basic restructuring was implemented only in 1580 when the *vilayet* of Bosna (Bosnia) was created out of certain western parts of Rumeli.[12]

In their Asian territories, whatever administrative variations they met with, the Ottomans established themselves largely in areas which had already been under Muslim overlordship for shorter or longer periods. In Europe, however, they had a more complex task to solve. They were confronted by a society which had previously had no direct contacts with Islam and was organised around the different laws, habits, customs and world view of Christianity. Pragmatism led to compromise. On the one hand, they introduced those institutions that were of elementary importance, such as the *timar* system, the *kadılıks*, and, in time, the provincial treasuries. On the other hand, they instinctively realised that to attempt a complete abrogation of all local usages and institutions would fail, and that it would be wiser merely to restrict their influence. Thus within a seemingly unified administrative complex, many small details could differ depending on the geographical position, the cultural background, the strength of traditions, and the length of occupation of any given smaller or larger entity.

Noteworthy are those institutions that were preserved by the Ottomans in the Balkans. A characteristic feature of their policy was not to interfere too much with the religious life of the local population, and they were far from eager to close down all Christian churches. Although Mehmed II had transformed the most important Byzantine church, the Hagia Sophia, into a mosque, he had also accepted a new patriarch for the Orthodox population of Istanbul and the Greeks, leaving them the second most venerated church, the Holy Apostles, as a cathedral.[13] In

---

10 For lists of the *sancaks* belonging to Rumeli in the 1520s, see M Tayyib Gökbilgin, 'Kanuni sultan Süleyman devri başlarında Rumeli eyaleti, livaları, şehir ve kasabaları', *Belleten* XX (1956), 251–61; İ Metin Kunt, *Sancaktan eyalete: 1550–1650 arasında Osmanlı ümerası ve il idaresi* (İstanbul 1978), 125–7.

11 Cf. A Galotta, 'Kapudan Pasha', *EI²*, iv, 1157.

12 Outside the boundaries of Rumeli lay the Ottoman vassal states of Dubrovnik, Moldavia, and Wallachia. See below, p. 88.

13 Steven Runciman, *The great church in captivity: a study of the patriarchate of Constantinople from the eve of the Turkish conquest to the Greek war of independence* (Cambridge 1968), 169–70. Some months later, however, the new patriarch Gennadios was allowed to transfer his seat to the Pammacaristos convent in a district fully populated by Greeks (Runciman, *Great church*, 184–5).

other parts of Europe, confiscation of Christian places of worship was also limited to a few isolated cases. Most often it occurred as a kind of punishment in towns taken by force of arms, but even in such cases several churches were left in the hands of the original population, unless they had fled completely. Further, the restoration of sacred edifices was also usually permitted, on condition that the buildings were not enlarged. More surprisingly, the erection of quite a number of completely new churches and monasteries was also allowed, or at least not hindered, in various Balkan regions, particularly in Bulgaria (near Sofia and the Rhodope mountains) and Serbia (the Fruška Gora monasteries). Christian religious art, above all wall-painting, produced several masterpieces during the centuries of Ottoman rule.[14] Church leaders were retained almost everywhere and their rights of taxation and jurisdiction in religious and civil matters recognised,[15] even if there were temporary lapses or the starting dates of Ottoman acceptance of some of these rights are not known.

On the other hand, it would be an exaggeration to speak here of religious toleration in the modern sense, particularly on the level of official or theoretical considerations. Non-Muslim subjects of the state were regarded as inferior citizens who had to wear different garments, refrain from using bells or worshipping their God loudly, who could not have a church in the vicinity of a mosque, and who were not equal before the *kadı*.[16] These restrictions, however, were felt mainly by Christians and Jews in Istanbul and certain other urban areas; the rural populations were almost untouched by them.

Another aspect of Ottoman policy was the settling of Muslim groups in Rumeli. Their most prominent representatives were the religious

14 This section is indebted to Machiel Kiel's *Art and society of Bulgaria in the Turkish period: a sketch of the economic, juridical and artistic preconditions of Bulgarian post-Byzantine art and its place in the development of the art of the Christian Balkans, 1360/70–1700* (Assen/Maastricht 1985), 167–205. For hundreds of Orthodox monasteries and churches in the patriarchate of İpek/Peć in the 16th century, see Olga Zirojević, *Crkve i monastiri na području Pećke Patrijaršije do 1683. godine* (Belgrade 1984), 39–207.

15 See, *inter alia*, Ladislas Hadrovics, *Le peuple serbe et son église sous la domination turque* (Paris 1947), 53–72; Josef Kabrda, *Le système fiscal de l'église orthodoxe dans l'empire ottoman* (Brno 1969); Branislav Djurdjev, 'The Serbian church in the history of the Serbian nation under Ottoman rule (till 1557)' in Jaroslav Cesar (ed.), *Ottoman rule in Middle Europe and Balkan[s] in the 16th and 17th centuries* (Prague 1978), 288–304; N J Pantazopoulos, *Church and law in the Balkan peninsula during Ottoman rule* (Thessaloniki 1967).

16 Cf. Karl Binswanger, *Untersuchungen zum Status der Nichtmuslime im Osmanischen Reich des 16. Jahrhunderts mit einer Neudefinition des Begriffes 'Ḏimma'* (Munich 1977).

elements, mainly dervishes, who founded convents in various places.[17] Soldiers also appeared in large numbers. Ordinary people – among them merchants and semi-nomads – arrived, some willingly, some within the framework of forced or state-initiated population transfer.[18] On the whole, however, Turkish infiltration was limited, since territorial acquisitions were larger than the demographic potentials of the conquering power.

By the time of Süleyman, we find a considerable Muslim population in the Balkans. Within an approximate total of five million inhabitants, the number of Muslims was about one million.[19] The question is: what was the ratio of 'original' Muslims as opposed to converts? Research has concentrated mainly on towns, gaining some ratios which are astonishingly high. About Tirnovo we learn that out of its 231 Muslims, 76 (33 per cent) were converts around 1500.[20] According to a more comprehensive survey, out of 9426 Muslim heads of families, 3310 (35 per cent) belonged to the same group in 24 towns of Macedonia in the period 1569–80, the highest value being that of Skopje with 701 apostates out of 1551 Muslims (45 per cent).[21] Several examples could be cited similar to that of Bitola, where in 1545 a quarter of its 123 Muslims were former Christians.[22]

Towns, however, are not really representative as far as the rate of conversion is concerned, partly because urban centres have always been more cosmopolitan, and in this case supported concentrations of Ottoman soldiers and tradesmen. It can also be assumed that many converts moved to towns from rural areas. The situation in villages therefore needs to be investigated also. This has been done so far only for those

---

17 Ö. L. Barkan, 'Osmanlı imparatorluğunda bir iskân ve kolonizasyon metodu olarak vakıflar ve temlikler. I. İstilâ devirlerinin kolonizatör Türk dervişleri ve zâviyeler', *Vakıflar dergisi* II (1942), 279–386.

18 M. Tayyib Gökbilgin, *Rumeli'de yürükler, Tatarlar ve evlâd-i fâtihân* (Istanbul 1957); Ö L Barkan, 'Osmanlı imparatorluğunda bir iskân ve kolonizasyon metodu olarak sürgünler' (İstanbul Üniversitesi İktisat Fakültesi mecmuası XI (1949–50), 524–69, XIII (1951–52), 56–78, XV (1953–54), 209–37. Barkan's hypothesis that it was state policy to resettle various groups from Anatolia to Rumeli remains to be fully tested.

19 Ö L Barkan, 'Essai sur les données statistiques des registres de recensement dans l'empire ottoman aux XVe et XVIe siècles', *Journal of the economic and social history of the Orient* I (1958), 9–36, esp. 32.

20 S Dimitrov, 'Za priemstvenostta v razvitieto na balkanskite gradove prez XV-XVI vek', *Balkanistika* 2 (1988), 13–14.

21 M Sokoloski, 'Aperçu sur l'évolution de certaines villes plus importantes de la partie méridionale des Balkans au XVe et au XVIe siècles', *Association internationale d'études du sud-est Européen, Bulletin* XII/1 (1974), 88.

22 Cvetkova, *Institutions ottomanes*, 72.

territories of Bosnia where Islamisation had been the most widespread.[23] Much lower values can be gained for the originally Christian villages of the *sancak* of Köstendil.[24] Such variation and uncertainty render any estimate of the ratio of converts extremely hazardous on present findings.[25]

What factors encouraged conversion? At one level, Islam attracted certain people simply because it was the religion of the powerful conqueror. There were also similarities between Bogomilism and Islam which induced others, mainly in Bosnia, to accept the Muslim faith (rather than Catholicism, which was also seeking converts).[26] The desire to protect family or community could also lead to conversion, albeit superficial.[27] There were also economic reasons. The Ottomans some-times granted tax exemptions, partial or full, for converts at least for short, unspecified periods (although few cases of this kind are documented),[28] and in view of the gradually decreasing number of Christian *timar* holders,[29] it must be assumed that the desire to maintain a position of local wealth and authority induced conversion at this level too.

Beside the comparatively light restraint on religious freedom, another factor enabling the original population to maintain a certain integrity was the preservation of a lower 'national' administrative stratum over

---

23 A Handžić, 'O islamizaciji u sjeveroistočnoj Bosni u XV i XVI vijeku', *Prilozi za orijentalnu filologiju* XVI–XVII (1966–67), 5–45.

24 *Turski dokumenti za istorijata na makedonskiot narod: Opširni popisni defteri od XVI vek za Kjustendilskiot sandžak* V/2 (trs M Sokoloski, Skopje 1980), 27–65, 77–286, gives the ratio of village Muslims as, e.g., 8.4 per cent in Kratovo *nahiye* and 5.5 per cent in Štip *nahiye* in 1570.

25 S Vryonis, 'Religious changes and patterns in the Balkans, 14th–16th centuries' in H Birnbaum and S Vryonis (eds), *Aspects of the Balkans: continuity and change* (The Hague/Paris 1972), 151–76, suggests that c.1520 around half those registered as Muslim (c.100,000 households) had originally been Christian. When contrasted with a *cizye* register for 1488/89 showing only 255 new converts, this implies a sus-piciously high ten-fold increase per annum in the conversion rate over the 30 years to 1520. Cf. Ö L Barkan, '894 (1488/1489) yılı cizyesinin tahsilâtına ait muhasebe bilançoları, *Belgeler* I (1964), 1–117, esp. 12, n.40.

26 Smail Balić, 'Der Islam zwischen Donau und Adria (sein Werden und Wesen)', *Anatolica* I (1967), 93–104. Srećko M Džaja, *Die 'bosnische Kirche' und das Islamisie-rungsproblem Bosniens und der Herzegowina in den Forschungen nach dem zweiten Weltkrieg* (Munich 1978), 99 and *passim*, is sceptical about the continuity of Bogomilism until the Islamic era. This issue again shows how little is known about the pre-Ottoman Balkans, and the consequent difficulty in formulating general views.

27 Cf. V L Ménage, 'The Islamization of Anatolia', in N Levtzion (ed.), *Conversion to Islam* (New York/London 1979), 64, including other factors leading to conversion.

28 Heath W Lowry, 'Changes in fifteenth-century Ottoman peasant taxation: the case of Radilofo' in A Bryer and H Lowry (eds), *Continuity and change in late Byzantine and early Ottoman society* (Birmingham/Dumbarton Oaks 1986), 29.

29 Cf. İnalcık, 'Stefan Dušan'dan Osmanlı imparatorluğuna', *passim*.

the larger masses. These *knezes* and *primikurs* had no easy task, since essentially they served the conqueror's interests as opposed to those of their own people. Moreover, their posts were hereditary (except for Bulgaria), which tended to make the holders rather antipathetic in the eyes of the common tax-payer. They were nevertheless valued as a continuation of pre-Ottoman local institutions, and it was due partly to this, and partly to rural conservatism, that a kind of self-government of village communities survived in the Balkans,[30] especially in moun-tainous regions. The special administrative measures taken against the Bulgarian Vlachs also show the diversity of methods the Ottomans were ready to follow when dealing with social groups at different levels of development or activity.[31]

Another interesting peculiarity is the existence of irregular local military contingents, *derbendcis* charged with the guarding of passes, and *voynuks* and *martoloses* performing other military services. These were all generally Christians,[32] and had their own leaders, with the same designations as the village principals. These non-Muslim military elements were sometimes more numerous in a *sancak* than the Muslim soldiers themselves. How far they might have succeeded in open revolt against the Ottomans is a moot point, since no serious anti-Ottoman movements can be observed among these Christian auxiliary troops in the sixteenth century.[33] Their loyalty can be partly explained by the fact that they received significant tax exemptions and often a piece of arable land (*baştina*) for life.

Another area where many earlier practices were almost everywhere retained was taxation. Ottoman *kanunnames* (collections of legal texts) for the European *sancaks* occasionally list taxes with non-Ottoman names, although these are not necessarily the most important ones. Some were connected with wine, definitely not a typical Muslim

30 See e.g. Elena Grozdanova, *Bălgarskata selska obština prez XV-XVIII vek* (Sofia 1979); Klára Hegyi, 'A törökök berendezkedése meghódított országaikban', *Történelmi szemle* (1981/3), 395–6.

31 Cvetkova, *Institutions ottomanes*, 62–3.

32 On the *derbendcis*, see Aleksandar Stojanovski, *Dervendžistvoto vo Makedonija* (Skopje 1974); on the *martoloses*, Milan Vasić, *Martolosi u jogoslovenskim zemljama pod turskom vladavinom* (Sarajevo 1967); on the *voynuks*, Yavuz Ercan, *Osmanlı imparatorluğunda Bulgarlar ve voynuklar* (Ankara 1986). For further privileged groups performing special services for the Ottomans, see Milan Vasić, 'Social structure of Yugoslav countries under Ottoman rule till the end of the 17th century' in Cesar (ed.), *Ottoman rule in middle Europe and Balkans*, 57–66. Cf. also Kiel, *Art and society of Bulgaria*, 74–86, 93–101.

33 Available literature gives little hard evidence of major peasant risings in Süleyman's time; vague references occur, e.g., 'running revolt round Mariovo and Prilep in 1564–5', Paul Coles' *The Ottoman impact on Europe* (London 1968), 115.

product. *Resm-i poçepina*, for instance, was a tax paid for tapping the barrels brought from another locality,[34] and almost certainly had a pre-Ottoman origin. Similarly, the *monopoliye* tax[35] allowed the landlord (usually the treasury or a *timar* holder) to sell his own, locally-produced wine, received as tax from the peasants, for a period of two months or seventy days, during which no one else was permitted to put wine on the market. Another remnant of pre-Ottoman times was the so-called *resm-i bojik*, or 'Christmas tax', concerned with the slaughtering of pigs before that feast. Ottoman sources indicate its existence mainly in Bulgaria, from Silistre to Sofia and Vidin,[36] but also along the former border between Hungary and Serbia, in the *sancak* of Sirem.[37] Considering that Islam neither observes Christmas nor accepts pork in the diet, the preservation of this tax is worthy of note. A modern totalitarian state would have banned both swine-keeping and the worship of a foreign God. For the Ottomans, however, it became a source of revenue, not spectacular, but easily recoverable, since it was an age-old practice and no one thought of disputing it.

HUNGARY

Ottoman progress in Hungary began with the fall of the key fortress of Belgrade in 1521, but it was only after twenty years and a series of complicated political events that the first Ottoman province was created, at Buda in 1541.[38] Buda seems initially to have been a remote outpost whose influence in the surrounding area was particularly fragile. This is evident from a list of *hasse*s accumulated by the first two governors of Buda and dated 1542.[39] Remarkably, the nearest settlements they

---

34 So far this has been attested on Hungarian territories only, despite the alien nature of the term; see G Dávid *A Simontornyai szandzsák a 16. században* (Budapest 1982), 95.

35 This was widespread throughout the Balkans, appearing in *kanunname*s of, e.g., Gelibolu, Niğbolu, Silistre, Tyrhala, İskenderiye (cf. Ö L Barkan, *XV ve XVI ıncı asırlarda Osmanlı imparatorluğunda ziraî ekonominin hukukî ve malî esasları. I Kanunlar*, Istanbul 1943, 236, 270, 283, 290, 291 resp.), Izvornik, Karadağ and Dukagin (cf. *Kanuni i kanun-name za bosanski, hercegovački, zvornički, kliški, crnogorski i skadarski sandžak*, Saopštavajn B Đurađev *et al.* (Sarajevo 1957), 106, 158, 174 resp.).

36 For Silistre and Sofia, see Barkan, *Ziraî ekonominin hukukî ve malî esasları*, 285, 252; for Vidin, cf. Dušanka Bojanić–Lukač, *Vidin i vidinskijat sandžak prez 15–16 vek. Dokumenti ot arhivite na Carigrad i Ankara* (Sofia 1975), 164, 182.

37 Bruce W McGowan, *Sirem sancağı mufassal tahrir defteri* (Ankara 1983), 2, and *passim*.

38 An outstanding new synthesis of this period is offered by Pál Fodor, 'Ottoman policy towards Hungary, 1520–1541', *Acta Orientalia Hungarica* 45/2–3 (1991), 271–345.

39 Başbakanlık Arşivi, İstanbul [BA], Maliye defteri 34, ff. 635v-40r.

possessed were at a distance of more than 150 miles. Bali Paşa's[40] annual income of over one million *akçe* came from the revenues of more than 450 villages scattered throughout an area covered by the *sancak*s of Pojega, Semendre, Vidin, İzvornik and Alaca Hisar. This huge sum was put together from the former possessions of no less than seventeen different *timar* holders, in addition to the existing possessions of the *beylerbeyi*. The improvisation of such financial arrangements shows clearly how unprepared the treasury was for the creation of the new *vilayet*, and thus that, in this case, political decisions did not necessarily harmonise with actual fiscal possibilities.[41] In other words, conquest was more important than any other consideration.

Compare this with data on the income of the *paşa* of Buda for 1546.[42] These are now included in a regular register, an *icmal* or *timar defteri*, reflecting a much more consolidated situation. In the space of about four years, the Ottomans had succeeded in obtaining large territories and were able to give the *beylerbeyi* quite a number of villages and seven towns in the *sancak* of Buda itself (of which only Buda, Óbuda and Pest, the three central places remained in their hands for the rest of the century),[43] to which others from more remote administrative units were added.

The territories conquered by 1546 underwent considerable change later, indicating that the borders of *sancak*s remained flexible. Significant redistribution was not rare,[44] but this was due only partly to new occupations. There were additional military and economic factors. The province of Buda, being the seat of the *beylerbeyi*, had to be extensive, and incorporated smaller or larger parts of eight former Hungarian counties. In other areas, particularly in western and northern Hungary, almost every castle of any importance became the centre of a *sancak*. However, these administrative units were sometimes so small that, in

---

40 For short biographies of the *paşa*s of Buda, see Antal Gévay, *A' budai pasák* (Bécs 1841). Bali Paşa is mentioned on p. 5 (no. 2), but erroneously identified with Küçük Bali Paşa (d. 1526/7). Cf. Hubert Neumann, 'Türkische Urkunden zur Geschichte Ungarns und Polens', *Der Islam* VIII (1918), 122.

41 Similar difficulties emerged when other officials of the *vilayet* centre were appointed, or when Bali Paşa's own men received *timar*s (cf. BA, Maliye defteri 34, ff. 641r, 684r, 688r, 689r, 697r, 698r).

42 BA, Tapu defteri 1044, 9–11. Most of the pertinent data were published by Gyula Káldy-Nagy, *Kanuni devri Budin tahrir defteri (1546–1562)* (Ankara 1971), *passim*.

43 Gyula Káldy-Nagy, *A Budai szandzsák 1546–1590. évi összeírásai. Demográfiai és gazdaságtörténeti adatok* (Budapest 1985), 158, 464, 492 resp.

44 E.g., 91 villages and *mezra'a*s were transferred to the *sancak* of Simontornya from Mohács between 1552 and 1563, while Anyavár *nahiye* was transferred from Simontornya to Szekszárd; cf. Dávid, *A Simontornyai szandzsák*, 18. Koppány was first a *nahiye* of Mohács and only later, by 1552, made the centre of a separate *sancak* (BA, Tapu defterleri 441, 412).

spite of the relatively dense population, the total revenue from taxation hardly exceeded 200,000 *akçe*, the minimum granted to a *sancakbeyi* on European territory at that time. The flexibility of the *sancak* boundaries suggests that at this level the Ottomans abandoned their earlier practice of retaining the territories of the old administrative units and naming them after their previous ruling families. While it is true that the *nahiye* boundaries occasionally followed the ancient Hungarian county frontiers,[45] this was not typical; no such correlation can be demonstrated in the *sancaks* of central and western Hungary.[46]

Transylvania and some counties east of the river Tisza were left by Süleyman in 1541 in the hands of John Sigismund, minor son of the deceased king of Hungary, John I of Szapolya, and his mother. Within these territories, the Ottomans initially made a distinction between 'Erdel' and 'the *sancak* of Petrovity'.[47] This suggests either that they envisaged developing two separate administrative units here, or that they made a distinction according to the existing power relations between the prince's tutor, George Martinuzzi, and the queen's main advisor, Peter Petrovics. The latter was also commander-in-chief of the southern confines, and the area under his control was the later Banat. Within a few years, a significant part of his holdings was attached to the *beylerbeyilik* of Temesvár (captured and made a *vilayet* centre in 1552), while the rest was added to Transylvania which became an Ottoman vassal state.[48]

Only by the treaty of Edirne of 1568 did the boundaries of the two Hungarian provinces of Buda and Temesvár become more or less stable. In spite of continuous skirmishing and the loss of certain fortifications on both sides, they remained so until the 'long war' of 1593–1606. A provincial appointment register for 1568–74 shows the *vilayet* of Buda

---

45 As suggested by Tibor Halasi-Kun for south-east Hungary in his 'Ottoman toponymic data and medieval boundaries in southeastern Hungary', in J M Bak and B K Király (eds), *From Hunyadi to Rákóczi: war and society in late medieval and early modern Hungary* (Brooklyn 1982), 243–50. However, the 6 maps accompanying this article appear insufficiently convincing, since relevant data from Hungarian sources are not shown in parallel.

46 See n. 44 above. Also, at different periods during the 16th century, the county of Tolna was shared among four *sancaks* (Simontornya, Szekszárd, Buda, and Mohács). Within the *sancak* of Simontornya, the *nahiye* of Endréd consisted of places mainly in Somogy, but also some further localities from Veszprém, Tolna and Fejér (cf. Dávid, *A Simontornyai szandzsák*, 137–42).

47 Mihnea Berindei and Gilles Veinstein, *L'empire ottoman et les pays roumains, 1544–1545: études et documents* (Paris/Cambridge 1987), 27–40.

48 Cf. B Köpeczi *et al* (eds), *Erdély története I. A kezdetektől 1606-ig* (Budapest 1986), 417–36.

containing twenty *sancak*s,[49] whilst that of Temesvár comprised only eight.[50]

An almost unbroken set of data can be assembled for the governors of the *sancak*s of Buda and partly for those of Temesvár. Material from two administrative units[51] confirms the principal tendencies already established for the empire as a whole in the period 1568–88,[52] namely that terms of office were quite short (24–28 months) and that *sancakbeyi*s were mostly transferred from and to nearby places. There was a certain hierarchy within the *sancak*s of the *vilayet* of Buda depending on the sums normally assignable to their governors. Beside Buda, the largest and wealthiest *sancak*, five other *sancak*s belonged to the rich category: Szendrő, Pécs, Szeged, Szigetvár, and Szolnok. *Bey*s nominated to these units generally received a revenue above 400,000 *akçe*, in comparison to 200,000 *akçe* and upward for the remaining *sancak*s. Where, as often happened, a *sancak* with appropriate revenue could not be found for a senior *sancakbeyi*, he would be appointed to a position of lesser value but with the addition of revenues from elsewhere.[53] Such reapportionment became more difficult as borders stabilised and, with increasing numbers of *sancakbeyi*s to accommodate, many were obliged to accept posts with less revenue than was their due officially.[54]

To obtain a new *timar* or an increase of existing income, a recommendation was necessary from a local military leader, usually the *alaybeyi*, as second-in-command within the *sancak* hierarchy.[55] In sixteenth-century Hungary, however, practice differed, and presentations

49 I.e., Buda/Budun, Szendrő/Semendre, İzvornik, Vulçitrin, Pozsega/Pojega, Pécs/ Peçuy, Székesfehérvár/İstolni Belgrad, Esztergom/Östörgon, Szeged/Segedin, Szerém/Sirem, Simontornya/Şimontorna, Koppány/Kopan, Fülek/Filek, Szekszárd/ Seksar, Szigetvár/Sigetvar, Szécsény/Siçen, Nógrád/Novigrad, Szolnok/Solnik, Szekcső/Sekçöy; see BA, Maliye defteri 563, 46–56. Cf. Kunt, *Sancaktan eyalete*, 134–5.

50 I.e., Temesvár/Temeşvar, Lippa/Lipova, Vidin, Alaca Hisar, Csanád/Çanad, Arad with Gyula/Göle, Modava, Pankota; cf. Kunt, *Sancaktan eyalete*, 135–6.

51 I.e., Simontornya (Dávid, *A Simontornyai szandzsák*, 27–30); and Gyula (Géza Dávid, 'The *Sancakbegis* of Arad and Gyula', *Acta Orientalia Hungarica* XLVI (1992/93), 143–62.

52 Kunt, *Sultan's servants*, 57–76.

53 E.g., in Dec 1575, Ali, *bey* of Esztergom, received only 324,263 *akçe* of an annual income of 426,802 *akçe* from his own *sancak*. The remainder came from the *sancak*s of Szendrő, Szeged and Pozsega, that from Szeged, at least, having been in his possession earlier. Cf. BA, Ruznamçe 42, part Esztergom, 16–18.

54 E.g., Ferhad Bey, governor of Szeged, entitled to 530,000 *akçe* in 1584, but in receipt of only 340,000; BA, Kepeci 325, 500–1.

55 H A R Gibb and H Bowen, *Islamic society and the west*, I (Oxford 1950), 51, 146–7; Halil İnalcık, 'Osmanlı bürokrasisinde aklâm ve muâmelât', *Osmanlı araştırmaları* I (1980), 2 (also for *beylerbeyi* or *serdar* submitting collective lists of this kind). Examples for non-Hungarian territories, see Klaus Röhrborn, *Untersuchungen zur osmanischen Verwaltungsgeschichte* (Berlin/New York 1973), 34, n.26.

were written mainly by the *sancakbeyi*s, occasionally by the *beylerbeyi*.[56] The *sancakbeyi*'s role thus increased in importance in this respect, at the expense of the *alaybeyi*. It should also be noted that such recommendations were often sent by another governor than that of the province wherein the *timar* or *zeamet* was granted. By this method, the possibility that a *sancakbeyi* could gather around himself a group of obligated clients diminished, in line with central state policy.[57]

REGIONAL ADMINISTRATIVE VARIATIONS

The fact that in former Hungarian lands there were both directly-governed regions and a vassal state facilitates comparisons of Ottoman administration in a wider sense with the Balkan provinces on the one hand, and with the Rumanian principalities on the other.

In contrast to the situation in the Balkans, in the directly-governed Hungarian provinces there are very few non-Muslims listed as *timar*-holders. Some of those who were belonged, in fact, to other ethnic groups – Slavs or Jews[58] – and as such probably came with the Ottomans. Further, few of the genuine Hungarian *timar*-holders had held fiefs earlier. Rather, they appear to have been mainly village or town judges who were rewarded for their services to the Ottoman state.[59] Such favour was infrequent and temporary; later Hungarian judges were merely exempted from the *cizye* (poll tax) and *resm-i kapu* (gate tax).[60] Contrary to their Balkan counterparts, the *knez*es and *primikur*s, their position was not hereditary, and they appear not to have played such an important role as mediators.

In addition to the Hungarian judges, the Ottomans also installed their own *kadı*s throughout their Hungarian province. These were

56 Evidenced by innumerable *ruznamçe* [daybook] entries, and a treatise, *'Ilm-i muhasebe* ('The science of book-keeping') written in Buda in 1587 (Nationalbibliothek, Vienna, Türk. Mss. Flügel 1999).

57 Several registers of recommendation survive, listing *sipahi*s and fortress troops, and their place of service. E.g. BA, Mühimme defteri 25, p. 144, no. 1505; Kepeci 5000 (unpaginated); Kepeci 342, ff 18v–19r (dated 1574/75, 1583, and 1594 resp.).

58 Antal Velics and Ernő Kammerer, *Magyarországi török kincstári defterek I: 1546–1635* (Budapest 1886), xxvi; Káldy-Nagy, *Kanuni devri Budin*, 34, (n.23), 56 (n.60), 63, (n.73) (all referring to the same person, Yovan Zabrag); 66 (n.89), 68 (n.97) (both refer to Nikola veled-i Yurin).

59 E.g. the judge of Buda, Péter Nagy, was a *timar* holder in 1547 (cf. L Fekete, 'Buda and Pest under Turkish rule', *Studia Turco-Hungarica* III (Budapest 1976), 27. For the rare example of a Hungarian fief-holder preserving his status, see BA, Mühimme defteri 1, p. 272 (252), no. 1542.

60 An unusual case is that of György Kuti, the judge from Tolna who possessed a *timar* for almost 25 years (cf. Dávid, *A Simontornyai szandzsák*, 79–81).

usually active mainly in the *sancak* centres, where the small Muslim population was concentrated and where they could be supported by military force if necessary. However, there were three important towns (Jászberény, Kecskemét and Ráckeve) with no Muslim inhabitants, where, as in the Balkans, *kadılıks* were created exclusively for the Christian, civil, population. Although the *kadıs* of these three towns appear to have done little other than supervise the continuing Hungarian courts and collect taxes and dues, the fact of their existence suggests that they might have had a more substantial role in local affairs had the Ottomans been able to secure a final victory over the Habsburgs. In the event, these *kadılıks* were terminated in the early seventeenth century.[61] This marked a turning point in Ottoman policy: with the withdrawal from the purely civil administration of the Christian population, they took a step backwards in the implementation of their original aim.

Most of the leading Hungarian landlords had fled to the Habsburg-dominated portion of the country following the Ottoman conquest; only the less wealthy remained. The departure of these nobles had far-reaching consequences. Since they never accepted the Ottoman presence, they continued to claim (in theory, at least) their former serfs' taxes and services.[62] Whether they could actually collect any dues is another question. There were undoubtedly certain regions – the farther from the borders the more in number – where it was practically impossible to realise their claims. There were nevertheless areas, some well behind the Ottoman military line, where the peasants accepted the dues as lawful and paid taxes (symbolic, perhaps) to their former Hungarian landlords or their successors. A partial explanation for this may be the element of reassurance it gave the peasantry that they had patrons on the other side of the frontier who would, they hoped, bring forces to bear to expel the Ottomans. It is certain, however, that there was always a border zone where double taxation was heavy, and that this was borne in addition to the ravages of life on a military frontier. Ottoman official protestations against Hungarian taxes were of no avail, although there is evidence that local commanders from each side made specific agreements to try to prevent the exploitation of their own subjects.

In contrast to Rumeli, and perhaps for security reasons, no irregular

61 Klára Hegyi, *Egy világbirodalom végvidékén* (Budapest 1976), 122–4.
62 Ferenc Szakály, *Magyar adóztatás a török hódoltságban* (Budapest 1981), *passim.*

military forces were recruited in Hungary; though some non-Muslim *martolos*es served in the fortresses, none of these was Hungarian.[63] Only certain auxiliary services were expected from the local population, principally for minor repairs to fortresses within the framework of the *cerehor* institution (locally-recruited Christian militia).[64] The inhabitants of villages carrying out such tasks were exempt from emergency taxes and large-scale fortification activities. Ordinary subjects were occasionally compelled to carry out these works, for which they were paid.[65]

Differences in adminstrative practice occur also with regard to the survival of pre-Ottoman taxes. In Hungary, in contrast to the Balkans, even such fundamental taxes as the *cizye* and the *ispence* were collected according to previous usage. The *cizye* was imposed only on persons above a certain level of wealth, a limit fixed so as to agree with the value above which the Hungarian *subsidium* (a tax to cover mainly military expenses) had been levied by the treasury.[66] The *ispence* is even more peculiar. It was termed *resm-i kapu* (gate tax) by the Ottomans, this being the Hungarian name for the basic land tax paid by serfs to the landlord.[67] The amount was fixed according to local traditions, to the extent that the inhabitants of Buda and Pest were exempt from it on the ground that 'they were not paying it during their kings' time'.[68] This or a similar phrase occurs at least once in almost every law book of the Hungarian *sancak*s, referring to either the sum of a tax or the method of its collection.[69] Sultanic decrees sometimes mention when the king's laws had been examined.[70] When imposing taxes,

63 Velics and Kammerer, *Magyarországi török kincstári defterek*, I, 6, 9, 17, 19–21, 48, 50–2, 56, etc.
64 Pál Fodor, 'The way of a Seljuq institution to Hungary: the *cerehōr*', *Acta Orientalia Hungarica* XXXVIII (1984) 367–99.
65 For a list of those participating in the repair of Székesfehérvár, see Nationalbibliothek, Vienna, Türk. Mss. Flügel 1400 (summarised ed. in Velics and Kammerer, I. 251–64).
66 Gyula Káldy-Nagy, 'Bevölkerungsstatistischer Quellenwert der *Ğizye*-defter und der *Tahrir*-defter', *Acta Orientalia Hungarica* XI (1960), 251–64.
67 On these taxes, see István Bakács, 'A dicalis összeírások', in J Kovacsics (ed.), *A történeti statisztika forrásai* (Budapest 1957), 51–81; and in the same volume, Bálint Ila, 'A dézsmajegyzékek mint a történeti statisztika forrásai', 82–118.
68 L Fekete, *Az Esztergomi szandzsák 1570. évi adóösszeírása* (Budapest 1943), 187,
69 Barkan, *Kanunlar*, 301, no. 14; 303, no. 1; 318, no. 1; 320–1, no. 10; 322, no. 1; 323, nos 8–11.
70 Gyula Káldy-Nagy, 'The administration of *ṣanjāq* registrations in Hungary' *Acta Orientalia Hungarica* XXI (1968), 193. Barkan, *Kanunlar*, 304, cites a very interesting *mühimme defteri* entry which well reflects Ottoman thinking about the preservation of former taxes: if they were acceptable to the population, they could survive; if not, they should be changed.

the previous practice of a town or a group of localities was often taken into consideration.[71]

Although the Ottomans did not interfere to any great extent with religious matters in Hungary, the cardinal and higher clergy abandoned the occupied territories in much the same way as did the higher nobility. Knowledge about the functioning of the Catholic church in Hungary for the remainder of the sixteenth century is limited. Names of priests preserved in *tahrir defterleri* (census registers) sometimes show high concentrations in towns, perhaps reflecting the presence of monastic communities,[72] while sporadic notes show that earlier religious foundations did survive for a time.[73] *Cizye* lists and other registers may further indicate surviving churches.[74] The number of churches transformed into mosques was again limited, confiscations taking place only in administrative centres. This nevertheless meant that some of the most prominent places of worship – the Holy Virgin church in Buda, the cathedrals of Esztergom, Pécs and Székesfehérvár became mosques, dealing a considerable blow to church organisation.[75] While little is known about how, if at all, new priests were supplied, the need for them clearly diminished since Catholicism lost ground almost everywhere in the country. This fact is reflected in certain registers where married priests appear in some settlements. The Ottomans neither hindered nor supported either of the confessional groups; they remained impartial in conflicts between Catholic and Protestant[76] and left them to share the churches.[77] As for converts to Islam, these constituted an extremely insignificant number among Hungarians.

---

71 E.g. the tax liabilities of Gyöngyös and the so-called 'Jász-towns' were fixed in lump sums based on ancient usage: 600 *filoris*, 2,500 *kile* of wheat, and 2,500 *kile* of barley totalled 67,500 *akçe* (BA, Mühimme defteri 2, p. 55, no. 504). For a useful collection of Hungarian words occuring in Ottoman documents, see Lajos Fekete, *Die Siyāqat-Schrift in der türkischen Finanzverwaltung I* (Budapest 1955), 57–65.

72 In one of the *mahalles* of Gyöngyös (with 118 heads of families) 10 priests were registered in 1546 (Lajos Fekete, *A Hatvani szandzsák 1550. évi adóösszeírása* (Jászberény 1968), 41. BA, Tapu defteri 441, ff. 66v-7v, 67v-8r, 149v-50v, 157v-8r, 158r-8v, 179v-81r, shows 6 towns in the *sancak* of Mohács with 7–10 priests each in the same year; by 1552, these numbers show a slow diminution (BA, Tapu defteri 443).

73 E.g. in Pécs, the monastery of St Francis had some pieces of arable land, 2 meadows, a house, and a vineyard in its possession in 1546 (BA, Tapu defteri 441, f. 8v). Less clear is its position in 1570 (BA, Tapu defteri 1012, p. 1).

74 Lajos Györffy, *Adatok az Alföld törökkori településtörténetéhez* (Szolnok 1956). Out of 131 settlements, 106 are registered as having a church.

75 A similar tendency can be detected in other areas also: see Binswanger, *Untersuchungen zum Status der Nichtmuslime*, 100.

76 M. Tayyib Gökbilgin, 'Hatvan kadılığının iki sicilli', in Gyula Káldy-Nagy (ed.), *Hungaro-Turcica. Studies in honour of Julius Németh* (Budapest 1976), 315–16, 318.

77 Lajos Fekete, 'Osmanlı Türkleri ve Macarlar, 1366–1699', *Belleten* XIII (1949), 738.

There were new Muslims in the cities, but these had different backgrounds and travellers reported that many of them spoke Slavonic.[78] At village level the population remained intact; Muslims appear exceptionally.[79]

With regard to the general effects of Ottoman conquest upon the original populations in towns which became administrative centres, there is considerable difference between the situation in the Balkans and that in Hungary. In the former (with few exceptions, and characteristically in cases of newly-occupied towns) both non-Muslim and Muslim populations grew, although the number of Muslims shows a more rapid increase.[80] In Hungary, however, the general tendency was the other way round. Compared to the first registrations, the Christian population diminished in these cities, without exception. In some it decreased continuously and quite significantly, as in Koppány[81] and Mohács;[82] in some there was a period of stagnation, as in Szeged;[83] in some, like Simontornya,[84] there were smaller ups and downs. This happened in a period when in most of the towns concerned there was almost no civilian Muslim population. The castles, however, bristled with Ottoman soldiers, and it was probably under these circumstances

78 Fekete, 'Buda and Pest under Turkish rule', 20. It should be noted that the Muslim civilian population is scarcely documented throughout the century, the largest numbers being registered in Bács (T Halasi-Kun, 'Sixteenth-century Turkish settlements in Hungary', *Belleten* XXVIII, 1964, 24–8), Gyula (Káldy-Nagy, *A Gyulai szandzsák*, 14, 41–57), Lippa (BA, Tapu defteri 457, pp. 11–14, Tapu defteri 578, pp. 9–14) and Temesvár (BA, Tapu defteri 364, pp. 12–25, Tapu defteri 579, pp. 17–32). It is remarkable, however, that no Muslim civilian was entered in any Buda register, except for some converted gypsies of Slavonic origin (Káldy-Nagy, *A Budai szandzsák 1546–1590*, 150–2).
79 Halasi-Kun, 'Sixteenth-century Turkish settlements', *passim*, gives 20 villages in the *sancak* of Szeged with varying proportions of Muslim inhabitants. However, it is noteworthy that none of these places had a single Hungarian inhabitant, and that nowhere else within the territory of the *vilayet* of Buda are Hungarian village converts documented.
80 E.g., Niğbolu had 446 Christian and 308 Muslim households in 1425; 100 years later there were 775 Christian and 468 Muslim hearths. In Plovdiv, 119 Christian and 761 Muslim heads of families were enumerated c. 1520–1530, rising to 153 and 1019 respectively by 1571–1580. Ruse had 574 Christian and 81 Muslim households in 1520–1530, increasing to 875 Christian and 824 Muslim families by the second half of the 16th century. See Nikolai Todorov, *The Balkan city, 1400–1900* (Seattle/London 1983), 66–7.
81 The number of married Hungarian men here was 109 in 1546, 90 in 1562, 51 c. 1570, and only 35 some 10 years later.
82 The Ottomans found 324 Christian households here in 1546, 437 in 1552, 105 in 1580, and 90 in 1590.
83 There were 1322 Christian heads of families here in 1546, decreasing to 691 by 1560. In 1570, 701, and in 1578, 703, married Hungarians are shown.
84 The 6 registers of this *sancak* give the following numbers: 1546 (34); 1552 (36); 1565 (56); 1570 (51); 1580 (41); 1590 (20).

that the Hungarian inhabitants of administrative and military centres moved to other places where they felt less threatened by the Ottoman presence. In two of the *sancak* seats (Esztergom and Nógrád) Hungarians disappeared altogether; some ten or twelve other former towns which had become *nahiye* centres with considerable garrisons, are also shown in certain registers to have had no civilian population. This was especially true just after a centre had been conquered, but there is evidence that only a small proportion of the original inhabitants returned later.[85] In contrast, the number of residents in towns without Ottoman military contingents was more stable, with occasional increases. It is worthy of note that of the sixteen largest urban settlements in Ottoman Hungary (i.e. those possessing more than 400 non-Muslim households), only four were administrative centres[86] and one other had a garrison,[87] while eleven were not subject to these burdens.[88]

EUROPEAN VASSALS

Since no direct Ottoman administration was introduced in the vassal principalities, we can confine ourselves to the most important differences in the position of Transylvania and the Rumanian territories (Moldavia and Wallachia) in the sixteenth century. Briefly, these are five. First, whereas Ottoman troops continued to be stationed in the capital cities of the Rumanian voyvodes (princes), none were located in Transylvania. Second, whereas the voyvodes of Moldavia and Wallachia were often directly appointed by the sultan, the princes of Transylvania were elected (at least in theory) by the diet, whose decision had only to be confirmed by the sultan. Third, the Rumanian princes were often compelled to send their sons to Istanbul as hostages, a practice that was not introduced in Transylvania. Fourth, the yearly tax imposed on Moldavia and Wallachia respectively was higher than that of Transylvania, although the economy of the latter was more developed. Fifth, in addition to these fixed annual sums, the Rumanian voyvodes were obliged to send certain agricultural products and livestock to Istanbul, partly for sale; no such quotas were imposed on Transylvania.[89]

---

85 It is not surprising that somewhere like e.g., Babócsa was initially left empty, since c. 600 soldiers were stationed there. A couple of families did return later.
86 Buda, Mohács, Pécs, and Szeged.
87 Békés.
88 Debrecen, Gyöngyös, Jászberény, Kecskemét, Laskó, Makó, Mezőtúr, Miskolc, Pásztó, Ráckeve, and Tolna.
89 Similar comparison is offered by Klára Hegyi, *A törökök berendezkedése, 400–3.*

It is not entirely clear how Transylvania managed to attain such greater independence and fewer burdens. One reason may be that vassal status had begun much earlier in the Rumanian principalities, and had become more onerous with time. Moreover, the fact that the Black Sea region was vital for the provisioning of Istanbul probably necessitated more direct interference. It may also be significant that the first ruler of Transylvania, John Sigismund, was the son of a former king of a large country and that Ottoman traditionalists respected this. Politically, a stable vassal state in Transylvania, however loosely controlled, was preferable to a Habsburg confederate.

CONCLUSION

Perhaps the principal reason for the differences in administrative practice between Ottoman Hungary and Rumeli during Süleyman's reign was the length of time each had been incorporated into the empire. While parts of Rumeli had been integral to the Ottoman state since the fourteenth century and by 1500 the entire *beylerbeyilik* was well established under Ottoman rule, Hungary constituted a completely new conquest, and one which was only partial, covering 40 per cent of the territory of the country. Moreover, due partly to remoteness from the main Ottoman centres, the occupation of Hungary remained unconsolidated throughout, thus encouraging variations in procedure.

These differences in the time factor and in the extent and thoroughness of territorial occupation also suggest reasons for the variations in the general outcome of Ottoman rule for the areas under discussion.

What did these imply in the case of Hungary? The above account attempts an objective portrayal of the administrative framework of the sixteenth century. It shows a relatively flexible, pragmatic, and in some respects tolerant practice, some elements of which were in harmony with the principles of Muslim law. On the other hand, serious damage was caused partly by recurrent periods of warfare – Hungary now being the principal Ottoman land frontier in Europe – and partly by the simple fact of lengthy foreign rule from a distant and different centre. In Ottoman Hungary the previous political system disintegrated, economic development slowed down or stagnated. The population suffered a considerable decrease in certain regions (mostly in those that had been purely Hungarian), but remained static or increased slightly in others; overall, however, it lost the natural increase to be expected for a period of 150 years. This went side by side with the transformation of the ethnic composition of the country, where the Hungarian element lost ground to Slovakian, Serbian and Rumanian. However, vital contacts were maintained with both Habsburg Hungary and with Transylvania, and trading links were preserved with important commercial centres in western Europe, for the sale of goods in both directions. Consequently, after the end of Ottoman rule in the late seventeenth century, Hungarian political reorientation towards the mainstream of European development was considerably eased.

The Balkans, on the other hand, had reached a lower level of political and economic progress by the time of the Ottoman conquest. The improved administrative system introduced by the Ottomans in the early stages of their rule was in some respects positive and beneficial. However, by the end of Ottoman rule in the nineteenth century the relationship had become largely negative and damaging; the Balkan lands were left at a significant distance developmentally from western Europe. Many of the current problems of the recently defunct Yugoslavia can be interpreted as consequences of the Ottoman era.

SURAIYA FAROQHI

Politics and socio-economic change in the Ottoman Empire of the later sixteenth century

Establishment historiography in the Ottoman realm came in for its first serious spate of criticism during the late 1960s and early 1970s, when sociologists, economists and finally historians discussed the applicability of feudalism and the Asiatic Mode of Production (AMP) to Ottoman history of the 'classical period'.[1] This latter category, which Marx experimented with but did not elaborate in his later work, involves a model of village communities established on the soil owned by a central state. The model probably attracted social scientists concerned with the Ottoman realm because of its emphasis on an overpowering central government, which seemed conspicuously absent from feudalism as understood at the time. In addition the existence of a village community consisting of peasants who were not serfs, managing its everyday life without much interference from the central power, equally recommended this model to researchers anxious to show that Ottoman society did not share some of the more glaring historical disadvantages of European feudalism.[2] Yet the changes which the feudalism-AMP debate brought to the writing of Ottoman history were less dramatic than might have been expected. In particular, the old assumption that the

1 For an overview of this debate, cf. Halil Berktay, 'Tarih çalışmaları', in *Cumhuriyet dönemi Türkiye ansiklopedisi* (1983).
2. One of the most interesting and influential articles in this debate is Huri İslamoğlu-İnan and Çağlar Keyder, 'Agenda for Ottoman history', *Review* I/1 (1977), 31–55 (repr. in H İslamoglu-İnan (ed.), *The Ottoman empire and the world economy* (Cambridge 1987), 42–62. Compare İslamoğlu-İnan's more recent contribution: 'Introduction: Oriental despotism in world-system perspective', in H İslamoğlu-İnan (ed.), *The Ottoman empire* (1987), 1–26; and also H Berktay, 'The "other" feudalism. A critique of 20th-century Turkish historiography and its particularisation of Ottoman society', unpubl. PhD thesis, University of Birmingham (1990). On AMP in general, cf. Perry Anderson, *Lineages of the absolutist state* (London 1974), 473–549.

Ottoman Empire went through a long period of political and cultural decline after 1550, 1566 or 1584–85 was not challenged by this debate, quite the contrary. The last of these three dates approximately coincided with the entry of English merchants into the Mediterranean, and the notion of an Ottoman collapse due to European interference fitted in well with the anti-colonial thrust of Turkish 'New Left' historians. A very narrow understanding of what constitutes cultural florescence also reinforced the 'decline' paradigm, for florescence was equated with the notions of originality and national style. Borrowings from other cultures were *ipso facto* suspect, and borrowings from Europe even more suspect than others.[3] Unfortunately for their reputation among orientalists and nationalist historians alike, Ottoman savants and artists from the seventeenth or early eighteenth century onward had indulged in an interest in European geography, clocks and architecture. They were thus often regarded as purely imitative epigones, and the notion that sixteenth-century Ottoman florescence was rapidly followed by long-term decline emerged unscathed from this first round of critical revisionism.

In recent years, a new wave of revision-minded historiography has been gathering force. Given the 'culturalist' climate of the 1980s, sixteenth-century Ottoman culture was studied more intensively than had been true during the past half-century, and the 'decline' paradigm was challenged for the first time from the cultural angle. The postmodern ambience of this decade allowed historians to appreciate the sophistication involved in the handling of several different cultural traditions at the same time; this was certainly one of the major merits of Mustafa Ali as perceived by Cornell Fleischer.[4] Previous studies on cultural borrowing, long familiar in neighbouring disciplines, exerted an impact in Ottoman history writing. Ali's borrowings from Arabic, Iranian and eastern Turkic traditions could now be regarded as an act of conscious choice, rather than a lack of originality; and it became possible to discuss Mimar Sinan's creative encounter with the Aya Sofya, without either making him into an epigone of Byzantine art, or else denying that he took a close look at a major building which he had before his eyes.[5]

Economic historians have other reasons to be unhappy with the

---

3 Marshall Hodgson, *The venture of Islam: conscience and history in a world civilization* (Chicago 1974), v. 3, 14.

4 Cornell Fleischer, *Bureaucrat and intellectual in the Ottoman empire: the historian Mustafa Ali (1541–1600)* (Princeton 1986), 240–1, and elsewhere.

5 A Kuran, *Sinan the grand old master of Ottoman architecture* (Washington DC/Istanbul 1987), 19; Gülrû Necipoğlu, 'The life of an imperial monument: Hagia Sophia after Byzantium', in R Mark and A Çakmak (ed.), *The Hagia Sophia: form, structure and meaning from the age of Justinian to the present* (Cambridge 1992), 195–225.

'decline' paradigm. Some of these reasons have to do with findings concerning not the period with which we are at present involved, but rather the seventeenth and eighteenth centuries. If townsmen inhabiting cities such as Ankara or Kayseri were able to build increasingly elaborate houses in the course of the seventeenth century, if many branches of Ottoman craft production flourished between approximately 1700 and 1760–70, it becomes difficult to maintain that the economic crisis of the late sixteenth and early seventeenth centuries inaugurated irreversible decline.[6] If the notion of a centuries-long economic crisis is rejected, it is immaterial whether we place the blame for this crisis upon European intruders or a supposed 'lack of dynamism' on the part of Ottoman society. But then we need to take a hard second look at some of the main 'crisis areas' of the Ottoman polity during the second half of the sixteenth century, namely the changing relationship between provincial and government elites, the prevalence of smuggling and the rebellions of mercenaries. The present essay attempts to do just this.

CENTRAL AND PROVINCIAL ELITES

According to the more old-fashioned histories, Ottoman florescence and decline on the central level had neat and immediately discernible corollaries in the sphere of provincial government.[7] During the period of Ottoman apogee, in the late fifteenth and early sixteenth centuries, centralisation was the order of the day, while decline and decentralisation constituted the two sides of another coin, minted sometime between 1550 and 1584–85. The only inconsistency within this neat pattern was due to the understanding that Ottoman methods of conquest involved no radical abolition of pre-conquest modes of local government and taxation.[8] But the history of Ottoman empire-building was mainly studied with respect to the Balkans, and the Balkans apart from Hungary were conquered during the fourteenth and fifteenth centuries. Therefore it was easy to regard the gradual integration of conquered territories as a feature characterising the empire's early history, and no longer of great importance during the 'classical' period of the sixteenth century.

---

6 Suraiya Faroqhi, *Men of modest substance: house owners and house property in seventeenth-century Ankara and Kayseri* (Cambridge 1987), 113–15; Mehmet Genç, 'Osmanlı ekonomisi ve savaş', *Yapıt, toplumsal araştırmalar dergisi* 49/4 (1984), 52–61 and 50/ 5, 86–93.

7 Bernard Lewis, *The emergence of modern Turkey* (Oxford 1968), 36–8.

8 Halil İnalcık, 'Ottoman methods of conquest', *Studia Islamica* II (1954), 104–29.

Recent research on Ottoman provincial history has disturbed this tidy picture, showing that gradual integration occurred much later also. In sixteenth-century Syria certain families prominent during Mamluk times continued to exercise political power until well after 1600.[9] Some local chiefs were awarded tax farms in order to give them a stake in the Ottoman system, so that they would hopefully oppose other chiefs inclined to rebel against the central government. The Ottoman administration of mid- and later sixteenth-century Syria was suspicious of Druze chiefs and even more of Shi'ites, who often entered into secret contacts with the Safavid Shah of Iran. As a result, considerable room for manoeuvre was allowed Sunnite chiefs. This policy was not a consequence of decentralisation resulting from Ottoman decline, but corresponded to a stage in provincial history during which the central government was still building up its power. Full central control in Syria was only achieved in the 1630s, after the elimination of the Ma'an dynasty. Thus the history of centralisation and decentralisation in sixteenth- and seventeenth-century Ottoman Syria in no way coincides with the conventional stages of Ottoman 'rise and decline'.

A similar statement can be made about Ottoman Egypt. The province was conquered in 1517, a year later than Syria. For several decades, Mamluks who had thrown in their lot with the Ottoman administration were influential in the political life of the province, even though the abortive rebellion of Hain Ahmed Paşa ultimately strengthened the impact of the Ottoman central administration. But by allowing the recruiting of Mamluks to continue, and by conceding Mamluks an important share in the business of tax-collecting, the Ottoman administration – even during the reign of Süleyman – permitted a significant sector of provincial government to remain outside its immediate control. The political crisis which shook Istanbul and Anatolia from the 1590s onward did not apparently result in a loss of central government control over Egyptian revenues. Only in the seventeenth century, particularly its last quarter, did the Mamluk elite retain an increasing share of provincial revenues in its own coffers.[10] Before this time, there is no one-to-one correspondence between political crisis in Istanbul and high or low points of Ottoman control over Egypt.

Even more drastic are the discrepancies where Eastern Anatolia is concerned. This area had been wrested from Safavid control by Selim I,

9 Abdul-Rahim Abu-Husayn, 'The *iltizam* of Mansur Furaykh: a case study of *iltizam* in sixteenth-century Syria', in Tarif Khalidi (ed.), *Land tenure and social transformation in the Middle East* (Beirut 1984), 250–1.

10 Stanford Shaw, *The financial and administrative organisation and development of Ottoman Egypt, 1517–1798* (Princeton 1962), 5.

after the battle of Çaldıran in 1514. But local principalities (*beyliks*), often under Kurdish dynasties, continued to exist in the region. Since these rulers were for the most part Sunnis, the Ottoman administration saw them as a political and military bulwark against the Shi'ite rulers of Iran.[11] As late as 1632–33, the memorialist Aziz Efendi, who looked back on a long period of service and incorporated sixteenth-century administrative wisdom into his work, recommended that local Kurdish *beys* should receive official support.[12] Throughout the sixteenth and seventeenth centuries Ottoman governors-general and tax farmers administered that part of the countryside which was more or less accessible from Erzurum and Diyarbakir, leaving Hakkâri, Cizre and Bitlis under the control of local rulers. Attempts at administrative centralisation were made in the second half of the sixteenth century, when tax registers (*tahrir*) were prepared for quite a few localities which had not been surveyed before. Centralising policies were often connected with the presence of an Ottoman army, a not altogether rare event given the frequency of Ottoman–Iranian wars down to the treaty of Kasr-i Şirin in 1639. But whenever the armies withdrew, local princes reasserted themselves.[13] Permanent centralisation did not happen until the 1830s, when Sultan Mahmud II had the principal *beyliks (beys)* overthrown by military force. Once again Ottoman power waxed and waned during the sixteenth and seventeenth centuries, according to a rhythm which had relatively little to do with the conventionally recognised stages of Ottoman expansion and decline.

At the same time, our understanding of political and administrative history in the centre of Ottoman power has also changed. With only mild exaggeration, we can say that for the first time, we now conceive of the Ottoman ruling class as having an authentic history. In the course of the period between about 1480 and 1620, major changes occurred in the relationship between the sultan and the palace-bred elite of *devşirme*-recruited high officials, between janissaries and provincial *sipahis*, between the descendants of the old Turkish aristocracy and the 'new men' recruited both through the *devşirme* and the later households of major *paşas* and *vezirs*. Many long-cherished generalisations have gone by the board: we now know that there never existed two

---

11 Rhoads Murphey (ed.), *Kânûn-nâme-i sultânî li Azîz Efendi: Aziz Efendi's Book of sultanic laws and regulations: an agenda for reform by a seventeenth-century Ottoman statesman* . . . (Cambridge, Mass. 1985), vii.

12 Murphey, *Kânûn-nâme*, 15 ff.

13 M M van Bruinessen, *Agha, Scheich und Staat: Politik und Gesellschaft Kurdistans* (Berlin 1989), 190, claims that Kurdish dynasties prospered under Ottoman domination, while previously the Akkoyunlu had attempted to eliminate them.

rigidly separate 'institutions', one exclusively manned by *devşirmes* and running a far-flung empire, and the other composed of free-born Muslims, concerned with teaching and administering the law.[14] Until a separate bureaucratic career evolved in the middle of the sixteenth century, men of *ulema* background frequently entered administrative service.[15] Most of the newly created positions were in financial administration; after the middle of the sixteenth century, these new officials produced previously unheard-of masses of documentation, but also after some gropings, an *esprit de corps* and a discourse on Ottoman politics.

The emergence of a highly organised central administration generated new tensions. After the death of Süleyman in 1566, no sultan succeeded in playing the role of a major conquering hero until Murad IV assumed personal power in 1632. Traditionally, the 'declining calibre' of the sultans has been regarded as one of the fortuitous, ancillary factors which hastened the decline of the Ottoman empire.[16] However it has recently been suggested that this claim makes more sense when stood on its head: because Ottoman central officialdom had become institutionalised and powerful, charismatic sultans were often a hindrance to the smooth functioning of the bureaucracy, and an education which ensured that most Ottoman sultans ascended the throne without previous political experience was not necessarily a disadvantage from the high officials' point of view.[17]

Other tensions concerned the linkage of central and provincial administrations. Toward the end of the sixteenth century, there were major rebellions in Anatolia, the so-called *celali* revolts. In response the central administration attempted to secure its grasp over provincial revenues by appointing palace-trained officials to ever more junior positions within the provincial administration, thereby blocking the advancement of those men who had begun their careers in the provinces.[18] Whether this process constituted an instance of centralisation or of decentralisation is open to debate. I would submit that both were involved: the now consolidated administration used centralising

14 Norman Itzkowitz, 'Eighteenth-century Ottoman realities', *Studia Islamica* XVI (1962), 73–94. However, Carter Findley, *Bureaucratic reform in the Ottoman empire: the Sublime Porte 1789–1922* (Princeton 1980), 46–7, defends a modified version of the 'ruling institution – religious institution' dichotomy. See also, Fleischer, *Bureaucrat and intellectual*, 216 ff.
15 Fleischer, *Bureaucrat and intellectual*, 219 ff.
16 Lewis, *Emergence of modern Turkey*, 23.
17 Rifa'at 'Ali Abou-El-Haj, *Formation of the modern state: the Ottoman empire, sixteenth to eighteenth centuries* (Albany, New York 1991), 38.
18 İ Metin Kunt, *The sultan's servants: the transformation of Ottoman provincial government 1550–1650* (New York 1983), 95 ff.

measures to control unrest. But blocking the careers of provincial officials incited the latter to rebellions, which in turn led to a loss of central control. Thus quite against official intentions, the Ottoman central bureaucracy acted as a major instigator of the *celali* rebellions.

Moreover centralisation at the appointment level was counterbalanced by decentralisation where finances were involved. Increasing demand for liquidity caused the central administration to whittle away at the emoluments of provincial governors. The latter were now expected to raise the needed funds on their own initiative, which gave them a political leeway they had not possessed down to the reign of Süleyman. In certain provinces, provincial treasurers were instituted in an effort to limit the governors' room for manoeuvre.[19] But these were scarcely powerful enough to curb the governors' independence, particularly since a variety of 'office-purchasing' had been surreptitiously introduced at about this time.

Further shifts in the balance of power were connected with the *timar*-holders (*sipahis*), who during the empire's formative period, had constituted the backbone of the army and secured local control of the peasantry. It has long been known that the central administration's need for cash led to the conversion of *timar* revenue grants into tax farms.[20] Tax-farming supplied the central administration with the means of planning its expenditures, even though this short-term advantage was compensated by long-term financial losses. Official motivation to protect *timar*-holders from the effects of inflation, which was making it increasingly difficult for the poorer *sipahis* to equip themselves for campaigns, was further diminished by the fact that *sipahis* served on horseback. By the late sixteenth century warfare based upon a preponderance of cavalry was becoming more and more obsolete, as technical advance in hand-guns led to a growing demand for musketeers.[21] *Sipahis* rapidly lost prestige, not necessarily in the political tracts of the time, whose authors frequently dwelt on the need to restore this former mainstay of Ottoman greatness, but in real life.[22] In the first half of the seventeenth century, janissaries who did not provide satisfactory service

19 Fleischer, *Bureaucrat and intellectual*, 313.
20 Bistra Cvetkova, 'Recherches sur le système d'affermage (*iltizam*) dans l'Empire Ottoman au cours du XVIe-XVIIIe s. par rapport aux contrées bulgares', *Rocznik orientalistyczny* XXVII/2 (1964), 111–32.
21 H İnalcık, 'Military and fiscal transformation in the Ottoman empire, 1600–1700', *Archivum Ottomanicum* VI (1980), 283–337; see esp. 292 ff.
22 Yaşar Yücel (ed.), *Osmanlı devlet teşkilâtına dair kaynaklar: Kitâb-i müstetâb; Kitâbu mesâlihi'l müslimîn ve menâfi' i'l-müminîn; Hirzü' l-mülûk* (Ankara 1988), section 'Kitâb-i müstetâb', xxv.

were awarded a *timar* and packed off to the provinces as a punishment. This practice further increased the pressure on old *sipahi* families.[23]

A decisive change was connected with the increasing employment of musketeers of peasant background. The situation of these people was anything but secure. Governors hired a significant number of armed bands, presumably for specific short-term purposes, and turnover was high. In the late sixteenth century the chiefs of mercenaries armed with muskets frequently attempted to gain political power for themselves. Kalenderoğlu and other rebels conquered major cities such as Bursa, and set siege to others.[24] In 1608, Grand Vezir Kuyucu Murad Paşa won decisive victories against the rebel chiefs and thereby ended the first stage of the provincial mercenaries' rebellions. Even though this did not mean the end of the movement as a whole, the early seventeenth century constitutes a watershed.[25] From now on mercenary chiefs no longer attempted to seize power on their own behalf, but attached themselves to governors duly appointed by the Istanbul authorities. In this sense, the movement toward administrative centralisation had won a semi-victory, and the Ottoman political class was fully victorious. From now on 'nobodies' of *reaya* background could not hope to penetrate the higher levels of the Ottoman political establishment, and since the separation of *reaya* and governing class formed part of the 'order of the world' as understood by the latter, this world order continued to prevail.

Seen from a distance, the Ottoman political crisis of the later sixteenth century is marked by the tension between an increasingly formalised and professionalised administrative service and a militarised provincial administration. The former's decisions on the day-to-day level were probably in many sectors more routine and predictable in 1590 than they had been in 1520, and even more regular in 1640 than in 1590. On the other hand, random violence by mercenary bands was probably a greater risk in the mid-seventeenth century than it had been a hundred years earlier. Of course the lack of sources for the early sixteenth century may result in some distortion; for once documentation increased as dramatically as happened between 1520 and 1570, the number of disputes, robberies and minor uprisings coming to light was bound to grow in proportion.

---

23 Murphey, *Kânûn-nâme*, 7.
24 William Griswold, *The great Anatolian rebellion, 1000–1020/1591–1611* (Berlin 1983), 157 ff.
25 Griswold, *Great Anatolian rebellion*, ends his account in 1611.

TRADE, WEALTH AND POLITICS

Toward the end of the fifteenth century, commercial wealth on Otto-man territory had apparently been limited to a few centres such as Bursa, and even in Bursa medium-level members of the political class controlled as much wealth as an affluent merchant was able to amass over a lifetime.[26] It is probable that very wealthy merchants were not common in the later sixteenth century either, although no monographs have covered this topic. But the overall volume of internal trade grew. Markets sprang up in villages where none had existed before, and peasants paid a sizeable proportion of their taxes in money. Doubtless demands for cash were often a burden on the taxpayers, but if the money had been totally unavailable, it would not have been paid. In Thessaly local fairs expanded, and began to generate so much revenue that sultans and grand vezirs began to annex them to newly established pious foundations.[27] Fabrics and leathers manufactured in many small towns of Anatolia and Rumelia were traded interregionally. Very prob-ably urban growth, which occurred throughout sixteenth-century Anatolia, is also linked to the increase in internal trade; for while the towns contained a sizeable agricultural population, so many new khans and covered markets were also built that an appreciable share of the growing urban population must have made a living in crafts and trade.

For the most part, the composition and economic background of sixteenth-century urban elites remains little known. While craftsmen were strictly supervised by market inspectors and on paper were allowed only a very limited rate of profit, certain guildsmen managed to circum-vent the impediments intended to block business expansion.[28] During the decades following the Ottoman conquest of Jerusalem, well-placed butchers branched out into trade, became market inspectors and mar-ried into office-holding families.[29] Merchants were certainly better placed than craftsmen in terms of economic opportunities, but they were not the only townsmen to benefit from sixteenth-century com-mercial expansion.

Merchant activity was facilitated by the manner in which Ottoman bureaucrats defined their relationship to what in nineteenth- and

---

26 H İnalcık, '15. asır Türkiye iktisadî ve ictimaî tarihi kaynakları', *İstanbul Üniversitesi İktisat Fakültesi mecmuası* 15/1–4, 60–1.

27 S Faroqhi, 'The early history of the Balkan fairs', *Südost-Forschungen* XXXVII (1978), 57, 62.

28 H İnalcık, *The Ottoman empire: the classical age 1300–1600* (tr. N Itzkowitz and C Imber, London 1973), 154.

29 Amnon Cohen, *Economic life in Ottoman Jerusalem* (Cambridge 1989), 31.

twentieth-century parlance, we have become accustomed to call 'the economy'. Here a number of contrary tendencies can be discerned. On the one hand, the sixteenth-century state apparatus, particularly after its mid-century reorganisation, constituted a formidable nucleus of power. Compared to the weight of this apparatus, the empire's tax-payers appear weakly organised and incapable of resistance. Older studies of the Ottoman polity have sometimes given the impression that the state was a colossus in the 'economic' as well as the political field: prices were legislated from above; trade in basic foodstuffs was only possible if the Ottoman bureaucracy had given formal permission; large masses of artisans were drafted to serve on campaigns or on public construction sites at less than the wages they would have received if working for private employers.[30] The activities of private entrepreneurs look quite puny by comparison.

Historical *problématiques* always bear the stamp of the period in which they were devised. Modern historians working on the political and economic power of the Ottoman state often had *dirigiste* policies of the twentieth century in mind, and have thought particularly in terms of the mobilisation for total war which was attempted during the two world wars. Therefore it is not surprising that the disillusionment with state-directed economies, which surfaced during the 1980s in different parts of the world, should have led scholars now to play down the *dirigiste* activities of the sixteenth-century Ottoman state. There is a common-sense background to this tendency. Scholars such as Fernand Braudel and before him Lucien Febvre have discussed *in extenso* how the technical conditions of the sixteenth century, particularly the means of communication, placed stringent limits on what was possible or impossible at that time.[31] Nor is this a new discovery; for the statement that the productive forces constitute the basis of social and political history is also a fundamental tenet of historical materialism. To be *dirigiste* in the modern sense of the word, a polity needs (at the very least) railroads, the telegraph, and an organised police force; all these features were obviously lacking in the sixteenth century. Thus it is not surprising that a recent study of Ottoman luxury trades should have emphasised the impediments to *dirigisme* even in areas which closely

---

30 L Güçer, 'Osmanlı imparatorluğu dahilinde hububat ticaretinin tabi olduğu kayıtlar', *İstanbul Üniversitesi İktisat Fakültesi mecmuası* 13–14 (1951–52), 79–98; Ö L Barkan, *Süleymaniye camii ve imareti inşaatı (1550–1557)*, (Ankara 1972, 1979); Mübahat Kütükoğlu, *Osmanlılarda narh müessesesi ve 1640 tarihli narh defteri* (İstanbul 1983).

31 Lucien Febvre, *Life in renaissance France* (tr. M Rothstein, Cambridge Mass., 1977), 14 ff, 95 ff; Fernand Braudel, *La Méditerranée et le monde méditerranéen a l'époque de Philippe II* (2nd edn, Paris 1966), I, 326–60.

interested the Ottoman palace:[32] a scarcity of trained designers, and limited means of communication made the functioning of a central design office difficult if not impossible. Similarly, having studied in detail the imposition of administratively fixed prices, another historian has surmised that these prices may have been enforced largely when the central administration was the purchaser, leaving a considerable 'grey zone' in which the play of supply and demand asserted itself.[33] But quite apart from historiographical and political reasons for describing the role of the state as more limited than had hitherto been assumed, a simple everyday experience of present-day third world countries played a decisive role: the difficulty of enforcing governmental policies of any kind when locally established social structures operate in a radically different fashion.

But in addition to the technical limits encountered by potential sixteenth-century *dirigistes*, there were limits due to the social composition and political assumptions of the Ottoman ruling class. Researchers dealing with administratively imposed prices or the spread of cash-based pious foundations have shown that on these issues certain dissenting members of the political class expressed their protest in writing. In the seventeenth century, a grand vezir from the Köprülü family refused to concern himself with the enforcement of administratively determined prices, because he espoused the view that prices should be allowed to find their own level in the market.[34] This was a minority view within the Ottoman establishment, but since it found its way into the chronicles as the opinion of a grand vezir, it may also have been held by quite a few *kadıs* about whom we know nothing. The enforcement of administratively imposed prices may sometimes have been somewhat lax on account of the scruples of *kadıs* who opposed price-fixing as a matter of principle. Another example of dissension within the Ottoman political class concerns Birgevi Mehmed Efendi, who in the second half of the sixteenth century protested against the opinion, espoused by Süleyman's *şeyhülislam* Ebusuûd Efendi, that cash foundations should be tolerated to ensure the regular functioning of mosques, *medreses* and soup kitchens. Birgevi assumed that interest-taking was illegal no matter what the circumstances, and his opinions ultimately were taken up by

32 J M Rogers, 'Ottoman luxury traders and their regulation', in H G Majer (ed.), *Osmanistische Studien zur Wirtschafts- und Sozialgeschichte, in memoriam Vančo Boškov* (Wiesbaden 1986), 135–55.
33 Cemal Kafadar, 'When coins turned into drops of dew and bankers became robbers of shadows: the boundaries of Ottoman economic imagination at the end of the sixteenth century' (unpubl. PhD diss., McGill University, Montreal 1986), 128.
34 Kafadar, 'When coins turned into drops of dew', 134.

an influential segment of seventeenth-century public opinion. Again the question arises whether the official registration and administration of cash foundations was affected by this current of opinion among the *ulema*.[35]

Another 'ideological' limit to boundless *dirigisme* on the part of the central government was the manner in which the rights of property owners were understood by many members of the Ottoman political class. These rights were strongly legitimised by the fact that they were anchored in the *şeriat*. As an example indicating this tension between state claims and the rights of property owners, we might refer to a dispute concerning certain wealthy people of Cairo, presumably the Mamluk elite.[36] The latter were accustomed to the use of gilt decorations on their houses, a practice which the Ottoman government forbade in 1577–78 on account of the ensuing waste of gold; the financial administration always regarded the possible withdrawal of gold and silver from circulation as a matter of major concern. But the governor of Egypt hesitated to promulgate the relevant rescript; in his view, people should be permitted to use their property in whatever way they saw fit. This argument was not accepted by the Ottoman central administration; but we do not know whether the gilt wooden ceilings, which had become popular in Cairo after the Ottoman conquest in 1517, lost their brilliant ornamentation after 1578.

More important were the limitations which opinions prevailing within the Ottoman administrative apparatus placed on the commercial activities of its highly-placed members, particularly sultans and grand vezirs. Ottoman sultans tried to regulate the activities of merchants, but only in a limited number of cases did they enter the market as sellers: metals and minerals produced by Ottoman mines were sold by mining contractors who operated on behalf of the Ottoman sultan. But there existed no foreign trade monopolies comparable to those of fifteenth-century Mamluk rulers.[37] Nor did the Ottoman sultans invest in the trade supplying Istanbul. Certainly there were exceptions. Süleyman's grand vezir Rüstem Paşa possessed considerable business acumen, and invested money in one of the burgeoning Thessalian fairs, the active port town of Tekirdağ–Rodoscuk, the central district of Istanbul, and also the south-east-Anatolian town of Malatya. During his tenure as a

35 Jon E Mandaville, 'Usurious piety: the cash *waqf* controversy in the Ottoman empire', *International journal of Middle East studies* X/3 (1979), 289–308.

36 Başbakanlık Arşivi Istanbul [BA], Mühimme defterleri 33, p. 39, no. 82 (985/ 1577–78).

37 S Faroqhi, 'Towns, agriculture and the state in sixteenth-century Ottoman Anatolia', *Journal of the economic and social history of the Orient* XXXIII (1990), 125–56.

provincial governor in the 1630s grand vezir Mehmed Paşa also made a fortune for himself in trade.[38] But many members of the Ottoman establishment at least in theory subscribed to the view that members of the political class should refrain from involvement in money-making activities. Only if the subjects of the sultan earned money, would they be in a position to pay their dues. As competition from members of the political class thus remained within limits, Ottoman merchants were able to make a profit from the expanding volume of internal trade.

So far, we have looked at the limits imposed upon the Ottoman state's activity by the technical conditions of the times and the interests of the political class. However, it would be a mistake to assume that Ottoman merchants passively accepted the conditions imposed upon them by the central bureaucracy. Whenever late-sixteenth-century sources discuss merchants, they speak about contraband trade. Certain traders avoided sending their goods to Istanbul, where government supervision was strongest, and smuggled sheep, rice or iron to Bursa or Edirne instead.[39] Other merchants, sometimes with the aid and connivance of local administrators, exported grain to Venice or other territories of the western Mediterranean.[40] Contraband trade in cotton is frequently recorded for the Bursa and Izmir areas.[41] Throughout the mountainous borderlands between Iran and eastern Anatolia, which were almost impossible to police, Ottoman merchants did their best to dodge the customs farmers; sometimes they were assisted by Kurdish princes who lowered customs rates to merchants willing to travel through their respective territories. These merchants did not make public statements concerning their activities, or if they did, they have not come to light. Ottoman bureaucrats, on the other hand, were vocal about these matters: in their view, and sometimes in the eyes of crafts-men who saw their access to cheap raw materials endangered by increasing trade, smuggling was immoral and smugglers deserved dire punishment.[42]

Growing trade and expanding commercial wealth made political centralisation more difficult to maintain. Even though Ottoman merchants did not demand a share in political power, they must have offered the producers more attractive prices than the agents of the

---

38 İ Metin Kunt, 'Derviş Mehmed Paşa, vezir and entrepreneur: a study of Ottoman political-economic theory and practice', *Turcica* IX/1 (1977), 197–214.

39 S Faroqhi, *Towns and townsmen of Ottoman Anatolia: trade, crafts and food production in an urban setting, 1520–1650* (Cambridge 1984), 224.

40 Faroqhi, *Towns and townsmen of Ottoman Anatolia*, 85.

41 Faroqhi, *Towns and townsmen of Ottoman Anatolia*, 135 ff.

42 Faroqhi, *Towns and townsmen of Ottoman Anatolia*, 128 ff.

central administration, and thereby endangered the latter's control over supplies.[43] For the merchants of a developing region such as the province of Aydın, it was important to cultivate other customers than the officially licensed buyers whose job it was to supply the army, navy or capital.[44] Before the commercial expansion of the mid- and later sixteenth century, the Ottoman central administration had limited the activities of the Aegean port towns, in order to channel the products of this region toward Istanbul. With foreign merchants entering the area, this policy proved impossible to continue and seventeenth-century Izmir developed into the region's central city. But similar developments can be observed in central Anatolia, where domestic trade was much more important than foreign merchants. Local notables, wealthy through the expansion of trade, began to defend their political interests in the capital, and by the late sixteenth century, the Ottoman administration was obliged to negotiate with them.[45] Quite possibly the central administration's rationale for limiting private trade was not simply the fact that certain kinds of trade were dangerous to its own provisioning policies. In addition, the accumulation of even modest wealth in the provinces limited the possibilities for government by command alone.[46]

However, while the Ottoman central administration may have been on guard against merchants, sixteenth-century government could not have worked without trade. Even the *timar* system depended upon the functioning of local markets; if the latter had not existed, the peasants could not have paid the numerous cash dues they owed the *sipahi*. Although market dues, internal customs duties, bridge tolls and the like produced modest revenues in comparison to agriculture, the more powerful and highly-placed administrators, such as provincial governors, nevertheless often derived a disproportionate share of their income from dues levied upon trade. Certain localities, most prominently the capital, were provisioned by traders. This situation explains why the sixteenth-century Ottoman administration pursued a contradictory policy: trade was to be furthered and, moreover, left to people who were not members of the Ottoman administration, but at the same time, the power of merchants was feared and curtailed.

43 Faroqhi, *Towns and townsmen of Ottoman Anatolia*, 102–3.
44 Daniel Goffman, *Izmir and the Levantine world 1550–1650* (Seattle 1990), 54.
45 Özer Ergenç, 'Osmanlı şehirlerindeki yönetim kurumlarının niteliği üzerine bazı düşünceler', in *VIII. Türk tarih kongresi, Ankara 11–15 Ekim 1976: Kongreye sunulan bildiriler* (Ankara 1981), 1265–74.
46 Cf. İslamoğlu-İnan and Keyder, 'Agenda for Ottoman history', 41.

SOCIAL TENSIONS WITHIN THE OTTOMAN STATE

This brings us to the vexed question of social class and socio-political conflict in the sixteenth-century Ottoman empire, and to the relationship of the state apparatus to society at large. The state apparatus possessed enormous political power over Ottoman society, but the cultural aspect was significant as well. The officials who made up this apparatus were also the patrons who ordered the production of cultural artefacts, and in the case of historical and other literary writing, members of the Ottoman political class formed almost the totality of writers and a large proportion of all readers. Referring back to the political teachings of medieval manuals of Near Eastern statecraft, these officials imposed their view of a dichotomous society:[47] on the one hand, there were the taxpayers in town and country who were to be protected so that they could pay their taxes, and on the other the sultan's officials in the broad sense of the term, who paid no taxes and advanced according to more or less well-defined criteria within differentiated career lines (*askeri*).

In principle, membership of the *askeri* and *reaya* sectors was hereditary, with only a few exceptions. Anyone who had completed the requisite courses of study was considered a member of the *ulema*, and thereby became a recognised *askeri*; the same applied to young men entering the sultan's service through the levy of boys (*devşirme*). More precarious was the position of soldiers, particularly in frontier districts, who had been awarded *timars* for bravery. In the mid-sixteenth century, such *timar* holders of non-*sipahi* background were sometimes ferreted out and their *timars* taken away from them. Thus the sultan and his bureaucracy determined who was a member of the *askeri* and who was not; membership was awarded by political arbiters according to political criteria.[48]

Professional activity was only marginally significant in determining who was or who was not an *askeri*. Modest artisans and fishermen were included in this category, provided they worked for the Ottoman state.[49] But their case was clearly exceptional: for the most part Ottoman *askeri* fought and administered. Differently from the medieval European schema, the *oratores* were *askeri* only when they taught and administered

---

47 H İnalcık, 'Capital formation in the Ottoman empire', *The Journal of economic history* XIX (1969), 97 ff.

48 This means that a position in commercial life and the resultant wealth did not make a person a member of the *askeri*.

49 Ö L Barkan, 'Edirne askeri kassamına ait tereke defterleri', *Belgeler* III/5–6 (1966), 257–8.

(the *medrese* teachers and judges).[50] If they did nothing but pray, as was true of many dervish *şeyhs*, their *askeri* status was constantly in doubt, and they needed powerful protectors to maintain it.

In the eyes of the Ottoman establishment, the *reaya* were often viewed as a more or less undifferentiated mass. Ottoman writers did not often discuss the different categories of *reaya*. However, in an unsystematic way, they did recognise the existence of artisans, merchants, nomad herdsmen and mercenaries (*levend*). Wealthy merchants often enjoyed substantial privileges which furthered the accumulation of capital.[51] But in general the Ottoman political class considered that the *reaya* were, and were supposed to be, poor men; the expression *reaya fukarası* ('the poor taxpaying subjects') was frequently employed. Since *reaya* were poor, it behoved a proper member of the ruling class to protect them from the exactions of robbers and other rival claimants to the surplus they produced. It was not mentioned that the *reaya* were normally poor because so much of the grain and/or money they raised and earned was taken away as taxes.

We do not possess many coherent texts in which the *reaya* expressed their feelings concerning the upper class. Folk songs from the janissary and brigand milieu, which have not yet been studied in a systematic way, probably contain the most accessible statements of this type.[52] Even more difficult of interpretation are the brief phrases occasionally attributed to the accused in judicial documents. Whilst these utterances are often quite vivid, one must resist the temptation to regard them as straightforward expressions of *reaya* intentions.[53] Even if they are *verbatim* quotes (and there is no reason why that should always be the case) the context was obviously determined by the *askeri* bureaucrats who set up the documents – and everyday experience warns us what can be done with quotes out of context. When captured robbers and rebels made their statements, the officials often made them adopt a defiant stance *vis-à-vis* organised religion, *ulema* and tax collectors. Quite possibly the defiance was exaggerated to make the activities of these deviants seem

50 G Duby, *Les trois ordres ou l'imaginaire du féodalisme* (Paris 1978), gives an account of the medieval triad *oratores-bellatores-laboratores*. Concerning the status of *zaviye şeyhs* on the margins of the *askeri*, cf. S Faroqhi, 'Political activity among Ottoman taxpayers and the problem of sultanic legitimation', *Journal of the economic and social history of the Orient* XXXV (1992), 1–39.

51 İnalcık, 'Capital formation in the Ottoman empire', 137.

52 Cemal Kafadar gave a paper on this topic at the conference 'Legalism and political legitimation in the Ottoman empire and the early Turkish republic, ca. 1500–1940', Bochum, December 1988.

53 S Faroqhi, 'Towns, agriculture and the state in sixteenth-century Ottoman Anatolia', 125–56.

all the more reprehensible. But the documents in question can at least remind us that the officials' view of Ottoman society was by no means uncontested.

In the sixteenth century, there existed different varieties of opposition world-view. The Anatolian Kızılbaş, who were often nomadic tribesmen, but who might also be agriculturalists or even townsmen, thought in terms of a shah of Iran who was at the same time a dervish leader.[54] To claim allegiance to him was a religious as well as a political act, and quite a few people knowingly courted death by harbouring emissaries of the shah and accepting the insignia of the Safavi dervish order. Possibly there were also religiously inspired counter world-views current among Ottoman *reaya* which had nothing to do with the Safavids. The *zaviye* (dervish lodge) of Sarı Saltuk in present-day Roumania was regarded as a hotbed of heresy, but direct Iranian influence was probably weak. In 1576–77 an artisan from Amasya declared himself to be the Mahdi and found adherents, but unfortunately nothing is known about the manner in which he hoped to inaugurate the millenium.[55]

On the other hand, the protests of late sixteenth-century insurgent mercenaries contain no religious references whatsoever. The members of a robber band operating near the central Anatolian town of Çorum and captured in 1003/1594–95 had attacked the home of a *kadı*, and with their swords hacked to pieces the headgear by which the judge made visible his status as a religious scholar.[56] Supposedly, they also declared that if they had been able to lay hands on the *kadı* himself, he would have suffered a similar fate. Here, a feud with an individual *kadı* caused the robbers, some of whom claimed to be former soldiers, to voice open disrespect for the institution of *kadı*-ship in general.

Nor were other Ottoman officials held in much greater esteem by Anatolian insurgents. In 1594–95 a palace official travelling through the Anatolian countryside was set upon and murdered; the murderers cut off his head and displayed it in a public place.[57] It was customary to exhibit in this fashion the heads of people who had been executed

---

54 Hanna Sohrweide, 'Der Sieg der Safawiden in Persien und seine Rückwirkungen auf die Schiiten Anatoliens im 16. Jahrhundert', *Der Islam* 41 (1965), 95–223; C H Imber, 'The persecution of Ottoman shi'ites according to the *mühimme defterleri*, 1565–1585', *Der Islam* 56/2 (1979), 245–73.

55 Ahmed Refik, *On altıncı asırda rafizîlik ve bektaşîlik: on altıncı asırda Türkiye'de rafizîlik ve bektaşîliğe dair hazine-i evrak vesikalarını havidir* (Istanbul 1932), 16–17; BA, Mühimme defterleri 29, p. 96, no. 231 (984/1576–77).

56 These documents have been published as an appendix (pp. 29–47) to *Çorumlu*, journal of the Çorum *halkevi* ('people's house') published from 1939 to 1942.

57 BA, Mühimme defterleri 73, p. 159, no. 372 (1003/1594–95). This is a tentative interpretation. I am currently trying to decipher the ways in which Ottoman *reaya* expressed their dissatisfaction with their 'betters'.

by order of the sultan; and though we know very little about popular culture in the late sixteenth and early seventeenth centuries, it seems reasonable to assume that the murderers meant to say that they regarded the act as an execution, presumably in retaliation for the dead man's exigencies as a tax collector.

However, the most hated groups of Ottoman officials were usually the provincial governors and their retinues, known as the 'men of customary law' (*ehl-i örf*) in contradistinction to the *kadıs* and jurisconsults as representatives of religious law (*şeriat*). Any association with these people was regarded as *prima facie* evidence that the person seeking such contacts was planning to harm his neighbours, and gain an advantage at their expense. Most remarkably, the Ottoman central administration did not disagree with this view, for the phrase 'constantly associating with the *ehl-i örf*' became a standard phrase of reprobation in official documents. It would be interesting to know whether this negative view of the major provincial administrators had been equally strong in the 1490s or 1520s, or whether it was the consequence of the administrative crisis which shook Anatolia during the last quarter of the sixteenth century. No sources useful for judging this issue have so far come to light. But as a working hypothesis, we can surmise that while *reaya* disgust with the *ehl-i örf* became more intense at the end of the sixteenth century, the phenomenon itself was not totally new. Given the inclination of both *reaya* and administrators to justify their acts with precedent, a dramatic deterioration in the behaviour of the late sixteenth-century *ehl-i örf* would probably have resulted in complaints that things had been better under the saintly Sultan Bayezid or the world-conquering Selim the Grim. Certainly the employment of large numbers of mercenaries in the retinues of governors made matters worse, but the tension itself was probably permanent.[58]

Thus the view of certain Ottomanists, who see the 'classical period' as a time of universal justice and harmony, seems scarcely tenable. Social tension between those who paid taxes and those who collected them was quite visible, even though this tension did not lead to peasant rebellion.[59] Nor is it likely that Ottoman *reaya* of the sixteenth century paid their taxes more cheerfully because the *timar*-holders did not

---

58 Mustafa Akdağ, *Celalı isyanları (1550–1603)* (Ankara 1963), has given a vivid account of these tensions in the Anatolian countryside during the second half of the sixteenth century.

59 H İnalcık, 'Military and fiscal transformation', contains a discussion of this issue, and the as yet unpublished PhD dissertation by Karen Barkey, *Bandits and Bureaucrats, the Ottoman route to state centralization* (Ithaca, London 1994) arrived after the present article had gone to press.

intervene much in their daily round of tasks, but collected taxes when work on the farm had been completed. In fact, there is documentary evidence to the contrary. Peasants complained about having to spend a great deal of time transporting the *timar*-holder's or tax farmer's grain to the nearest market.[60] Certain provincial tax regulations (*kanunname*) accordingly determined the maximum distances which peasants were required to travel on this errand. However, it seems that when grain was required to feed a large city, *kadi* and tax assignee collaborated in order to oblige peasants to visit the urban market, contrary regulations notwithstanding.[61] Another occasion for disputes and foot-dragging on the part of the *reaya* was the division of newly-harvested grain in the field. In principle, peasants were not allowed to remove their grain before the tax collector had claimed his share; but what if the latter did not show up, leaving the grain to rot or be eaten by mice? Viewed from an opposing angle, a *timar*-holder who was not present in person when the harvest was divided was likely to suffer grave disadvantages. The Ottoman administration attempted to minimise this problem, by allowing *timar*-holders on campaign in a remote border region to delegate one of their number for tax-collecting purposes, an arrangement which lent itself to a good many abuses.[62]

The tensions between peasants and tax collectors did not lead to outright rebellion because Ottoman peasants had other options available. Given the huge distances involved, the modest resources of most *timar*-holders and the frequency of *timar*-holder absence due to campaigns, the limits on mobility laid down in the Ottoman *kanunnames* were often difficult to enforce. Even the famous tax registers (*tahrir*) were only of limited use to the *timar*-holder, *vakıf* administration or tax-farmer. If the *tahrir* was prepared once in thirty years, the absence of surnames and the generally low expectation of life, leading to frequent turnover, must have made it difficult to track down fugitives. If the latter had migrated to a town, they could often present witnesses who affirmed that the new migrants had lived in their midst for the number of years needed to establish official residence.[63] If the fugitive had become a theological student or a mercenary, the *timar*-holder might have even more trouble bringing him back. Thus peasants who were thoroughly dissatisfied with conditions in the village had alternatives available, and

60 S Faroqhi, *Towns and townsmen of Ottoman Anatolia*, 285.

61 Faroqhi, *Towns and townsmen of Ottoman Anatolia*, 285.

62 Gilles Veinstein, 'L'hivernage en campagne, talon d'Achille du système militaire ottoman classique, à propos des *sipahi* de Roumélie en 1559–1560', *Studia Islamica* 58 (1983), 126.

63 Faroqhi, *Towns and townsmen of Ottoman Anatolia*, 270.

as anthropological studies dealing with twentieth-century uprisings have shown, peasants will shun the dangers of rebellion as long as other, less risky options are available.[64]

CONCLUSION: THE *ASKERI* AS A CLASS

Up to this point, we have taken the division taxpayers–taxtakers, which is documented in the primary sources of the period, as given. Thus we have proceeded in a manner comparable to that practised by historians of late medieval and early modern Europe, who accept as given the 'estates', the basic subdivisions of society according to the primary sources of the time. But we can also try to apply one of the other versions of 'social class' as developed by social theorists of the nineteenth and early twentieth centuries to the historical information which we possess about the sixteenth-century Ottoman polity. Among historians dealing with France or Italy, this has given rise to heated disputes, which are often not devoid of a political colouring.[65] Conservative historians will generally consider such a proceeding as by and of itself illegitimate, while liberals or radicals may be willing to give it a try, or even to make the concept of class into an organising principle of their work.

In Ottoman history the situation is not very different. I would advocate experimenting with the term 'class', at least with respect to the *askeri*. By class I mean, in the Weberian tradition, a major group of people who share a common situation within the productive process, the possibility or impossibility of property accumulation and usually a degree of consciousness of their common status and prestige. When used in this fashion, classes are not necessarily determined by the market, as is normal under industrial capitalism, but occur in all societies in which there exists a state of more than nominal significance.[66]

---

64 James C Scott, *Weapons of the weak: the everyday forms of peasant resistance* (New Haven 1985), 298.

65 Thus a political disagreement was behind the dispute between Porchnev (*Les soulèvements populaires en France au XVIIe siècle*, Paris 1972), and Mousnier (*Peasant uprisings in seventeenth century France, Russia and China*, London 1971) concerning the character of French popular uprisings in the 17th century. Discussions concerning medieval uprisings have also been carried out against the background of a similar *problématique*.

66 As an interpretation of Weber's understanding of class, which is very useful to the practising historian, compare Hans Ulrich Wehler, *Deutsche Gesellschaftsgeschichte*, v. I, *Vom Feudalismus des Alten Reiches bis zur Defensiven Modernisierung der Reformära 1700–1815* (Munich 1989), 125–39. Needless to say, accepting Weber's notion of class does not entail acceptance of his notion of the Oriental city, which has been the source of very serious misunderstandings and is best discarded.

Moreover social classes are not permanent or monolithic. They form, re-form or split up many times in the course of the history of a given polity, and the formation and dissolution of social classes constitutes one of the main themes of social and economic history. There is a certain level of continuity between generations; sons follow their fathers even though new recruits are admitted. In a pre-industrial setting, a consciousness of common class interests and class-based 'honour' is overlaid with other loyalties, to village, tribe or patron. In fact even in industrial societies, class consciousness becomes the dominant focus of loyalty only in very specific situations.

Concerning the Ottoman empire of the later sixteenth century, we can argue that the *askeri* formed a class in this Weberian sense of the term. The *askeri* class was in no way monolithic, but constituted an alliance of differentiated groups whose members shared certain characteristics. Had it been otherwise, it would have made no sense for a writer such as Mustafa Ali to formulate criteria by which the life-style of an 'Ottoman gentleman' could be differentiated from the manner in which lesser beings conducted their lives.[67] *Timar* holders, *kadı*s or janissaries doubtless earned their respective livings in different ways, and opportunities for the accumulation of property differed accordingly. But they shared basic attributes, particularly the right not to pay taxes while living off the taxes paid by others. Moreover changes in mid-career from one administrative or military service to another were by no means unknown, and this must have strengthened the cohesion of the *askeri* as a whole.[68]

Intergenerational continuity poses more of a problem. When dealing with the Ottoman bureaucracy of the sixteenth century, scholars tend to emphasise the fact that *devşirme*s were normally of peasant background, while a significant number of *ulema* did not come from established *ulema* families, but had merchant or artisan fathers. *Timar* holders are also depicted as public officials, whom the central administration could transfer at will.[69] These observations can be used as an argument against the appropriateness of regarding the *askeri* as a class. But at the same time, measures to secure intergenerational continuity within the *askeri* were also of some significance: Mustafa Ali profoundly disapproved of sons of non-*askeri* families entering the service of the sultan,

67 Andreas Tietze, 'Mustafa 'Ali on luxury and the status symbols of Ottoman gentlemen', in *Studia turcologica memoriae Alexii Bombaci dicata* (Naples 1982), 577–90.

68 Fleischer, *Bureaucrat and intellectual*, 225.

69 Rifa'at 'Ali Abou-El-Haj, *Formation of the modern state*; Ö L Barkan, ' "Feodal" düzen ve Osmanlı timarı', in Osman Okyar and Ünal Nalbantoğlu (eds), *Türkiye iktisat tarihi semineri: metinler, tartışmalar . . .* (Ankara 1975), 17.

while the sons of *timar*-holders for whom no *timar* was available were not immediately assimilated to the *reaya*. Rather they were given the chance to perform special services, such as the procuring of saltpetre, which allowed them to maintain their tax-exempt status.[70] Even in the palace, where the royal road to advancement led through the school of pages and the personal service of the sultan, arrangements were made for the inclusion of a certain number of young men related to high-level officials.[71] The Ottoman *askeri* were not a closed group, even though official emphasis on rigid separation of *askeri* and *reaya* created pressures in that direction. But then a class need not be a closed group. In order to constitute a class, a certain level of intergenerational continuity is quite sufficient.

That the composition of the *askeri* changed over time, or rather that people attempted to change it, becomes most apparent during the *celali* rebellions. We may never know for sure whether Kalenderoğlu, the best-known rebel chief of the late sixteenth century, really intended to set up an independent principality.[72] But it is quite obvious that most rebel chiefs of the time, who rarely came from the inner circles of the Ottoman establishment, could be pacified by appointments as military commanders or pashas on the Rumelian frontier. Thus we can assume that many rebels had this possibility in mind when they first revolted, and can call this an attempt to change the composition of the *askeri* class from the outside. But how should we define the relationship of the *askeri* to the Ottoman state, the service of which was the primary duty of every Ottoman *askeri*? The 'continuance of the [sultan's] good fortune' or, differently translated, 'the continuance of the state' was secured by prayers both public and private, while 'religion and state' also became a set phrase in Ottoman official documents.[73] This manner of speaking and writing makes it seem likely that Ottoman *askeri*, or at least the more articulate among them, saw the Ottoman state as an abstraction, as something that existed outside of themselves. They did not regard themselves as identical with the Ottoman state, but saw themselves as servants of this state and of the sultan. Of course it is quite a different matter whether we are willing to accept this interpretation at face value. One could argue that the Ottoman *askeri* had created the abstraction of a state distinct from themselves the better to legitimise

---

70 Ö L Barkan (ed.), *XV ve XVI ıncı asırlarda Osmanlı imperatorluğunda ziraî ekonominin hukukî ve malî esasları, v. I: Kanunlar* (Istanbul 1943), 45, 54–5.

71 Kunt, *Sultan's servants*, 39–40.

72 Griswold, *Great Anatolian rebellion*, 169.

73 These formulas recur time and again in many documents recorded in the *mühimme defterleri* ('registers of important affairs').

their domination; after all, comparable ideological formulations are familiar enough from contemporary history. One could further make a case for the *askeri* as coterminous with the state. After all, the state structures with which the manuals of Ottoman history have familiarised us were for the most part manned by *askeri*, and ensured the recruitment, training, and emoluments of their members. I admit that I remain profoundly sceptical of the Ottoman state's ability to function in a manner contrary to the interests of its ruling class, and I would extend that scepticism to states in general. Rationalisation and bureaucratic procedures, whether by early modern or contemporary standards, result in certain limits being placed on the pursuit of short-term interests by the ruling class. But in the long run, these interests will again assert themselves.

PART II

Ideal sultan, ideal state

CHRISTINE WOODHEAD

Introduction

In 1826 Mahmud II abolished the janissary corps. No longer feared as the sultan's elite bodyguard, the janissaries and their adherents had degenerated into a reactionary political force of little military value which regularly blocked Ottoman attempts at modernisation. Immediately termed by Ottomans *vaka-i hayriye*, 'auspicious event', their removal had tremendous symbolic as well as practical significance, marking a determined break with the past and paving the way for an increasingly broad policy of internal reorganisation and centralisation. The last century of Ottoman rule – dominated by the *tanzimat* reforms, constitutionalism, and the gradual disintegration of the empire – has a momentum quite different from that of previous centuries. Though formally the final chapter in the history of the Ottoman empire, the nineteenth century is now commonly viewed also, and with equal validity, as the beginning of a new era, as the essential pre-history of the modern Republic of Turkey, without which many of Atatürk's reforms would not have been possible.[1]

However, for the pre-nineteenth-century era established interpretations of Ottoman history have been difficult to shake off. The sheer longevity of the dynasty; its survival despite attempted dismemberment of the sultanate by Timur in 1402 and despite periods of pronounced instability at the beginning of both the seventeenth and the eighteenth centuries; the dominant notions of order and conformity found in Ottoman historical sources – all encouraged broad generalisations on the nature and ideology of the pre-modern Ottoman state. Particularly influential was Wittek's *gazi* theory, which envisaged holy war and its

1 Bernard Lewis, *The emergence of modern Turkey* (London 1961; 2nd edn, 1968) is the standard account.

requirements as the principal *raison d'être* of the early Ottoman *beylik*, and later as the fatal flaw of the succeeding empire.[2] Lybyer's definition of the essentially separate and distinct 'ruling' (i.e. *devşirme*, originally Christian) and Muslim institutions of the 'classical' period provided a similarly tenacious model for the study of Ottoman administration.[3]

Ottoman historical development in the period before c. 1800 can thus appear veiled behind a smoke screen of (largely superficial) continuity in basic principles and practices. These were held responsible first for the state's rise to power and then, having seemingly failed to adapt to changed circumstances, for its gradual decline. The central concept of a sixteenth-century golden age, identified primarily with the reign of Süleyman, provided an essential focus for interpretation. This was presented as a time of unprecedented military success, of the establishment in more or less final form of the 'classical institutions' of Ottoman government, and of the attainment of a specifically Ottoman literary and artistic maturity. Surveys of Ottoman history projected an inevitably 'whiggish' view of achievements during the pre-Süleymanic era, and an increasingly doom-laden interpretation of events of the succeeding two centuries.[4] More detailed research which traces specific causes of Ottoman decline back from the late sixteenth century into the reign of Süleyman himself is largely a refinement of this simple rise-decline-fall paradigm.

That Süleyman's reign should appear an Ottoman golden age, and Süleyman himself the model for an ideal sultan, is hardly surprising, given the circumstances and achievements of his sultanate. In 1520, at the age of 26, he had succeeded his father Selim I without the disruption of fratricidal strife of the kind which had inaugurated the reigns of both Selim in 1512 and of Bayezid II in 1481. His reign of 46 years (or 48 according to the lunar *hicri* calendar) was longer than that of any other Ottoman ruler, before or after. The territorial extent of his empire, only recently doubled in size by Selim I's prestigious conquests

2 Paul Wittek, *The rise of the Ottoman empire* (London 1938, repr. 1971), and 'De la défaite d'Ankara à la prise de Constantinople', *Revue des études islamiques* 12/1 (1938), 1–34. Cf. Colin Imber, 'Paul Wittek's "De la défaite d'Ankara . . ." ', *Osmanlı araştırmaları* V (1986), 65–81 (analysis summarised in Imber's *The Ottoman empire 1300–1481*, Istanbul 1990, 12–13); Rudi Paul Lindner, 'Stimulus and justification in early Ottoman history', *Greek Orthodox Theological Review* 27/2 (1982), 207–24.

3 A H Lybyer, *The government of the Ottoman empire in the time of Suleiman the Magnificent* (Cambridge, Mass. 1913; repr. 1966). Cf. N Itzkowitz, 'Eighteenth-century Ottoman realities', *Studia Islamica* 16 (1962), 73–94; Joel Shinder, 'Early Ottoman administration in the wilderness: some limits on comparison', *International Journal of Middle East Studies* 9 (1979), 497–517.

4 E.g. S J Shaw, *History of the Ottoman empire and modern Turkey* (Cambridge 1976), vol. I: *Empire of the gazis – the rise and decline of the Ottoman empire, 1280–1808*.

of Syria, Egypt and the Muslim holy cities in the Hijaz, was by the 1540s further expanded to include Iraq and most of Hungary. Victories over Safavid Iran and the extension of Ottoman influence on the North African coast testified further to his ascendancy. Süleyman was the dominant symbol of the Muslim threat to Christian control of the Mediterranean and to the stability of Habsburg Europe; his was by far the largest and most powerful Muslim state in the Islamic world at the time. In contrast to most European princes, he had ready access to considerable wealth, and spent lavishly and easily on major architectural projects, on charitable endowments, in the support of cultural and artistic development, and in all aspects of imperial festivities and accoutrements.

Moreover, Süleyman was probably the first Ottoman sultan whose image registered widely among the courts and peoples of western Europe. Apart from the obvious repercussions of Ottoman military and naval encroachment in Hungary and the Mediterranean, Christian curiosity was fed by a variety of sources, including letters and reports from merchants and envoys visiting Istanbul, broadsheets carrying the latest news of Ottoman military and (sometimes) political events, and subsequently through the popularity of 'Turkish' themes and images in drama of the late sixteenth century. To Europeans, Süleyman richly deserved the Renaissance sobriquet 'the Magnificent'.

Details of Süleyman's reign below the level of textbook survey naturally reveal a less than ideal state, and also one in which, in the latter part of his reign, Süleyman felt sufficiently insecure to engineer the deaths of two of his sons in order to forestall his own deposition. Elderly and often ill, his military and political competence became increasingly open to question during the last two decades of his reign. His death in 1566, though no doubt sincerely mourned on a personal level, was perhaps a relief to those seeking an opportunity for a new impetus in state affairs. In this light it is proper to ask how Ottoman perceptions of Süleyman and his era changed over time, and for what reasons. At what stage did his reign take on for Ottomans the aura of a 'golden age', how was this expressed, and what was its significance both for the making of later Ottoman policy and for the writing of Ottoman history?

The four essays which follow attempt to set in comparative perspective the concepts of ideal state and ideal sultan, against which to assess Süleyman's reputation. They offer initial food for thought on a topic which requires further study. Peter Holt's analysis of the presentation of Saladin and the thirteenth-century Mamluk sultan Baybars as ideal rulers suggests certain conventions of style and format within Islamic literary and historiographical tradition which influenced contemporary Ottoman 'biographers' of Süleyman. The political imperatives behind such composition, principally the need to establish appropriate credentials for leadership, appear equally strongly in the Ottoman case. This theme is pursued by Colin Imber in his examination of the succession of legitimation theories present in Ottoman historical writing of the fifteenth and sixteenth centuries. The development of Ottoman political thinking can be traced through the notions of warrior king and champion of the Faith, of geneaological and hereditary right, and of religious sanction through the caliphate for a possible claim to universal sovereignty. Peter Burke discusses the range of meaning encompassed in western Europe by Renaissance understandings of the term 'golden age' – terminology which differed markedly from that used by the Ottomans themselves. There was, for instance, no comparable Ottoman concept associated with 'gold', just as there was no commonly-used Ottoman equivalent of 'the Magnificent'. There were, however, parallels in the purposes for which the notion of the ideal state could be used. Building upon these, the final essay assesses the image of Süleyman and his style of rule as presented in contemporary Ottoman historiography and as elaborated implicitly or explicitly in Ottoman political tracts of the later sixteenth and the seventeenth centuries.

As the European image of Süleyman is a topic of a rather different order, bound up with Christian perceptions of power, morality, and the self-image of the West, it has been deliberately excluded from detailed discussion here.[5] Nor has an attempt been made to examine Süleyman's image in the eyes of contemporary Muslim rulers, such as the Safavid shah of Iran or the Central Asian Uzbek khans. The effusively complimentary rhetoric of Shah Tahmasp's letter to 'Sultan Süleyman Shah Khan' on the occasion of the treaty of Amasya in 1555 appears to leave practically no variant of traditional encomia unused, and clearly signifies an appreciation of Ottoman power – as it perhaps would when suing for peace.[6] It is likely, however, that there was more to this than simply the rhetoric of the moment. The 'becoming respect' often shown towards the Ottomans by Persian historians[7] may be appropriately reflected in a late sixteenth-century Ottoman view of Tahmasp

---

5 Cf. M E Yapp, 'Europe in the Turkish mirror', *Past and Present* 137 (1992), 134–55.

6 Text given in Petra Kappert (ed.), *Geschichte Sultan Süleymān Kānūnīs von 1520 bis 1557, oder Tabakātü' l-memālik ve derecātü' l-mesālik von Celālzāde Muṣṭafā* (Wiesbaden 1981), ff. 491a–4b.

7 J R Walsh, 'The historiography of Ottoman-Safavid relations in the sixteenth and seventeenth centuries', in B Lewis and P M Holt (eds), *Historians of the Middle East* (London 1962), 204.

(shah 1524–76) as a sad figure struggling to retain control of an inferior system of government, a poor relation envying Süleyman his wealth, the good order, and the general prosperity of his empire.[8]

8 Christine Woodhead, ' "The present terrour of the world?" Contemporary views of the Ottoman empire c. 1600', *History* 72/234 (1987), 27.

P M HOLT

The sultan as ideal ruler: Ayyubid and Mamluk prototypes

> The more one reads and sifts the more dubious become all these chronicles,
> the more questionable becomes every assertion in them.
>
> Lord Rosebery, *Napoleon: the last phrase*

I

In Shawwāl 581/December 1185 Saladin was stricken with a prolonged
illness, so serious that his life was despaired of. Andrew Ehrenkreutz,
the least sympathetic of his modern biographers, has suggested in the
form of a rhetorical query, that if in fact he had died at this time, his
career would have presented an appearance remarkably different from
that which has been conventionally ascribed to it over the last eight
centuries.[1] At the time of Saladin's illness, to develop Ehrenkreutz's
point, the crowning mercies of the defeat of the Franks at Ḥaṭṭīn and
the restoration of Jerusalem to Islam lay nearly two years in the future.
The previous eleven years since the death of Saladin's lord, Nūr al-Dīn
b. Zangī, in 569/1174 had revealed a consistent and dominant purpose
in his policy and actions, namely to usurp the rule over the Zangid
possessions in Syria and Mesopotamia. To achieve this he was already
provided with a base in Egypt, which he had ruled since 564/1169 as
Nūr al-Dīn's viceroy. Saladin's bearing as an over-mighty subject had
aroused his lord's apprehensions, and only Nūr al-Dīn's death had ended
the growing tension between the two. In the ensuing decade, during

---

1 Andrew S Ehrenkreutz, *Saladin* (Albany 1972), 237.

which Saladin gained possession of the two Zangid capitals in Syria, Damascus in 570/1174 and Aleppo in 579/1183, his dealings with the Latin kingdom of Jerusalem resemble those of his predecessors – an unstable relationship of warfare alternating with truces between Muslim and Christian parties which were equally involved in the vicissitudes of regional politics.

If, then, Saladin had died in 1185, during, one may note, operations against Mosul, the capital of Zangid Mesopotamia, his career, as Ehrenkreutz suggests, would hardly have attracted more notice than those of other warlords of the period, who in striving to establish themselves might more or less incidentally become embroiled with the Frankish states, and thus sanctify a part of their blood-letting as holy war. The death of Saladin, had it occurred at this time, would moreover have denied him his most influential apologist, Bahā' al-Dīn Ibn Shaddād, whose short, well-written and persuasive biography, *al-Nawādir al-sulṭāniyya wa'l-maḥāsin al-Yūsufiyya* ('The rare merits of Sultan Yusuf') was used by later Arabic historians, and as published with a Latin translation in 1732 was the principal primary source on Saladin available to Gibbon and Stubbs. Bahā' al-Dīn was certainly acquainted with Saladin in 1185, but only because he had twice come to him as the ambassador of the Zangid lord of Mosul. It was not until 584/1188 that he changed masters. Returning from the pilgrimage to Mecca, he visited the newly recovered holy city of Jerusalem, and was dissuaded by Saladin from returning to Mosul. So at least he tells us.

Bahā' al-Dīn was therefore in Saladin's personal entourage only during the last five years of the sultan's life. He wrote *al-Nawādir* after Saladin's death but when he himself was still in Ayyubid service as the judge of Aleppo, having been appointed by Saladin's son, al-Ẓāhir Ghāzī. The structure of the biography is interesting and significant. In the published edition edited by the late Gamāl al-Dīn al-Shayyāl,[2] a short preliminary chapter, one page in length, covers Saladin's early years from his birth in 532/1137–8 to his participation in the expedition to Egypt led by his uncle, Shīrkūh, in 558/1163. This is followed by eight chapters dealing with his virtues, and taking up twenty-eight pages. Of the remainder of the book, forty pages cover events of the quarter-century from 558–83/1163–87, while no less than 170 pages are devoted to the following six years to Saladin's death in 589/1193. This chronological imbalance in itself imposes a certain perspective of events on the reader.

---

2 Bahā' al-Dīn b. Shaddād, *al-Nawādir al-sulṭāniyya wa'l-maḥāsin al-Yūsufiyya*, ed. Gamāl al-Dīn al-Shayyāl (Cairo 1964). Hereafter *Nawādir*.

The stage is set for the presentation of Saladin as the ideal ruler by the eight short chapters on his virtues – in effect a mirror for princes given specific personal application. These chapters represent him as displaying the primitive virtues honoured among the Arabs (although Saladin himself was, of course, not an Arab), the qualities of a pious Muslim, and the characteristics of a good ruler – notably generosity and courage, orthodox belief and devotion to the holy war, exemplary justice and magnanimity. Then follows the comparatively brief narrative of the years before Ḥaṭṭīn. Saladin's transcendent abilities are soon made apparent. Unwillingly accompanying his uncle on the three expeditions to Egypt in 558/1163, 562/1167 and 564/1169, he became the older man's indispensable adviser. He alone had the courage to capture the *wazīr* Shāwar, who was the obstacle to their plans to control Egypt. When, after this act of politic treachery, Shīrkūh succeeded to the wazirate, Saladin served as his omnicompetent deputy, and when Shīrkūh died a couple of months later, Saladin himself became *wazīr* (*de facto* ruler of Egypt under the Fatimid caliph). Bahā' al-Dīn hardly suggests the controversy which actually surrounded this succession, but says:

> ... matters went forward in the most orderly fashion. He lavished money, and won the men over. Caring little for the world, he ruled it, and thanked God for His grace.

This, however, is shown as the turning-point in Saladin's career. Bahā' al-Dīn goes on to say 'He gave up wine and renounced pastimes, putting on the garment of serious endeavour'.[3] It was at this time, so he told Bahā' al-Dīn, that God inspired him to undertake the conquest of the Frankish coastlands. The picture of Saladin as an ideal *wazīr* is rounded off with a reference to his re-establishment of Sunnī Islam in Egypt after the two centuries of the Fatimid caliphate. The tension between Saladin and Nūr al-Dīn in the last year of the latter's life is glossed over with the statement, attributed by Bahā' al-Dīn to Saladin:

> I heard that Nūr al-Dīn might march against us in Egypt. Some of our companions advised open rebellion against him, and armed conflict to repulse him, if his intention was verified. I alone withstood them, saying that was all wrong, and so we continued to dispute until the news of his death arrived.[4]

Bahā' al-Dīn goes on to present in the best light he can Saladin's activities in the following years. His operations against the Franks are

---

3 *Nawādir*, 40.
4 *Nawādir*, 47.

duly recounted, but it cannot be disguised that they were relatively insignificant, and usually unsuccessful. Of the defeat at al-Ramla in 573/1177 he says 'It was a great weakness, which God set right by the famous battle of Ḥaṭṭīn – God be praised!'.[5] The truces which Saladin made with the Latin kingdom in this period are not mentioned. His preoccupation with the elimination of Zangid power from Syria, and if possible from Mesopotamia also, could not be ignorerd, but it is carefully presented as an aspect of his devotion to the holy war. Nūr al-Dīn's son, al-Ṣāliḥ Ismāʿīl, was, we are told, 'a mere boy, who could not support the burdens of kingship, nor by himself repel the enemy of God from the land'. Saladin therefore came to him in Syria, 'so that he might be his guardian to control his situation and straighten out his business, which had gone awry'.[6] Hence he occupied Damascus. Aleppo, the northern capital, eluded him for another nine years, until eighteen months after al-Ṣāliḥ Ismāʿīl's death. Bahāʾ al-Dīn comments:

> Behold this zeal, which the triumphant capture of Aleppo could not distract from the Holy War! But his intention was to make use of the country for the *jihād*.[7]

The much longer final portion of the work, covering the six glorious years of unremitting holy war from the Ḥaṭṭīn campaign to Saladin's death, develops this portrait of the sultan as *mujāhid* (champion of Islam in the holy war).

This presentation was not the first of its kind. Saladin's secretary, ʿImād al-Dīn al-Iṣfahānī, who had held the same office under Nūr al-Dīn, was the author of a work entitled *al-Fatḥ al-Qussī fiʾl-fatḥ al-Qudsī* ('The eloquent exposition of the conquest of Jerusalem' – the Arabic title incorporating a pun which eludes translation). Although the earliest extant manuscript is dated 595/1199, D S Richards cites evidence that the work was 'already available in some form during Saladin's lifetime', and that a passage was read to him in 588/1192.[8] The chronological range of *al-Fatḥ* is more limited than that of *al-Nawādir*: it is not a biography of Saladin but an account of the period from Ḥaṭṭīn to Saladin's death. If *al-Fatḥ* was, as Richards believes, originally intended for presentation to Saladin, we have an explanation of the exalted

---

5 *Nawādir*, 53.
6 *Nawādir*, 50.
7 *Nawādir*, 63.
8 D S Richards, 'A consideration of two sources for the life of Saladin', *Journal of Semitic Studies* 25/1 (1980), 61. Hereafter Richards.

phraseology of the introduction, where Saladin's taking of Jerusalem is boldly compared to the Prophet's *hijra* (emigration) to Medina.

With such a eulogistic record available, why did Bahā' al-Dīn set to work to produce *al-Nawādir*? There were perhaps two reasons. The first is stylistic. Al-Iṣfahānī, a master of the high style of Islamic chanceries, writing to glorify his victorious master, couched his invaluable first-hand narrative of events in a rhymed prose of such elaboration that it has baffled readers, both eastern and western, from his own time to the present day. Al-Bundārī (fl. 624/1227), who made an abridgement of al-Iṣfahānī's major chronicle of Saladin, *al-Barq al-Shāmī*, admits in phraseology not unworthy of al-Iṣfahānī himself that 'I found the pearls of his intentions hidden in the seas of the clashing waves of his rhymes, and I saw that the highlights of his expressions were submerged in the flood of his host of successive epithets'.[9] The late Henri Massé, who translated *al-Fath* into French, made the same criticism in more mundane language: 'while admiring the author's verbal virtuosity, it must be admitted that the complications of style and vocabulary . . . often mar this masterpiece, the narrative and documentary merits of which are undoubted'.[10] The straightforward narrative and somewhat pedestrian prose of *al-Nawādir* contrast markedly with the rhetoric of *al-Fath*. Bahā' al-Dīn's work might appeal less to connoisseurs of Arabic style but it offered to the general public a clear and agreeable presentation of Saladin and his achievements.

There may also have been a second and political inducement for Bahā' al-Dīn to write as and when he did. Ibn al-Athīr, the spokesman of anti-Ayyubid opinion, produced a dynastic history of his own patrons, the Zangids. The project was, he says, formed in the time of the atabeg Nūr al-Dīn Arslān Shāh, who reigned from 589/1193 to Rajab 607/January 1211, and the work actually ends in 607/1211 at the start of his son's reign. Ostensibly Ibn al-Athīr's work is a history of the atabegs of Mosul, as promised by its title, *al-Bāhir fī ta'rīkh atābakāt al-Mawṣil* ('The splendid chronicle of the atabegs of Mosul'). In fact almost half the book is devoted to describing the deeds of Nūr al-Dīn b. Zangī, the Syrian atabeg who was Saladin's lord but who never ruled in Mosul. The account of Nūr al-Dīn is given in such detail that he completely overshadows his insignificant kinsmen in Mesopotamia. If this biography of Nūr al-Dīn is set beside *al-Nawādir*, it seems very likely that one is a counterblast to the other. The problem

---

9 Al-Fath b. 'Alī al-Bundārī, *Sanā al-Barq al-Shāmī*, ed. Fathiyya al-Nabarāwī (Cairo 1979), 12.

10 Henri Massé, 'Imād al-Dīn . . . al-Iṣfahānī', *EI*² III, 1158.

is to decide on chronological priority. The earliest extant manuscript of *al-Nawādir* is dated 625/1228.[11] However, internal evidence suggests that the work was composed before Jumādā II 613/October 1216, and there is one single reference which implies a date before Muḥarram 595/November 1198. If this last is disregarded,[12] it is possible that *al-Nawādir* appeared after *al-Bāhir*, and was a response to Ibn al-Athīr's idealised presentation of Nūr al-Dīn. But the evidence is not conclusive, and the question should perhaps remain open.

However this may be, the accounts of the two heroes offer a number of parallels. The narrative of Nūr al-Dīn's exploits concludes with an appendix on his exemplary virtues. He is presented as a paragon of justice, asceticism, piety and knowledge, only equalled by the Rightly-guided Caliphs and 'Umar b. 'Abd al-'Azīz; Ibn al-Athīr recounts anecdotes in support of these claims. This passage, twenty pages long, resembles the similar catalogue of Saladin's virtues in *al-Nawādir*. In places one appears almost a point-by-point reply to the other. For example, Nūr al-Dīn is particularly eulogised as the just ruler, and Ibn al-Athīr commemorates his most important institutional innovation in this field, the establishment of *dār al-'adl*, a fixed place in which by the exercise of his prerogative power, he could supplement and enforce the *sharī'a* justice of the *qāḍī's* court. This is given overtones of anti-Ayyubid polemic: Ibn al-Athīr asserts that *dār al-'adl* was set up because the *qāḍī* of Damascus dared not deal with wrongs committed by the military officers, especially Shīrkūh, 'who acted as if he were a partner in the kingdom'.[13] Nūr al-Dīn's justice, we are told in another anti-Ayyubid anecdote, made itself felt even after his death. A Damascene, wronged by one of Saladin's soldiers, could obtain no redress from the sultan. He invoked the memory of 'the just king', al-Malik al-'Ādil, and a mob gathered at Nūr al-Dīn's tomb. Thereupon Saladin granted him redress, and gave him a reward. The plaintiff

> . . . wept more bitterly than at first. Saladin said to him, 'Why are you weeping?' He said, 'I weep for a ruler who does justice among us after his death'. Saladin said, 'That is true. All the justice you see in me, I learnt from him.'[14]

The justice of the two rulers is the subject of a pair of parallel anecdotes, of which there are other examples. Ibn al-Athīr tells how,

11 MS. Wetzstein, II, 1893, Berlin.
12 Richards, 60, calls it 'a slender thread'.
13 *Recueil des historiens des croisades: Historiens orientales*, II/ii, 305–6. Hereafter *RHC: Hor.*
14 *RHC: Hor*, II/ii, 304–5.

when a subject raised a complaint concerning property against the atabeg, Nūr al-Dīn

> ... went to the *qāḍī* and said 'I have come to trial. Follow your usual procedure with me'. On his appearance, he treated him equally with his opponent, and interrogated him. The case against him was not established, and it was established that the property belonged to Nūr al-Dīn. Thereupon Nūr al-Dīn said to the *qāḍī* and those present, 'Has he invalidated my right of possession?' They said, 'No'. He said, 'Bear witness that I give him this property concerning which he brought me to court. I knew that he had no case against me, and I appeared with him only so that he should not think that I wronged him. Since it is apparent that right is on my side, I give it to him.'[15]

Bahā' al-Dīn recounts a similar incident which occurred when he himself was *qāḍī* in Jerusalem, a post to which he had been appointed by Saladin. A certain merchant, 'Umar al-Khilāṭī, complained that Saladin had unjustly deprived him of the estate of his deceased *mamlūk*, and he produced a legal document in support of his claim. Saladin agreed that the case should be heard, and descended from his royal seat to be on a level with the plaintiff. However, 'Umar al-Khilāṭī gained no advantage from this condescension. Saladin asserted that the *mamlūk* had been his, that he had manumitted him, and that on his death his estate passed to his heirs. He then produced a cloud of witnesses from among his own high officers to testify that at the alleged date of the document the *mamlūk* had been in his possession in Egypt. The plaintiff's case thus failed in this instance also, but Saladin (at the prompting of Bahā' al-Dīn) played the magnanimous ruler by giving the merchant a robe of honour and a considerable bounty.[16]

To conclude: whether or not he was replying to Ibn al-Athīr, the object of Bahā' al-Dīn in *al-Nawādir* is to present Saladin as an ideal ruler. He is shown as a paragon of all the virtues, and above all as a champion in the holy war against the Franks, his efforts being crowned by the recapture of Jerusalem and the beating back of the Third Crusade. But Bahā' al-Dīn was not merely composing an encomium for the gratification of Saladin's kinsmen – and in particular his own patron, al-Ẓāhir Ghāzī. He wrote to legitimise Saladin's usurpation of the Zangid patrimony, and thereby to legitimise Ayyubid rule as it continued after Saladin's death. *Al-Nawādir* is one of the most successful pieces of propaganda ever conceived, and it has coloured the writings of historians, Near Eastern and European, Muslim and Christian alike, for nearly 800 years.

15 *RHC: Hor,* II/ii, 302–3.
16 *Nawādir,* 14–16.

II

A second presentation of an ideal ruler is the biography of the Mamluk sultan Baybars (regn. 658–76/1260–77), *al-Rawḍ al-zāhir fī sīrat al-Malik al-Ẓahir*, written by his head chancery clerk, Muḥyī al-Dīn Ibn ʿAbd al-Ẓāhir. Although this is much longer than *al-Nawādir*, it is similarly structured and probably modelled on the earlier work. In the published edition by ʿAbd al-Azīz al-Khuwayṭir,[17] one can discern a tripartite construction resembling that of *al-Nawādir*: a preliminary section of twenty-eight pages dealing with Baybars's life to his accession as sultan, another of twenty-three pages on his virtues, followed by the remainder of the book, nearly 400 pages, providing a chronicle of his reign. Ibn ʿAbd al-Ẓāhir states that he was an eyewitness, in constant attendance on the sultan and enjoying his confidence, and that the work was written for the royal library. It was therefore a commissioned work, and there is evidence that it was even more than this.

Ibn ʿAbd al-Ẓāhir's problems of presentation were in some respects more difficult than those which had confronted Bahāʾ al-Dīn. Saladin came from a Muslim family of Kurdish immigrants who had voluntarily entered the service of the Zangids. Baybars, by contrast, was a first-generation convert to Islam, who had his origin among the Kipchak Turks, and who was recruited as a *mamlūk* into the military household of al-Ṣāliḥ Ayyūb, the last effective Ayyubid sultan of Egypt (regn. 637–47/1240–49). Baybars himself achieved the sultanate as the result of a double usurpation: first, the *coup d'état* of 648/1250, in which al-Muʿaẓẓam Tūrān-Shāh, al-Ṣāliḥ Ayyūb's son and successor, was killed, and which brought Ayyubid rule in Egypt to an end; secondly, the assassination in 658/1260 of Baybars's immediate predecessor, Quṭuz. The problem was to present this barbarian warrior, a *mamlūk* who had made his way red-handed to the throne, as a ruler whose ideal qualities would be manifest and acceptable to the sultan himself, to his Mamluk comrades, and to his Egyptian and Syrian subjects. It was a literary feat accomplished with tact and discretion, and duly rewarded by the sultan.

Whether the episode of slavery through which Baybars and other *mamlūks* passed was seriously regarded as a social blemish outside their own circle is not easy to say. At the beginning of the Mamluk sultanate, there was a tribal rising of the Arabs in Egypt, and one of the leaders declared:

---

17 Muḥyī al-Dīn b. ʿAbd al-Ẓāhir, *al-Rawḍ al-zāhir fī sīrat al-Malik al-Ẓāhir*, ed. ʿAbd al-ʿAzīz al-Khuwayṭir (al-Riyāḍ 1976). Hereafter *Rawḍ*.

We are the lords of the land. We are more worthy to rule than the Mamluks. It was enough to serve the Ayyubids, who were rebels and took the land by force, and they are only the slaves of the rebels.[18]

This was, however, an isolated incident and an unusual expression of feeling. The chroniclers and other historical writers make no distinction on this point between the Mamluk sultans and other rulers. From the point of view of the Mamluks themselves, their original status as slaves in the eyes of Islamic law seems to have been wholly unimportant – slavery was a preliminary phase in a military career which could lead to high office and even to the sultanate. Two things were important: first, the master (*ustādh*) who acquired, trained and ultimately emancipated the *mamlūk*; secondly, the military household composed of the *mamlūk*'s comrades (*khushdāshiyya*) in the service of the *ustādh*. These were the objects of the *mamlūk*'s primary loyalties, a loyalty towards the master which was virtually indefeasible but one towards the comrades which was sometimes less firmly assured.

It is in the light of these Mamluk social and ethical concepts that Ibn 'Abd al-Ẓāhir presents the early career of Baybars before his accession as sultan. Baybars is depicted as a close companion of al-Ṣāliḥ Ayyūb, whose royal qualities are eulogised. Here the biographer exercises a certain economy with the truth. Baybars is shown as patterning himself on al-Ṣāliḥ Ayyūb so that he became in effect the sultan's spiritual heir, 'and the sultanate shone in the face of his deeds, and his prowess declared what God would make of it'.[19] With Baybars thus preordained to the sultanate, al-Ṣāliḥ Ayyūb's heir by blood, al-Mu'aẓẓam Tūrān-Shāh, is adjudged incompetent and incorrigible. At the crisis of the campaign against St Louis, 'al-Malik al-Mu'aẓẓam could not bring himself to mount a horse for battle but sailed in a boat like a spectator'.[20] These and other defects of character and conduct, which threatened the ascendancy of the Ṣāliḥiyya (i.e. the military household formed by al-Ṣāliḥ Ayyūb) led to the successful assassination plot, in which (it is implied) Baybars took a leading part. Ibn 'Abd al-Ẓāhir continues to represent Baybars as pre-eminent among the Ṣāliḥiyya in the stormy events of the succeeding decade until in 658/1260 he set out with Quṭuz to confront the ever-victorious army of the Mongols in Palestine. At 'Ayn Jālūt 'there was the victory which God had ordained, and of which Baybars was the cause'.[21] Baybars is shown as wanting to press

18 Al-Maqrīzī, *al-Sulūk*,I, ed. Muḥammad Muṣṭafā Ziyāda (Cairo 1956), 386.
19 *Rawḍ*, 47.
20 *Rawḍ*, 49.
21 *Rawḍ*, 64.

on with the holy war, and being restrained by Quṭuz out of jealousy. This led to the murder plot, in which Baybars struck the fatal blow.

Having, after some controversy, been elected sultan by the Mamluk amirs, Baybars returned to Egypt, where

> ... he proceeded to restore the regime of al-Ṣāliḥ with its divine laws and human regulations, and he appointed for its affairs *mamlūks* of the deceased al-Malik al-Ṣāliḥ, whom he had chosen and selected.[22]

The true political significance of Baybars's coup is brought out in the next section of the biography, dealing with his policy towards his *khushdāshiyya*:

> When God gave him the kingdom, nothing distracted him from granting favours to the old and young among them. He promoted them after everyone of them had believed that he would never again find a supporter. . . . When God graciously permitted the advent of the sultan's regime, he gathered the fugitives, brought in those afar off, promoted those who lacked advancement, appointed those who had been dismissed, and returned to them the possessions, chattels and benefits of which they had been deprived. He appointed the deserving to amirates, promoted those worthy of promotion, and set up a special treasury department for them.[23]

Clearly the golden days of al-Ṣāliḥ Ayyūb had returned for the veterans of his household!

The Baybars who is presented in this portion of the biography is therefore essentially a paragon of the Mamluk virtues, who models himself on his *ustādh*, and assists his *khushdāshiyya* in times of hardship and prosperity alike. His accession to the sultanate is shown as being in the first place the triumph of one Mamluk household over another to the advantage and benefit of the Ṣāliḥiyya. There is, however, a further implication. Since Baybars demonstrated by his qualities and character that he was the true heir of al-Ṣāliḥ Ayyūb, there was no usurpation. The two murders in which Baybars was involved, that of Tūrān-Shāh and that of Quṭuz, merely opened the way to the throne for the rightful sultan. Thus his legitimacy as the successor to the Ayyubid dynasty is established.

With Baybars on the throne, Ibn 'Abd al-Ẓāhir begins the second part of his work, in which the lineaments of the ideal sultan prevail over those of the ideal Mamluk. Like Bahā' al-Dīn with Saladin, Ibn 'Abd al-Ẓāhir sets to work to recount Baybars's virtues with appropriate illustrative anecdotes, which, however, are set in the limited circle of Mamluk military society. First comes his bravery, which is demonstrated

22 *Rawḍ*, 71.
23 *Rawḍ*, 74.

by his proficiency in horsemanship and warfare, 'and also by the taking of the kingdom with his sword and single-handed'![24] Next come his readiness to pardon and his forbearance, shown above all in his clemency towards his former comrade, Sanjar al-Ḥalabī, who proclaimed himself sultan in Damascus at the start of Baybars's reign. His lavish generosity is then extolled. As an exile and chief of mercenaries before the coming of the Mongols, he had been richly remunerated by the Syrian Ayyubids, 'yet of all that he kept only an outer garment, a sword and a horse'.[25] After becoming sultan, relates Ibn 'Abd al-Ẓāhir on Baybars's own authority, he spent over a million gold dinars on the forlorn hopes sent against the Mongols under the shadow-caliph and the princes of Mosul.

Ibn 'Abd al-Ẓāhir has several chapters presenting Baybars as the just ruler of tradition. His abolition of uncanonical taxes, his restoration of *dār al-'adl* (palace of justice), and his insistence on payment being made for goods purveyed for him on campaign are given as instance of this function. A chapter on his maintenance of the *sharī'a* is illustrated by a familiar type of anecdote. Long before he became sultan, Baybars had commenced the sinking of a well for the benefit of the poor – or possibly dervishes (*al-fuqarā'*). While he was in exile, the work was completed by an ordinary soldier, who quarrelled with the intended beneficiaries. Baybars, now sultan, summoned the man, who demanded judgment according to the *sharī'a*, apparently over the ownership of the well. By order of the *atābak*, who presided in *dār al-'adl*, the case was referred to the sultan, who set up a show trial conducted before the chief judge. When the soldier appeared,

> . . . the *atābak* said to the sultan, 'Let my lord betake himself with him to the Holy Law'. So the sultan arose, ungirt his sword, and placed himself on an equality with his opponent, standing before the chief judge, who was seated.

The outcome was that the *imāms* of the four law schools declared that the sultan was the owner of the well, but should compensate his opponent for his part of the construction and fittings. The case thus ended amicably with the sultan bestowing robes on the *atābak*, the chief judge and his servant, and the sultan's opponent.[26] The incident resembles the anecdotes told about Nūr al-Dīn and Saladin, but with a notably more elaborate *mise en scène*, characteristic of the greater institutional formality of Mamluk government.

24 *Rawḍ*, 75.
25 *Rawḍ*, 76.
26 *Rawḍ*, 84–6.

The chapter dealing with Baybars's loyalty offers some points of interest. Much of it is taken up with an account of his treatment of the Ayyubid refugees, who had fled from the Mongols in Syria when Quṭuz was sultan. Quṭuz, distracted by military affairs, neglected them, but when Baybars came to the throne he provided for their needs, and allowed the two leading Ayyubid princes to ride with him in state processions – the equivalent of a 21-gun salute! The chapter begins, however, with a very different instance of his loyalty, 'the vengeance for his brother-in-arms, the Amir Fāris al-Dīn Aqṭāy, upon al-Malik al-Muẓaffar'.[27] Al-Muẓaffar Quṭuz, while in the service of his *ustādh*, the sultan al-Muʿizz Aybak, had murdered Aqṭāy, the chief of the Ṣāliḥiyya household, and in due course Baybars brought about the murder of Quṭuz. At this point the mask of the Muslim sultan slips to reveal the Turkish tribesman. It is quickly resumed some pages later, when Ibn ʿAbd al-Ẓāhir goes on to enumerate Baybars's public works: on the Prophet's mosque at Medina and the Dome of the Rock at Jerusalem, the restoration of misappropriated estates belonging to the *awqāf* (pious endowments) at Hebron, the construction and refurbishment of fortifications, the building of fighting-ships, and other items designed to enhance the security and prosperity of the Muslim inhabitants of his realm. It is unnecessary to follow Ibn ʿAbd al-Ẓāhir into the annals of Baybars's reign, in which he appears above all as a champion of Islam. The Turkish warrior is transformed into the *mujāhid*, holding back the heathen Mongols from Syria, and continuing with notable success the holy war against the diminished Frankish states. He dies in the odour of sanctity after his last campaign into the Mongol protectorate of Rūm, during which he is enthroned as successor to the Seljuk sultans at Kayseri – the most impressive and least durable of his military and political achievements.

III

There was to be a sequel to this well-laboured official royal biography. Ibn ʿAbd al-Ẓāhir had a nephew, Shāfiʿ b. ʿAlī al–ʿAsqalānī, who like other members of the family was employed in the sultan's chancery. He was born in 649/1251–2, had the misfortune to lose an eye in the battle of Ḥimṣ against the Mongols in 680/1281, but lived until 730/ 1330, continuing his literary, if not his official, activities. He tells us that his uncle discussed with him the preparation of an abridgement of

27 *Rawḍ*, 79.

al-Rawḍ al-zāhir, but he did not undertake this during Ibn 'Abd al-Ẓāhir's lifetime 'out of respect to him in asserting what he denied, and denying what he asserted'. However, Ibn 'Abd al-Ẓāhir died in 692/1293, sixteen years after Baybars himself, and between this date and 716/1316 (as indicated in the colophon of the unique manuscript), Shāfiʿ produced his own contribution to the biography of the great sultan.

The title is innocent enough, *Ḥusn al-manāqib al-sirriyya al-muntazaʿa min al-sīra al-Ẓāhiriyya* ('The excellence of the recondite virtues extracted from the biography of Baybars').[28] Innocent also is the statement in which Shāfiʿ announces his intention:

> I have abridged it desiring brevity, which is the soul of good style, the sweet and potable waters of eloquence. I have recorded the more important leading matters from it, so that it may be delightful to read, and returned to with pleasure.[29]

But *Ḥusn al-manāqib* is not a mere abridgement of *al-Rawḍ al-zāhir* but rather a revised version. Shāfiʿ indicates very clearly the limitations within which his uncle wrote:

> Let it be his excuse, if he extolled [the sultan], enhancing his importance, treating his policy at excessive length, that [the sultan] told him about his career, showing his commendation by a series of robes and gifts, depending on him for grammar and for setting it down, remunerating him for producing this beautiful biography with its high style, listening with a smile of approval to its phrases. When [Ibn 'Abd al-Ẓāhir] had completed a portion of it, [the sultan] would take his seat, and bid him be seated so that he might hear it. He would recompense him with precious robes and so forth as a reward for the enjoyment of this remarkable creation.[30]

From this it would seem that *al-Rawḍ al-zāhir* is not so much a biography of the sultan as Baybars's memoirs.

Baybars's achievements after he became sultan were, of course, matters of common knowledge, and were indeed both real and substantial. In campaigns in Syria almost every year he had kept the Mongols at bay, and had brought unremitting pressure to bear on the Frankish states. Several of the great Crusader castles were taken, and in 666/1268 the northern city of Antioch, the capital of the principality, fell to him. Where these events are concerned, Shāfiʿ is mainly content with the straightforward abridgement of his original. His work as a revising editor is noticeable rather in his treatment of Baybars's career

---

28 Shāfiʿ b. 'Alī b. 'Abbās al-Kātib, *Kitāb ḥusn al-manāqib al-sirriyya al-muntazaʿa min al-sīra al-Ẓāhiriyya*, ed. 'Abd al-'Azīz al-Khuwayṭir (al-Riyāḍ 1976). Hereafter *Ḥusn*.

29 *Ḥusn*, 26–7.

30 *Ḥusn*, 166.

before he became sultan. He specifically notes that Ibn 'Abd al-Ẓāhir does not mention that Baybars was first a *mamlūk* of the Amir 'Alā' al-Dīn al Bunduqdār, having been taken into the military household of al-Ṣāliḥ Ayyūb when his master fell into disfavour, and that he bore the *nisba* 'al-Bunduqdārī' until he became sultan. The second point on which Shāfi' explicitly corrects Ibn 'Abd al-Ẓāhir's narrative is in the account of Baybars's accession to the sultanate. In *al-Rawḍ* Baybars is shown as killing his predecessor, Quṭuz: 'The sultan al-Malik al-Ẓāhir did what he did by himself, and attained his aim alone.' By contrast Shāfi' gives a full account of the fatal hunting party, the plot to isolate the doomed sultan, and Baybars's delivery of the *coup de grâce* after Quṭuz had first been wounded by his own swordbearer. 'The account', says Shāfi', 'was not related thus by [Ibn 'Abd al-Ẓāhir] out of regard to the time and the sultan's honour.'[31]

The production of a revised version of events continues for the following episode, the actual accession of Baybars. In Ibn 'Abd al-Ẓāhir's account Baybars and his companions return to the royal pavilion, and discussion arises among the assembled amirs over the election of a new sultan. The *atābak*, the senior Mamluk amir, says that the killer of Quṭuz 'did not risk his life and put it in jeopardy so that the power to command and forbid might pass to another. He who slew him is most worthy of his place.' Baybars is accordingly enthroned. 'This', says Ibn 'Abd al-Ẓāhir, 'is what the *atābak* told me.'[32] Shāfi', an inartistic writer, gives at different places in his text two slightly variant accounts of this episode.[33] These put rather a different complexion on events. He states that the consultation of the amirs had reached a conclusion with the decision to enthrone the amir Balabān al-Rashīdī, when the *atābak* (who had been detained in the antechamber of the pavilion) broke in on the assembly. He insisted that 'the custom of the Turks is that he who kills the king is himself king',[34] and that the throne thus passed to Baybars by right of regicide. Whatever the grounds of the *atābak's* assertion of an old Turkish custom, this passage gives evidence of a factional division among the Mamluk amirs. The first Mamluk sultan, al-Mu'izz Aybak, had broken the power of the Ṣāliḥiyya household in 652/1254 by procuring the murder of Aqṭāy by Quṭuz. Many

31 *Rawḍ*, 68; *Ḥusn*, 31.
32 *Rawḍ*, 68–9.
33 *Ḥusn*, 22–3, 155–6.
34 I have rendered *asat al-Turk* as 'the custom of the Turks' on the assumption that *asa* represents *yasa*. I have not discovered any evidence that this was a Turkish custom. Haarmann has found something of a precedent in the murder of the Kurdish Marwanid, Abū 'Alī, at Āmid in 397/998; see Ulrich Haarmann, *Quellenstudien zur frühen Mamlukenzeit* (Freiburg 1970), 146, n. 6.

of the Ṣāliḥiyya, including Baybars, fled to Syria; others were impris-
oned in Alexandria. The most senior of the latter group was Balabān
al-Rashīdī. The *atābak*'s unsought intervention was effective, but Baybars had to swear to give the amirs assignments (*arzāq*), dignities and
security before they would swear allegiance to him as sultan.

In addition to this revised account of Baybars's earlier career, there
are various additional anecdotes of events in his reign which are not
given by Ibn 'Abd al-Ẓāhir. At one point Shāfiʿ is extremely critical
both of the sultan and of his uncle as biographer. This is in connection
with the episode when Baybars sent the newly-installed 'Abbasid puppet
caliph, al-Mustanṣir, with a military force to recover Baghdad from the
Mongols. He comments:

> The Master Muḥyī al-Dīn said, 'The sultan said to me, "In equipping the
> caliph and the princes of Mosul, I spent 1,060,000 dirhams" '. I say that I
> have never seen anything stranger than this notion, or stranger than the
> agreement of a sensible and well-advised person with it. A horde that had
> seized the country through their numbers and preparedness, their fortitude
> and the abundance of their forces – how could this pitiful little band set
> out against them? Truly it did not equal a thousand of them. It was nothing
> but money thrown away and souls doomed to die. If the whole Egyptian
> army and the Syrian army with its bedouin and foot-soldiers had set out,
> they would have been in the utmost jeopardy.[35]

This apart, however, the additional material supplied by Shāfiʿ is generally favourable to Baybars. It includes, for example, instances of his
upright behaviour in *dār al-'adl*, and an account of a near-miraculous
landslip into the Jordan, which enabled his men to build a bridge at
an otherwise impossible site.

IV

Two questions remain. First, what is the portrait of Baybars which
emerges from the pages of *Ḥusn al-manāqib*? Secondly, why did Shāfiʿ
b. 'Alī undertake this critical reworking of *al-Rawḍ al-zāhir*? The answers
are connected. The Baybars of *Ḥusn al-manāqib* is still an impressive,
even an heroic figure, whose military achievements secured the future
of Islam in Syria against the threats from the Mongols and the Franks.
He appears, further, as an autocratic but just ruler, who was (to use a
cliché) the true founder of the Mamluk sultanate. What he has lost is
the aura of legitimacy as the true heir of al-Ṣāliḥ Ayyūb, by which Ibn

35 *Ḥusn*, 46.

'Abd al-Ẓāhir sought to disguise his twofold usurpation. But when Shāfiʿ wrote, Ayyubid legitimacy had long ceased to be a political issue, and Baybars could stand justified by his deeds. So his image in this later work is that of a more human ruler than that on which Baybars set the seal of his personal approval.

This does not mean that Shāfiʿ b. ʿAlī was a Lytton Strachey of the fourteenth century, seeking to set the record right or to vent his spleen on greater men than himself. The forty years which elapsed between the death of Baybars and the completion of *Ḥusn al-manāqib* were a period of important political changes. In 675/1279 the sultanate was usurped from the sons of Baybars by Qalāwūn, another veteran of the Ṣāliḥiyya, who established a dynasty that lasted after a fashion for over a century. Shāfiʿ b. ʿAlī completed *Ḥusn al-manāqib* when Qalāwūn's son, al-Nāṣir Muḥammad, was ruling as a vigorous autocrat. The Frankish states had long ceased to exist, the Mongols had conducted their last campaigns into Syria. From the standpoint of the Qalawunid dynasty, Baybars can be shown, not unsympathetically, as a great warrior and ruler in a vanished age. It is significant that Shāfiʿ, inartistic as ever, pads out his biography of Baybars with episodes from the reign of Qalāwūn. He even gives an anecdote prophetic of Qalāwūn's ultimate supremacy, and closes it with the words:

> ... it is the fates which cause the victor to be vanquished, the seeker to be sought, the last to be first, and the judged to be the judge.[36]

36 *Ḥusn*, 175.

COLIN IMBER

Ideals and legitimation in early Ottoman history

By the end of the reign of Süleyman in 1566, the Ottomans had created an ideology which not only justified the Ottoman sultan's rule in his own territories, but also bestowed on him a claim to universal sovereignty. These claims, and the beliefs which supported them, had developed between the late fourteenth and mid-sixteenth centuries, becoming ever more grandiose with the continuing growth in Ottoman power. They did not derive from a single source or a single coherent set of ideas, but rather from an accretion and coalescence of myths and ideals, each of which had emerged at a different time to answer a particular political need or to appeal to a particular group of the sultan's subjects. However, all the elements in this complex ideology served the single purpose of justifying the rule of the Ottoman dynasty. This complexity to serve such a simple end perhaps reflects the political nature of the Ottoman empire. Its sheer size and ethnic, religious and geographical diversity meant that the principle of its unity was extremely simple: loyalty to the Ottoman dynasty. This loyalty is what Ottoman ideology sought to promote. The Ottoman dynasty, like a large percentage of its subjects, was Muslim and Turkish and it was from within Muslim and Turkish tradition, both popular and learned, that it derived its claims to rulership and sovereignty.[1]

---

1 However, many Ottoman subjects were neither Muslim nor Turkish, and it seems likely that alternative devices to legitimise Ottoman rule would have grown up within these communities. For example, the story which appears in the 16th century depicting the sultans as descendants of the Byzantine Comnene dynasty probably reflects a spurious Ottoman genealogy whose purpose would have been to legitimise their rule in the eyes of their Greek subjects. For stories of this 'Comnene' descent, see Théodore Spandouyn Cantacasin (ed. C Schéfer), *Petit traicté de l'origine des Turcqz* (Paris 1896),11–13; Pseudo-Sphrantzes [Makarios Melissenos] (ed. I Bekker), *Georgius Phrantzes. Ioannes Cananus, Ioannes Anagnostes* (Bonn 1838), 69–71.

The most celebrated of these legitimising ideals was the notion that the sultans and their armies were *gazi*s, warriors of the faith, whose wars against Christians represented an Islamic holy war against infidelity. The ultimate source of this idea was the *şeriat*, the holy law of Islam, which, to simplify greatly, makes the prosecution of holy war an obligation on the Islamic community. By invoking the *şeriat*, Ottoman rulers were able to project their wars against Christian neighbours and their subjects' raids on Christian territories as the necessary fulfilment of a divinely imposed obligation, a claim which gave them legitimacy in the eyes both of their own subjects and of other Muslim sovereigns.[2]

The first person to give a literary formulation to these claims was the poet and moralist Ahmedi (1334?-1412) who, probably in the 1390s, appended to a much longer work a section which he entitled *The History of the Ottoman kings*[3] for presentation to Emir Süleyman, the son of Bayezid I (1389–1402). The work is in fact a panegyric and not a history, lacking any chronology apart from the sequence of Ottoman rulers, and recounting these rulers' deeds within a conventional framework of exemplary virtues: how they were 'just and equitable', 'a refuge and support for men of learning', how 'they built mosques and *mihrabs*', and so on. However, the predominant virtue which Ahmedi attributes to the Ottomans is their prosecution of the holy war. He in fact describes his 'history' as a *Book of holy wars* and prefaces it with an idealised description of a holy warrior:

A *gazi* is one who is God's carpet-sweeper
Who cleanses the earth of the filth of polytheism
Do not imagine that one who is martyred in the path of God is dead
No, that blessed martyr is alive.

He portrays all the Ottoman rulers as *gazi*s, from the time when Ertuğrul, the father of Osman, first set foot in Sultan Öyüğü, the territory from which, in Ottoman tradition, they began their career of conquest:

From there they sent an army to the abode of infidelity
To ravage the lands and slaughter infidels.

2 The potency of *gaza* as a source of Ottoman dynastic legitimation in the eyes of foreign rulers is apparent as early as the first decade of the fifteenth century, in the panegyric history of Timur by Nizam al-Din Shami. When describing Timur's campaign against Bayezid I in 1402, Nizam al-Din is careful to portray Timur as reluctant to attack Bayezid, whom he acknowledges as a great *gazi*; Nizam al-Din Shami (ed. F Tauer), *Zafarnameh* (Prague 1938), I, 248.
3 Text in N S Banarlı, 'Ahmedi ve Dâsitân-i tevârîh-i mülûk-i âl-i Osmân', *Türkiyat mecmuası* 6 (1936–39), 111–35.

This image was to become typical of all later literary portrayals of the Ottomans.

By the time Ahmedi presented his poem to Emir Süleyman, the Ottoman rulers had probably themselves already adopted the title *gazi*.[4] However, a line in Ahmedi's poem suggests that the words *gazi* (holy warrior) and *gaza* (holy war), and perhaps also the ideals which these words embody, were not widely current among Ottoman subjects, and that the formulation of these ideals perhaps owed much to Ahmedi himself. In his section on the deeds of the second Ottoman ruler, Orhan, he writes

> Those servants of religion made raids (*aktılar*) against the infidels
> For that reason they called holy war (*gaza*) *akın*

This line strongly suggests that the words which Ahmedi heard in daily use were not the Arabic terms *gaza* and *gazi*, but rather *akın* (raid) and *akıncı* (raider). These are Turkish words with no religious connotations and it seems to have been Ahmedi himself who substituted for them the Arabic forms. At one level, therefore, these two terms, which appear so frequently in Ottoman texts from the time of Ahmedi, are simply manifestations of a general tendency in Ottoman Turkish from the fifteenth century onwards to replace Turkish terms with Arabic ones. In some fifteenth-century texts, the terms *akın/akıncı* and *gaza/gazi* appear interchangeably.[5] This change in terminology was, however, of greater import than the many parallel shifts from Turkish to Arabic vocabulary, where the change in the word produced no alteration in meaning. In this case, the change represents a conscious sanctification of the activity. Mere 'raiders' become 'holy warriors'. The shift in vocabulary seems here to represent an ideological development.

4 Two scraps of epigraphical evidence suggest this. An inscription in Bursa bearing the date 1337/8 describes the second sultan, Orhan, as 'sultan of the *gazis*, *gazi* son of a *gazi*'. However, R C Jennings, 'Some thoughts on the *gazi*-thesis', *Wiener Zeitschrift für die Kunde des Morgenlandes* 76 (1986), 153–61, has convincingly argued that the inscription does not in fact date from 1337/8, but is a late addition/restoration, possibly dating from 1417. A second inscription bearing the date 1375, on a bridge in Ankara, includes *gazi* among the titles attributed to Murad I (1362–89).

5 E.g., the chronicler Aşıkpaşazade describes a raid into Hungary in 1440, in which he participated, in these terms; '. . . they crossed the river [Danube] and made an *akın* on the district. The *gazis* took much booty . . . They say there had not been such a *gaza* since the foundation of Islam.' Aşıkpaşazade, (ed. Ali), *Tevârîh-i âl-i Osmân* (Istanbul 1914), 125. Similarly, a sultanic decree of 1493, regulating the distribution of booty taken by the Rumelian *akıncıs*, in its preamble uses the terms *gazi* and *gaza*, whereas in the body of the text it uses *akıncı* and *akın*; I Beldiceanu-Stenherr, 'En marge d'un acte concernant le *pengyek* et les *aqıngı*', *Revue des études Islamiques* 37 (1969), 21–46.

The unlearned version of this 'holy war' ideology found its expression in a popular Turkish literature of the fifteenth and sixteenth centuries, where *gazi*s play the role of epic heroes whose antagonists are 'infidels', and where religious motifs, notably the appearance of the Prophet Muhammad in dreams or at the head of Muslim armies, often play an important part in the development of the plot.[6] The purpose of these works was primarily, it seems, entertainment. Their stories of heroic deeds, 'countless virgins' seized as booty, and other epic clichés play a more important part than religion, but their religious motifs and religious ethos nevertheless made them bearers of popular *gazi* ideology. Similarly, the predominantly religious *menakıb* literature – popular stories relating the exemplary deeds of saints – frequently contains episodes where the saint-hero appears in the guise of a holy warrior, and sometimes in association with the Ottoman sultans. An example of this kind of *gazi*-saint is Sarı Saltuk, whose *menakıb* a certain Ebu'l-Hayr Rumi collected, apparently at the command of the Ottoman prince Cem in 1473. Woven into the narrative of the legendary Sarı Saltuk's heroic deeds against the infidels are references to real places, events and persons (notably to Osman, the first Ottoman sultan), but historical realities are subordinate to epic and religious motifs.[7] A somewhat similar example, this time dating from the middle years of Süleyman's reign, is Enisi's *menakıb* of the saint Akşemseddin. Akşemseddin was a historical figure, a spiritual mentor to Mehmed II (1451–81) and present at the conquest of Constantinople in 1453. This historical event in fact features in Enisi's work, but is transformed to comply with the conventions of popular *gazi* and *menakıb* literature. In Enisi's tale, it is the saint Akşemseddin who prophesies the exact hour of city's fall and, as the Muslim army enters Constantinople, the sultan sees a host of saints 'clad in white raiment' leading it to victory.[8]

These epics and *menakıb* with their persistent motif of Islamic militancy evidently served, through the medium of entertainment, to propa-

---

6 The earliest Anatolian example of this kind of literature appears to be the *Book of Melik Danişmend*, not originally an Ottoman work, but one which survives in an Ottoman recension of a version written down in 1245. An example of a typical popular religious motif in this work is where the hero, Melik Danişmend, marries the Christian Gülnuş Banu after the Prophet had converted her to Islam in a dream; I Mélikoff, *La geste de Melik Danişmend*, v. 1 (introduction and translation), v. 2 (critical edition), Paris 1960.

  For a study of another typical *gazi* motif, see Paul Wittek, 'The takıng of Aydos castle, a ghazi legend transformed' in G Makdisi (ed.), *Arabic and Islamic studies in honour of Hamilton A R Gibb* (Leiden 1965), 662–72.

7 For extracts from the *menakıb* of Sarı Saltuk, see Fahir İz, *Eski Türk edebiyatında nesir*, 268–318.

8 Extracts in İz, *Nesir*, 345–6.

gate popular *gazi* ideology,[9] but the 'historical' materials embedded in them, such as Enisi's story of the conquest of Constantinople, must also have served to form a popular view of the Ottoman past. It is not surprising therefore that the earliest Ottoman dynastic chronicles draw heavily on these materials and conform more to the genres of epic and *menakıb* than they do to historiography. Their importance is perhaps not so much as a source for dynastic history as marking a stage in the development of dynastic ideology.

The earliest Ottoman 'histories', by Ahmedi (1390s), Şükrullah (c. 1460) and Enveri (1465) were not independent works, but simply short additions to longer books. The first chronicles dealing solely with the Ottoman dynasty – the Anonymous Chronicles, and those by Aşıkpaşa-zade (1484) and Oruç (c. 1500) – did not appear until the reign of Bayezid II (1481–1512),[10] probably with this sultan's active encouragement. Their appearance is important firstly because it marks the point in time, almost two centuries after the state's foundation, when the Ottoman sultans came to occupy a position in the Ottoman literary imagination of equal or greater importance than that of earlier Islamic dynasties. By the end of Bayezid's reign, Ottoman dynastic historiography had become virtually an independent literary genre.[11] Secondly, these early histories created a popular image of the sultans.

An important feature of this image is its presentation of the sultans and their followers as *gazi* heroes. This is true above all of the chronicles' accounts of the legendary or semi-legendary exploits of the fourteenth-century Ottomans. These display many of the features of *gazi* epics: for example, the stories of the conversion of the Christian Köse Mihal to Islam, after the Prophet had appeared to him in a dream and directed him to join Osman. The several variant stories of how Süleyman Paşa, the son of the second sultan Orhan (c. 1324–62), and his men made the first Ottoman conquests in Europe after crossing the Dardanelles on rafts, are equally typical of the epic-*gazi* tradition. The stories of saints which sometimes appear embedded in this heroic material – in particular the legend of Osman's marriage to the daughter of the dervish Edebali – add motifs from the tradition of *menakıb*. In this way, the Ottoman 'histories' of the late fifteenth century draw on

9 A 20th-century analogy might be the spy-thriller genre which has served to propagate cold war ideology, or Hollywood films, where figures such as John Wayne have created a popular American self-image.

10 See V L Ménage, 'The beginnings of Ottoman historiography' in B Lewis and P M Holt (eds), *Historians of the Middle East* (London 1962), 168–79.

11 A landmark in this development was Bayezid II's commissioning the scholar Kemal-paşazade's multi-volume Ottoman history. See Ibn-i Kemal (ed. Ş Turan), *Tevârîh-i âl-i Osmân. I defter* (Ankara 1970), 35–6.

popular literary traditions to project an image of the sultans which conformed to popular ideals of heroism, holy war and piety. It was an image too which seems to have continued into the sixteenth century and later.

The narratives which make up these early Ottoman histories probably acquired their present form in the circle of active *akıncıs*,[12] for whom *akın* and *gaza*, raiding and holy war, were one and the same. In fact, the autobiographical materials which enliven Aşıkpaşazade's chronicle reveal him to have been an *akıncı* in the following of Ishak Bey of Skopje in the 1430s and 1440s. The image of the sultans that they project is clearly one that would appeal to active warriors. It is, however, quite different from another view of *gaza* which, also from the late fifteenth century, was to become a dominant theme of dynastic ideology. This is the learned view, which derived not from popular religion but from the canonical texts of the *şeriat*.

The earliest to promote this theme in an Ottoman context was Ahmedi. In his *History of the Ottoman kings* he not only transforms *akın* into *gaza*, but also presents the Ottomans as pursuing *gaza* solely for the sake of religion and not in pursuit of epic deeds of valour. Elsewhere in his verse, he deplores those who pursue *gaza* for plunder. This, he says, is mere brigandage; *gaza* should be pursued as a sincere act of worship for the sake of God alone.[13] The same pious promptings occur again in Şükrullah's chapter on the Ottomans which he appended to his *Universal History* of c. 1460. For example, although his section on the conquests of Süleyman Paşa obviously depends on an oral source and contains many motifs familiar from popular Turkish epics,[14] he

---

12 E.g., the stories of the conversion of Köse Mihal perhaps originated among the *akıncıs* of Rumelia. The probably legendary figure of Köse Mihal is presented in these as the ancestor of the historical Mihaloğlu family which, from the late 14th century to the early 16th, provided the hereditary leaders of the *akıncıs* on the border with Hungary. The stories of Köse Mihal in the chronicles give prophetic sanction to the Mihaloğlu family's claim to leadership in the holy war and thus to their activities as leaders of the *akıncıs*. They also give the Mihaloğlu family, and thus also the *akıncıs*, a privileged position in relation to the Ottoman dynasty.

13 Tunca Kortantamer, *Leben und Weltbild des altosmanischen Dichters Ahmedī* (Freiburg 1973), 236. Ahmedi's pious rejection of plunder as a motive for *gaza* is in sharp distinction to Aşıkpaşazade, for example, whose personal memoirs inserted into his chronicle show just how important a motivation the acquisition of plunder really was.

14 Examples are Şükrullah's stories of how Süleyman Paşa with his 'forty followers' crossed the Dardanelles on a raft; and how, with twenty men, he defeated an infidel army by sending a group of five men under cover of dark, to each side of the enemy force, beating drums and crying 'God is great', thus convincing the infidels that they faced a large Muslim army; Th. Seif, 'Der Abschnitt über der Osmanen in Şükrullāh's persischer Universalgeschichte', *Mitteilungen zur Osmanischen Geschichte* 2 (1923–26, repr. Osnabrück 1972), 63–128.

nevertheless introduces it with a scene where Süleyman Paşa's father, Orhan, instructs his son 'If, with the grace of God, you cross (the Dardanelles), first of all invite the infidels to accept Islam. If they do not accept, go forward to war.' This instruction reflects precisely the rules of warfare as the *şeriat* prescribes and, in including it, Şükrullah is portraying the sultans as pursuing *gaza* in accordance with the canonical rules. This tendency to portray Ottoman warfare in terms no longer deriving from the popular epic tradition but from the *şeriat*, became particularly evident during the reign of Bayezid II, and finds a typical formulation in a phrase in Tursun Bey's *History of (Mehmed) the Conqueror* (c. 1490) composed during this reign: 'Victory and conquest are . . . proper to the decrees of the luminous *şeriat*.'[15] This canonical view of holy war became dominant during the sixteenth century, as the *ulema* and *medrese*-trained bureaucrats came to dominate the intellectual life of the empire, and it was henceforth in canonical terms that the wars of the Ottoman sultans usually find their literary manifestation. This interpretation of Ottoman warfare as the fulfilment of a canonical obligation on behalf of the entire Islamic community justified, in the eyes of the learned, the sultans' claims to be leaders of holy war, in the same way as the popular epic tradition of holy war justified it in the eyes of the unlearned.

A second literary development of the late fifteenth century was to transfer almost the entire merit of *gaza* onto the figure of the sultan. A comparison between Ahmedi in the late fourteenth century, and the Ottoman history by Neşri in the late fifteenth (1485), demonstrates this change. Ahmedi opens his chapter on the 'Ottoman kings' with a eulogy on the merits of the *gazi*s, where he comments that they 'came at the end of time', because 'that which comes at the end of time is better than that which comes at the beginning', just as the Koran is the last and most perfect of God's revelations and Muhammad the last and most perfect of God's Prophets. Neşri repeats this assertion, but with a significant alteration. It is no longer, in this version, the *gazi*s in general who are best because they come at the end of time, but the Ottoman sultans, whom he now characterises as 'the pre-eminent *gazi*s and *mucahid*s after the apostle of God and the rightly-guided caliphs'.[16] It is this view of the sultan as pre-eminent *gazi* that characterises the literary accounts of the sixteenth-century reign of Süleyman and figures prominently among the titles which this sultan adopted. For example, in a

15 Tursun Bey (ed. A M Tulum), *Târîh-i Ebü'l-Feth* (Istanbul 1977), 170.
16 Mehmed Neşri, (ed. F Unat and M Köymen), *Kitâb-i cihânnümâ* 1 (Ankara 1949), 55.

list of sultanic titles[17] composed by the *şeyhülislam* Ebussuûd[18] Süleyman appears as 'the lord of *gazi* wars, famous among mankind . . .'. The great conquests of the first twenty years of his reign gave a particular force to this claim.

The ideology of holy war provided two justifications for Ottoman rule. Firstly, it portrayed the sultans as fulfilling a canonical obligation; secondly, it gave them a canonical right to rule the territories which they had conquered from the infidels. The first to give a clear formulation to the idea that holy war bestowed territorial rights was Neşri who, in his account of the reign of Osman, writes: 'The mighty sultans and noble kings recognised Osman's virtues and sincere intent and said . . . "Let whatever he takes from the infidels be lawful to him" '.[19] Neşri clearly intended the same rule to apply to the conquests of all the Ottoman sultans.

However, in promulgating holy war as a basis for territorial legitimacy, Ottoman ideologists faced a problem in that the sultans had acquired many of their lands in wars against fellow Muslims, and it was difficult to present these hostilities as *gaza*. They adopted several devices for circumventing the problem. Firstly, the Ottoman chronicles of the late fifteenth century tend to present Ottoman conquests in fourteenth- and early fifteenth-century Anatolia as peaceful acquisitions without force of arms, and thus exonerate the Ottoman dynasty from the charge of waging war against Muslims. A second device which these chronicles adopted was to justify such wars as a religious obligation, on the grounds that the other Muslim rulers of Anatolia had cooperated with the infidels, and thus distracted the Ottomans from their sacred task of *gaza*. An anonymous chronicle of c. 1485 justifies all Ottoman conquests in Anatolia on these grounds.[20] Another technique was to portray the sultans' Muslim enemies as 'oppressing' Muslims, thus making the 'removal of oppression' obligatory for the Ottomans. Tursun Bey, for example, describes Mehmed II's campaign against the Akkoyunlu ruler Uzun Hasan in 1473 within this kind of moralistic framework. In 1472 Uzun Hasan attacked the Ottoman city of Tokat, committing 'terrible oppression and clear injustice'. It therefore 'became obligatory

17 This list of sultanic titles appears at the head of Ebussuûd's introduction to the cadastral survey of Buda, made after 1541. See Ö L Barkan, *XV ve XVI asırlarda Osmanlı imperatorluğunda zirai ekonominin hukuki ve mali esasları* (Istanbul 1943), 296.
18 Ebussuûd held the post of *kazasker* of Rumelia from 1537 to 1545, and of *şeyhülislam* from 1545 until his death in 1574. His influence on the formation and systematisation of Ottoman law and ideology is immeasurable. For his career, see R C Repp, *The mufti of Istanbul* (Oxford 1986), 272–96.
19 Neşri, *Kitâb-i cihânnümâ*, 52.
20 Bodleian Library, Oxford, MS Marsh 313, ff. 5r–7v.

by *şeriat* and custom, by reason and by transmitted authority' for Mehmed to 'remove this harm from the Muslims and to cut off the head of evil'.[21] Tursun Bey depicts Mehmed II's subsequent campaign and victory over Uzun Hasan as a necessary and religiously sanctioned revenge for the sack of Tokat.

Another justification for Ottoman rule in Anatolia, which became current in the late fifteenth and sixteenth centuries, was that the Ottomans were the legal heirs to the earlier Seljuk sultans of Anatolia (c.1071–c. 1300), and that the other dynasties that had come to occupy former Seljuk territories and whom the Ottomans subsequently displaced were mere usurpers. Fifteenth-century Ottoman tradition contains many stories linking Osman and his father Ertuğrul with the Seljuks, but it was Neşri who conflated these to form a coherent story which 'proved' Ottoman claims. In Neşri's account, which became a source for sixteenth-century historians, it was the Seljuk sultan Alaeddin I (1220–37) who granted lands in north-western Anatolia to Ertuğrul. His descendant, Alaeddin II (1282–1303) sent Ertuğrul's son Osman a drum, standard and sword, as symbols of authority and, before his death, made Osman his heir, as he himself was childless. Neşri is careful to describe Osman as never acting disloyally to the Seljuks so long as this dynasty survived, and as enlarging his realms only through *gaza*:

> And that is why Osman and his descendants were called *gazi*, for his principle of action was not to bear sway by usurpation over the lands of the believers, but solely through *gaza* and *cihad*.[22]

The Ottomans are thus presented as acquiring Anatolia as a legal inheritance, the rulers whom they displaced in the process being simply 'usurpers'. The popular chronicles do not invariably reflect this tradition, which appealed to the learned rather than to the warrior classes, but from Neşri's time onwards it was to remain an important strand in official Ottoman claims to legitimacy.

The Ottoman claim to be legal heirs to the Seljuks crystallised in the late fifteenth century and reflected the historical fact that the Muslim lands which the Ottomans had conquered during the fourteenth and fifteenth centuries comprised, more or less, the realms of the former Seljuk dynasty. The legal claims justified these conquests retrospectively. After 1500, however, the territories of the Ottomans' most powerful rivals in the Muslim world lay outside Anatolia, and this new political and strategic situation gave rise to new forms of Ottoman propaganda and a new set of Ottoman dynastic claims.

21 Tursun Bey, *Târîh-i Ebü'l-Feth*, 157.
22 Neşri, *Kitâb-i cihânnümâ*, 52.

During the sixteenth century, the Safavid shahs of Iran were the Ottomans' most dangerous Muslim enemies. Dynastic hostility led to open warfare between 1514 and 1536, 1548 and 1555, and finally between 1578 and 1590. Even during the years of peace, the fact that the Safavid shah's claims to religious legitimacy found many adherents among the subjects of the Ottoman sultan, especially in Anatolia, led to a constant fear of pro-Safavid rebellions.[23] The political threat of the Safavids and their claims on the loyalties of many Ottoman subjects required effective Ottoman counter propaganda.[24] Since the Safavids were Muslims, albeit *şii* rather than *sunni*,[25] it was not easy to maintain straightforwardly that war against them was *gaza*. This is nevertheless what the Ottomans did. The claim required first of all that they portray the Safavids not as 'believers' but as 'infidels' against whom it was a religious obligation to fight.

The first clear record of this process is a long legal opinion which a scholar known as Hamza Sarı Görez issued, apparently as a justification for the wars of Selim I (1512–20) against the Safavid shah İsma'il. In it, he characterises the followers of the shah as 'belittling the *şeriat* of our Prophet . . . the religion of Islam . . . and the manifest Koran . . . and saying that what God has forbidden is licit'. He concludes that

> by decree of the *şeriat* and the transmitted authority of our books . . . the said group are infidels and heretics. It is an obligation and a religious duty to kill them and to scatter their congregations.[26]

In these circumstances, war against the Safavids would constitute *gaza*, and the notion that it did so became commonplace during the reign of Süleyman, finding perhaps its ultimate formulation in the writings of the two *şeyhülislam*s Kemalpaşazade (held office 1526–34) and Ebussuûd (held office 1545–74). Kemalpaşazade succinctly described the Safavids as having 'the outward form of Muslims, but the inward nature of infidels', and elaborated on this view in an Arabic treatise enumerating their largely imagined misdemeanours:

---

23 On this topic in general, see H Sohrweide, 'Der Sieg der Safaviden und seine Rückwirkung auf die Schiiten Anatoliens im 16. Jahrhundert'. *Der Islam* 41 (1965), 95–223.

24 See Elke Eberhard, *Osmanische Polemik gegen die Safawiden* (Freiburg 1970).

25 Ottoman propaganda was not, however, directed against the Safavids as shiites. To do so would have incriminated shiites in the Ottoman empire who were not Safavid adherents and who presented no opposition to Ottoman rule. Ebussuûd in fact opens a long formulation of Safavid heresy with the assertion 'they are not shiites'; M E Düzdağ, *Şeyhülislâm Ebussuûd Efendi fetvaları* (Istanbul 1972), no. 481.

26 For text of Hamza's *fetva*, see S Tansel, *Yavuz Sultan Selim* (Ankara 1969), 35–6. For further discussion, see Repp, *Mufti of Istanbul*, 218–20.

They claim that what the shah makes licit is licit, and what the shah makes forbidden is forbidden. If the shah makes wine licit, then it is licit.[27] In short, the varieties of their unbelief, transmitted to us through what is common knowledge, cannot be numbered... We have no doubt about their unbelief and apostasy...

In a legal opinion quoted at the end of the treatise, Kemalpaşazade replies to a question on the legality of war against the Safavids, that such a war would be 'a major *gaza*'.[28] A series of Ebussuûd's legal opinions, dating from between 1548 and 1555, the years of Süleyman's second campaign against Iran, gives a yet more elaborate formulation to the same ideas.[29] In this way, Süleyman was able to project all his wars, not only against Christian Europe, but also against Safavid Iran, as holy wars.

The ideological need to portray the Safavids as 'infidels' produced a corresponding need to portray the Ottoman sultans as pious orthodox Muslims, and the only defenders of true orthodoxy against such infidelity. This need arose at a time when the *ulema* had come to dominate the intellectual life of the empire, and the result was a reformulation of Ottoman claims to legitimacy in terms of orthodox, canonical Islam.

It was not that the Ottoman sultans had not claimed a religious legitimacy before the sixteenth century, but rather that their claims had sprung from folk religion and not learned Islam. The chronicles of the last quarter of the fifteenth century in fact all contain episodes which serve to show that God had foreordained the rule of the dynasty. The most famous of these remained embedded in Ottoman historiography down to this century. This is Aşıkpaşazade's story of how the first sultan, Osman, was the guest of a dervish called Edebali, and how he had a dream which the holy man interpreted as showing that God had bestowed rulership on him and his discendants. After interpreting the dream, Edebali betrothed his daughter to Osman, making her an ancestress of the future sultans.[30] In this tale and in several typologically related narratives, the dream motif reflects the popular belief that God speaks to man directly in his sleep, and the dreams in these stories are therefore divine prognostications of the future greatness of the dynasty. The tale of Osman's marriage to Edebali's daughter also gave a popular

---

27 The Ottoman authorities in the 16th century came to define a heretic as a person who regarded what the *şeriat* forbids (notably wine-drinking and fornication) as lawful. Kemalpaşazade is here portraying the Safavid shah as claiming that his own authority supersedes that of the *şeriat*.

28 Quoted in Ş Tekindağ, 'Yeni kaynak ve vesikaların ışığı altında Yavuz Sultan Selim' in Iran seferleri', *Tarih dergisi* xvii/22 (1968), 49–78.

29 Düzdağ, *Şeyhülislam Ebussuûd Efendi fetvaları*, nos. 479–89.

30 Aşıkpaşazade, *Târîh-i al-i Osmân*, 6–7.

religious legitimation to the Ottoman sultans. The inclusion among the dynastic ancestors of the saint Edebali who, in popular belief, would have a spiritual lineage linking him directly to the Prophet, bestowed the same spiritual ancestry on the dynasty.

By the accession of Süleyman in 1520, canonical Islam had come to replace folk religion as a source for dynastic legitimation. This change reflects not only the growing importance of the *ulema* and the need to portray the sultans as defenders of true religion against Safavid infidelity, but also a developing notion of universal sovereignty. During the fifteenth century, the Ottoman sultans had claimed pre-eminence over neighbouring Turkish dynasts, but no more than this. The conquests of Süleyman's father, Selim I, enlarged their ambitions. In 1516–17, Selim defeated the Mamluk sultan and annexed Mamluk territories in Syria, Egypt and the Hijaz, giving him the most extensive realms of any Islamic monarch. Furthermore, these realms now included the holy cities of Mecca and Medina, conferring on the Ottoman sultan the prestigious role of possessor and defender of Islam's holiest shrines. Henceforth, 'servant of the two holy sanctuaries' or similar phrases regularly appear among the titles of the Ottoman sultans.[31] This new view of the sultan as defender of the holy cities and guarantor of the faith against infidelity and heresy, required new forms of legitimation. It required in the first place a 'historical' justification for Ottoman claims to pre-eminence among Islamic sovereigns.

During the fifteenth century, the Ottomans had in fact already created a historical fiction which gave them a 'right' to rulership. This was not a religious claim, but one which they based on a spurious genealogy, which survives in many versions, but which received its definitive form in Neşri's history (1485).[32] This genealogy draws on materials from the epics, written and oral, of Oğuz Khan, a legendary great ruler and ancestor of the Turks. In its various manifestations, it shows the Ottoman sultans as descending in the senior line from the great Oğuz Khan himself. In the fifteenth century, this genealogy sufficed to 'prove' that the Ottomans were superior to neighbouring Turkish dynasties, who are depicted as descendants of Oğuz Khan in the cadet lines, and to legitimise the Ottoman sultans' rule to their

---

31 In Ebussuûd's formulation, Süleyman was 'protector of the holy ground of the two sacred sanctuaries'. Selim I's conquests also gave the sultan guardianship of Jerusalem, sacared to Muslims, Jews and Christians alike. In a letter to the Habsburg emperor Ferdinand, dated 1554, Süleyman described himself as ruler of '. . . Mecca, Medina and Jerusalem . . .', reflecting a consciousness of Jerusalem's status as the third holiest city.

32 Neşri, *Kitâb-i cihânnümâ*, 54–6.

Turkish subjects, who would be familiar with the Oğuz epics on which the genealogy is based.[33] Dynastic histories of the sixteenth century and later retain this genealogy, but by then it must have lost its impact. The Oğuz epics represented a popular Turkish literary tradition which must have become unfamiliar to educated Ottomans as they adopted the literary tastes of a cosmopolitan Muslim elite. In consequence, the sixteenth century saw the replacement of genealogical 'proofs' of the Ottomans' historical rights to rulership, with 'proofs' adduced from the canonical texts of Islam.

These 'proofs' appear, probably not for the first time, in the Ottoman history composed after 1541 by the former grand vezir, Lutfi Paşa. In support of Ottoman claims to rulership, Lutfi Paşa quotes a saying of Muhammad from one of the canonical six books of prophetic tradition: 'At the beginning of each century, God most high will send to the (Muslim) community someone who will renew its faith and sovereignty.' Lutfi Paşa interprets this saying as a prophecy of Ottoman rule. The most recent 'renewers of the faith' had been the Ottoman sultans: Osman, who had restored Islam at the beginning of the Islamic eighth century after the conquests of the pagan Mongols; Mehmed I who, at the beginning of the ninth, had restored the faith after the ravages of Timur; and Selim I who, at the beginning of the tenth, had defeated the Safavid infidels. Lutfi Paşa continues the Safavid theme, which was directly relevant to the period when he was writing, by quoting spurious letters from the '*ulema* of Transoxania', praising Selim I as 'the shah on the throne of the caliphate', who alone had defended the good order of the *şeriat*. Lutfi Paşa also provides a tendentious summary of Islamic history, showing that since the days of the four 'rightly-guided' caliphs who succeeded the Prophet, the only dynasties to remain untainted by 'heresy' or 'rebellion' were the Ottomans and their 'exemplars and guides', the Seljuks.[34] The prophetic traditions from which Lutfi Paşa quotes are one source of canonical authority. The other is the Koran, the pre-eternal word of God. Here too dynastic eulogists found prophecies of Ottoman rule. One of these was the imperial tutor and historian, Sadeddin who, in the preface to his *Crown of histories*, composed for presentation to Murad III (1574–95), quotes a Koranic verse:

---

33 On this genealogy, see Barbara Flemming, 'Political genealogies in the sixteenth century', *Osmanlı araştırmaları* VII–VIII (1988), 123–39.

34 Lutfi Paşa, (ed. Ali), *Tevārīh-i āl-i Osmān* (Istanbul 1922), 11–16. Lutfi Paşa's introduction contrasts strongly with the contents of his history, which derive from a popular Anonymous Chronicle, and reflect the popular and not the learned tradition of Ottoman historiography.

God will bring a people whom He loves and who love Him, humble towards believers, but mighty towards the infidels, fighting in the path of God and fearing no one.[35]

This 'people', in Sadeddin's exegesis, was the Ottoman dynasty.

These examples show that, by the mid-sixteenth century, canonical Islamic texts and a canonised view of Islamic history had ousted folk religion and the Turkish epic tradition as sources for dynastic legitimation. The mid-sixteenth century also saw a systematic attempt to define and justify Ottoman rule in terms of the Islamic juristic tradition. This was, above all, the work of the great Ebussuûd in the years between his appointment as *kazasker* of Rumelia in 1537/8 and his death in 1574. For Ebussuûd, what justified the sultan's rule was his promulgation and protection of the *şeriat*, the canonical law of Islam; what defined a Muslim was adherence to this law. By attempting to redefine governmental practice in canonical terms, Ebussuûd sought to create an image of the Ottoman sultan as a truly orthodox sovereign whose rule was in effect indentical with the rule of the *şeriat*. During his period of office, 'Ottoman rule' and '*şeriat*' became almost interchangeable concepts. In his list of sultanic titles, he even describes Süleyman as 'the one who makes manifest the exalted word', a phrase implying that it is through the sultan that God makes known his commands to mankind, and disobedience to the sultan is therefore also disobedience to God. An example of this doctrine in a severely practical form appears in a sultanic decree of 1537/8 requiring governors throughout the sultan's realms to make Muslim villagers build mosques in their villages if none existed already and to attend prayer regularly. Failure to do so would incur punishment.[36] The sultan and Ebussuûd no doubt justified this decree simply as an enforcement of the divine will, since prayer is an incumbency of the *şeriat*. However, failure to observe it would be a defiance not only of God, but also of the sultan's command, and hence it must have acted as a test of loyalty to the sultan as much as to orthodox Islam.

However, the systematic formulation of the idea that the sultan was God's agent in promulgating the divine ordinances of the *şeriat* required great ingenuity. In the first place, there were many groups within the Ottoman empire whose Islam was heterodox, but who clearly were not disloyal to the Ottoman sultan. Secondly, and more importantly, many, if not most, Ottoman laws and administrative practices clearly did not derive from the *şeriat*. The solution to the first problem was simply to

---

35 Koran, *sura* 5, v. 59, quoted in Sadeddin, *Tāc et-tevārīh* I (Istanbul 1861/2), 6.
36 Düzdağ, *Şeyhülislam Ebussuûd Efendi fetvaları*, no. 282.

permit heterodox practices, so long as they were not made public, and so long as their adherents, outwardly at least, professed loyalty to the şeriat.[37] The justification of non-canonical laws was more difficult.

Part of Ebussuûd's solution to this problem is apparent from his list of sultanic titles, one of which describes Süleyman as 'the one who makes smooth the path for the precepts of the manifest şeriat'. This phrase embodies the idea that the rule of the sultan is necessary in order to establish the good order of the world, without which the rule of the şeriat would not be possible. Ottoman laws, in this formulation, although not themselves deriving from the şeriat, became a necessary precondition to its enforcement. A second solution was to redefine Ottoman practices in canonical terms. Non-canonical taxes, for example, such as sheep-tax and customs duty, Ebussuûd justified as representing the canonical impost of *zakat* (alms). He achieved this by invoking the legal fiction that the taxpayer paid these levies with the 'intention' of paying *zakat*.[38] More coherently, in the preface to the lawbook of Skopje and Salonica of 1568/9, he not only gives a formalised description of the system of land tenure and taxation in operation, but also 'harmonises' it with the şeriat by equating the fiscal and administrative terms actually in use, with terms in the canonical texts.[39] These measures were steps in bringing Ottoman law, in terminology if not in substance, into harmony with the holy law.

Ebussuûd's efforts to sanctify Ottoman secular law seem to parallel his attempts during the second half of Süleyman's reign to promulgate a notion of the sultan as caliph, and thus as supreme head of the Islamic community. His intention is clear from his list of sultanic titles, which includes the attributes

> caliph [i.e. 'successor'] of the apostle of the Lord of the worlds [i.e. the Prophet Muhammad] . . . the shadow of God over all peoples . . . possessor of the supreme imamate . . . heir to the great caliphate . . .

Ebussuûd was not in fact the first to describe the sultan as 'caliph'. The title 'caliph of God' appears as early as 1421 on the title page of an almanac for presentation to Mehmed I (1413–21).[40] He seems, however, to have been the first to use it in a defined juristic sense. This he derived, in all probability, from the jurist al-Mawardi (d. 1097) who, although a marginal figure in the Islamic legal tradition, was one

---

37 This becomes clear from a number of heresy trials held during Süleyman's reign.
38 Düzdağ, *Şeyhülislam Ebussuûd Efendi fetvaları,* nos 216, 217. In Islamic law, 'intention' is normally necessary to establish the validity of an act of worship.
39 Text in Barkan, *Zirai ekonominin hukuki ve mali esasları,* 297–9.
40 Ç N Atsız, *Osmanlı tarihine ait takvimler* (Istanbul 1961), 9.

of the few jurists to provide a theory of the caliphate. By adopting this theory, Ebussuûd could perhaps claim for the sultan authority over all Muslims. An example of this occurs in the questions put on Süleyman's behalf to Ebussuûd, concerning the legitimacy of the war against the Safavids. These describe Süleyman as 'sultan of the people of Islam' and the Safavids as 'rebels', implying that Süleyman had a right to universal rulership and that all Muslims who denied his authority belonged to the juristic category of 'rebels'.[41] A second function of al-Mawardi's theory of the caliphate was to justify *de facto* government offices and practices as falling within the boundaries of the *şeriat*, and to give sultanic decrees a legitimacy in modifying the *şeriat*, at least to the extent of choosing definitively between the options available within it, and promulgating this choice as an administrative decree.[42] An example of the sultan's use of this right, and one which appears to have caused controversy, was a decree of 1544, evidently drawn up by Ebussuûd as *kazasker*, forbidding women to marry without the consent of a male guardian. An opinion within the canonical tradition does in fact permit such a marriage, but the sultan's decree of 1544 closed the option, and Ebussuûd, when questioned, justified the decree partly on the grounds of the sultan's authority as caliph.[43]

Ebussuûd appears in fact to have been working towards the construction of a theory that the Ottoman sultan, as caliph, had universal sovereignty and that his decrees had the force of ordinances of the *şeriat*. He never produced a definitive formulation of this idea. He was probably too busy ever to do so. Furthermore, the promulgation of this notion required a public perception of the sultan's majesty. Süleyman's great conquests between 1520 and 1540 undoubtedly fostered such an image, but the increasing and visible infirmities[44] of his old age and, above all, the revolt of his son Bayezid, between 1559 and 1561, must have destroyed his aura of greatness. When Ebussuûd died in 1574, the theory of the Ottoman caliphate died with him.

41 Düzdağ, *Şeyhülislam Ebussuûd Efendi fetvaları*, no. 479. In Islamic law, the term 'rebel' describes a Muslim who abjures the authority of a legitimate Muslim sovereign, and against whom that sovereign may legitimately fight. More normally, Ottoman propaganda described the Safavids not as 'rebels' – which would be an admission that they were in fact Muslims – but as 'infidels'.

42 See Norman Calder, 'Friday prayer and the juristic theory of government: Sarakhsī, Shīrāzī, Māwardī', *Bulletin of the School of Oriental and African Studies* XLIX/1 (1986), 35–47.

43 P Horster, *Zur Anwendung des Islamischen Rechts im 16. Jahrhundert* (Stuttgart 1935), 28–9.

44 See the comments on Süleyman's appearance in 1555 by the Habsburg ambassador Busbecq, in E S Forster (trs), *The Turkish letters of Ogier Ghiselin de Busbecq* (Oxford 1972), 65–6.

PETER BURKE

Concepts of the 'golden age' in the Renaissance

The *reaya* no longer obeyed the sovereign's commands: the soldiers turned against the sultan . . . the old order and harmony departed

Selanıki[1]

The order of the world has been destroyed; men can neither enforce the ordinances of rulers, nor maintain the true daily price [of goods]

Mustafa Ali[2]

It is a long time since the high-chambered household of the lofty Sultanate . . . was served by solicitious, well-intentioned, worthy *ulema* and by obedient, self-effacing, willing slaves

Koçu Bey[3]

If a 'golden age' is simply a period in the past, recent or remote, which the speaker or writers prefers to the present, then the concept can be found in many parts of the world. The Hindus have a tradition of four world ages, or yugas, each worse than the one before. The first is known as '*Krita Yuga*', the age of perfection.[4] A similar theory of four ages, beginning with the best, '*Varivira Cocharuna*' was held by the Peruvians before the arrival of the Spaniards.[5] Chinese Confucians looked back with nostaglia to a time of harmony they associated with the rule of the Sages. In Japan, in the age of the Shinto revival (eighteenth and nineteenth centuries) the age of harmony was situated before the introduction of Chinese learning. In those days, according

1 Quoted in H. İhalcık, *The Ottoman empire, the classical age, 1300–1600* (London 1973), 46.
2 Quoted in C Fleischer, *Bureaucrat and intellectual in the Ottoman empire: the historian Mustafa Ali (1541–1600)* (Princeton 1986), 306.
3 Quoted by B Lewis, 'Ottoman observers of Ottoman decline' *Islamic studies* i (Karachi 1962), 71–87, repr. in his *Islam in history* (London 1973), 199–216.
4 H Zimmer, *Myths and symbols in Indian art and civilization* (New York 1962), 13 ff.
5 Recorded by the historian Felipe Guaman Poma de Ayala.

to one scholar, the Japanese people were literally giants.[6] For their part, Ottoman observers of Ottoman decline in the seventeenth century dated the golden age of the empire to Süleyman, whilst in his day reformers were already looking back to the age of Mehmed II.[7]

I

In one culture, that of the West, the phrase 'age of gold' had a more precise meaning, or rather, a whole range of meanings.[8] It seems to have been on the tip of many European tongues during the fifteenth and sixteenth centuries, or rather – to keep closer to the surviving evidence – it flowed easily from many European pens, including those of such celebrated figures as the humanists Marsilio Ficino and Desiderius Erasmus, the novelist Miguel de Cervantes Saavedra, and the poets Ludovico Ariosto, Joachim Du Bellay, Pierre Ronsard and Torquato Tasso.

However, the meaning of this recurrent phrase is more ambiguous that it appears. It was polysemic. The golden age was viewed and described in a number of diverse, indeed contradictory ways. The term was most commonly used to refer to a period in the past which was believed to be in some sense superior to the present. However, different writers stressed different aspects of that superiority. For some the golden age was a time of peace, for others a time of justice, a time of prosperity, or a time when art and literature flourished. For most writers, the golden age was a phenomenon of the past, usually the remote past, but some (like Ficino and Erasmus) claimed that it would return in the future, possibly in the near future, almost the present. The writers who placed the golden age in the remote past sometimes imagined it in terms of a simple, austere, (and even on occasions a vegetarian) life, an image characterised by recent historians of ideas as 'hard primitivism'. An Islamic parallel to this hard primitivism might be Ibn Khaldun's nostalgic evocation of the nomadic way of life. Others, on the other hand, described life in the golden age as rather more comfortable, when the earth bore fruit spontaneously and in abundance in a manner

---

6 C Blaker, 'Two Shinto myths', in S Henry and J-P Lehmann (eds), *Themes and theories in modern Japanese history: essays in honour of Richard Storry* (London 1988), 64–77.

7 Lewis, 'Ottoman observers'.

8 A useful survey is to be found in H Levin, *The myth of the golden age in the Renaissance* (London 1970). Cf. E Lipsker, *Der Mythos vom goldenen Zeitalter* (1933), and W Veit, *Studien zur Geschichte des Topos der Goldenen Zeit* (Cologne 1961).

reminiscent of the glutton's paradise, the Land of Cockaigne ('soft primitivism').[9]

The dominant conception of the golden age was one of a society characterised negatively by the absence of conflict, private property, money, and even agriculture; and more positively, as an arcadian society of happy shepherds and shepherdesses, contrasted with more recent ages of 'iron' (in the sense of war) and 'gold' (in the sense of money).[10] One might describe such a society as a utopia (or conversely, one might read Sir Thomas More's description of the imaginary island of Utopia as an evocation of the golden age).

Three comments may be worth making at this point. The first is to note the implication that private property and war are connected, an implication which contrasts with the conventional wisdom of the period. In the second place, since intellectuals in industrial societies so often regard the age of agriculture as golden, it may be salutary to be reminded that in that age (which of course included the Renaissance), the object of nostalgia was not the peasant but the shepherd. In the third place, it is worth stressing the dependence of the idea of the golden age on the cyclical view of history current in ancient Greece and Rome (and revived at the Renaissance), a view which justified the hope that the golden age might return.

Did the writers and scholars of the Renaissance really believe in the golden age or did they regard it as a metaphor, a myth or a poetic fiction? The question is a difficult one to answer, not only because attitudes varied but also because the distinctions between myth and history, fact and fiction were less sharp in the Renaissance than they became in the age of positivism.[11] Even in the age of positivism (indeed, even today), it would be unwise to ignore the importance of myth and metaphor (including the image of the golden age) in the work of professional historians.[12]

In the case of some at least of the scholars, thinkers and writers of the Renaissance, I am prepared to assert that the idea of the golden age was more than a myth or a metaphor. At the literal-minded end

9 On hard and soft primitivism, A O Lovejoy and G Boas, *A history of primitivism and related ideas in antiquity* (Baltimore 1934). A reference to vegetarianism by Lorenzo de' Medici is quoted in G Costa, *La leggenda dei secoli d'oro nella letteratura italiana* (Bari 1972), 50.

10 M G Flaherty, 'Money, gold and the golden age in Germany' in D Daiches and A K Thorlby (eds), *The old world: discovery and rebirth* (London 1974), 363–41.

11 W Nelson, *Fact or fiction: the dilemma of the Renaissance story-teller*, (Cambridge, Mass. 1973).

12 H V White, *Metahistory* (Baltimore 1973); A Demandt, *Metaphern für Geschichte* (Munich 1978).

of the spectrum we find Jean Bodin, in his book on historical method, first published in 1566, arguing against a belief in the golden age which he attributes to other scholars, while the Flemish humanist Abraham Ortelius wrote a treatise called *The image of the golden age* (1596), which deals with what would now be called the 'prehistory' of Germanic society.[13] Cervantes, on the other hand, treats the notion in ironic manner by putting the praises of the golden age into the mouth of Don Quixote. Noticing a handful of acorns, he launches into a lecture to the goat-herds, full of the usual commonplaces: 'In that blessed age all things were held in common. . . . All was peace then, all amity, all concord', and so on.[14] In the case of poets such as Ronsard and Tasso, the modern tendency to assume that they dealt exclusively in myth and fiction needs to be resisted; for Renaissance writers frequently treat narrative poets (the classical writers Homer, Virgil and Lucan in particular), as historians. The Elizabethan poet Arthur Golding assimilated golden age and paradise in the introduction to his translation of Ovid as if the ancient writers had had intimations of Christian doctrine.[15]

According to some people in this period, Paradise was a real place with a location on the earth's surface which might be discovered if voyagers searched hard enough. Similarly, the golden age was a real period in the history of the world. For others, both these notions had to be interpreted symbolically, not literally. Yet others were less certain, or at any rate expressed themselves more ambiguously. It might be best to regard the Renaissance idea of the golden age as one which does not easily fit the modern categories of 'history' (as opposed to 'myth') or 'literal' (as opposed to 'metaphorical'), but floated somewhere between the two. Its ambiguity was a source of its power.

II

This idea of the golden age was not new (or better, these various ideas of the golden age were not new) in the Renaissance. They were commonplaces in ancient Greek and Roman times, as the humanists well knew. Histories of the idea usually begin with Hesiod, in the

---

13 J Bodin, *Method for the easy comprehension of history* (1566; English trans. New York 1945), ch. 7; cf. Naldi, quoted in Costa, *La leggenda*, 49. A Ortelius, *Aurei saeculi imago: sive Germanorum veterum vita, mores, ritus et religio* (Antwerp 1596).

14 Cervantes, *Don Quixote*, pt. 1 (1605), ch. 11

15 A Golding, *The metamorphoses* (London 1567).

eighth century BC or thereabouts, and his reference to the four races of men, first the 'golden race' (*chruseon genos*), and then those of silver, bronze and iron. However one might well ask whether the Greeks might not have taken the idea over from Hindu tradition. In any case, the classic formulations, most frequently quoted in the Renaissance, are the descriptions of the *aurea secula* by Ovid and Virgil. According to Ovid,

> In the beginning was the Golden Age, when men of their own accord, without threat of punishment, without laws, maintained good faith and did what was right . . . there were no judges, men lived securely without them . . . The peoples of the world, untroubled by any fears, enjoyed a leisurely and peaceful existence, and had no use for soldiers. The earth itself, without compulsion, untouched by the hoe, unfurrowed by any share, produced all things spontaneously, and men were content with foods that grew without cultivation.[16]

The second famous formulation comes from Virgil's *Fourth Eclogue*, describing the birth of a wonderful child in whose time 'the great line of the centuries begins anew' and Astraea goddess of justice returns to earth. Under the rule of this child, 'a golden race (*gens aurea*) will spring up throughout the world . . . the soil will not feel the harrow, nor the vine the pruning-hook', for the earth will bear fruit spontaneously. From the days of the early Christians onwards, this passage of Virgil was often interpreted as a prophecy of the coming of Christ. In the writings of the fathers of the early Church, such as Lactantius, men who lived in two cultures, the classical and the Christian, the pagan idea of the golden age was fused with the Judeo-Christian (and later Muslim) idea of the millennium. In the thirteenth century, the figure of a Just World Emperor who would restore the golden age was integrated into this complex of ideas.[17] The Florentine poet Giovanni Nesi, a disciple of the prophet Girolamo Savonarola, associated the golden age and the millennium, and his *Oracle of the New Age* (1496) announced that they would arrive in the year 1500.[18] Attempts were made to integrate the figure of Antichrist as well. The Protestant humanist Celio Secundo Curione suggested that there would be a golden age of peace before Christ returned to judge mankind. The Dominican friar Tommaso Campanella added a number of details to

---

16 Ovid, *Metamorphoses*, Book 1, English trans. (Harmondsworth 1955), 31–2.
17 E L Tuveson, *Millennium and Utopia* (Berkeley and Los Angeles 1949); N Cohn, *The pursuit of the millennium* (London 1957); F Yates, 'Charles V and the idea of the Empire' [1960], repr. in her *Astraea* (London 1975), 1–28.
18 D Weinstein, *Savonarola and Florence* (Princeton 1970).

this picture of a *seculum aureum*. There would be one ruler for the whole world, men would live longer, and the sciences would flourish.[19]

The idea of the golden age can also be found in the Middle Ages (from Boethius to the *Roman de la Rose*), but references to it are far more frequent in the Renaissance, whether because the classical tradition was much more widely known in the fifteenth and sixteenth centuries or because the contrast between iron and golden ages seemed more relevant to experience at that time. The concept was also used in new ways.

At this point I should like to return to the problem of the meaning of the concept, attacking it from a somewhat different angle. The meaning of a concept is defined by some linguistic philosophers as its use. The uses of this particular concept are extremely various, but they are at least classifiable.

(i) Flattery or propaganda (according to the intended audience, prince or people). During the Renaissance we find many addresses to princes telling them that the golden age has returned or at any rate that it will return under their beneficient rule. This is what the Italian humanist Poggio Bracciolini wrote to Alfonso of Aragon, king of Naples (1445); the poet Lorenzo Pulci to Lorenzo de' Medici (1483); the German humanist-poet Conrad Celtis to the emperor Maximilian; Ariosto (1516) and Erasmus (1517) to pope Leo X; Ariosto (1532) to Charles V (replacing the pope by the emperor after expectations had been disappointed); Du Bellay to Henri II of France; Ronsard to Charles IX of France; and so on.[20]

The idea of a returning age of gold was sometimes dramatised in the form of a festival, like the one devised in Florence in 1513, by the humanist Jacopo Nardi and the painter Jacopo Pontormo, to celebrate the election of a Florentine pope, Leo X. The golden age was represented in the form of a small boy who was gilded for the occasion (*il putto dorato*). Unfortunately, and ironically, he died a few days later, poisoned by the gilding.[21]

(ii) We must not be too quick to write off these addresses to princes, which belonged to the traditional genre of eulogy, as empty or servile. They expressed or insinuated genuine hopes and tactful advice.[22] They

19 M Reeves, *The influence of prophecy in the Later Middle Ages* (Oxford 1969), esp. 431, 451, 482.
20 On Poggio and Pulci, see Costa, *La leggenda*, 35, 55. Cf. Costa, *La leggenda*, 60, 67, 69, on Boiardo, Cariteo, Sannazzaro; and E Armstrong, *Ronsard and the age of gold* (Cambridge 1968).
21 G Vasari, 'Life of Pontormo', in his *Vite* (1550: many editions and translations).
22 Cf. D J Gordon, *The Renaissance imagination* (Berkeley 1975), and M McGowan, *Ideal forms in the age of Ronsard* (Berkeley 1985), ch. 1.

were a form of prince-management. References to the golden age might also express political and social criticism, as utopias so often do. In the Italian poet Petrarch, for example, they are associated with a critique of the papacy and with support for the unsuccessful reform movement of Cola di Rienzo in the middle of the fourteenth century.[23] In the French poet Ronsard, writing at a time of bitter civil wars between Catholics and Protestants, references to the golden age suggest not only his nostalgia for the period before 1562, when the wars began, but also his support for the peace movement of the so-called '*politiques*' and for the religious policies which would make peace possible.[24] The frequent contrasts between the golden age and the 'age of gold', in other words money, offer a contemporary critique of what we call capitalism.[25] In the early seventeenth century, one can even find a reference to the golden age in the manifesto of a popular rising, in Normandy in 1639, in which hostility to the taxes introduced by Louis XIII was expressed in the form of nostalgia for the regime of Louis XII and his '*siècle d'or*'.[26] In similar fashion, Hungarians living under Ottoman rule looked back to the golden age of Matthias Corvinus as a time of peace and justice.

III

It may seem a contradiction, but stereotypes and commonplaces have a history. The words may be repeated *ad nauseam*, but their meaning and their associations change as they are employed in different contexts. In the course of the fifteenth and sixteenth centuries, the European idea of the golden age gradually changed its significance as the schema was used to interpret new events and experiences.

In the first place, there was the discovery of America. The wish for a golden age or a paradise was projected on to the newly-discovered continent. To humanists like Pietro Martire d'Anghiera, who knew his Ovid well, the inhabitants of Cuba and Hispaniola seemed to be living in the golden age before the introduction of law (*aurea aetate viventes, sine legibus*).[27] The traveller Amerigo Vespucci, after whom 'America' takes its name, also perceived the newly-discovered continent in terms of the stereotype of the golden age, stressing the fertility of the soil

23 Costa, *La leggenda*, 17.
24 Armstrong, *Ronsard*.
25 Flaherty, 'Money, gold and the golden age in Germany'.
26 M Foisil, *La révolte des Nu-pieds* (Paris 1970).
27 S Buarque, *Visão do Paraíso* (São Paulo 1958; 3rd edn 1969), 179–80.

and the lack of private property. The acquisition of Mexico and Peru made Charles V much more of a world ruler than his medieval predecessors had been, and so encouraged Ariosto and other poets to see him as the Just World Emperor and to predict that the time was at hand when the rest of the prophecy would be fulfilled, in other words that the Church would be reformed, that the Turks and the Jews would be converted, that the millennium would arrive and that the golden age would return. As the Spanish poet Hernando de Acuña put it in a famous sonnet, addressed to his king, there would be 'only one flock and one shepherd on earth . . . one monarch, one empire and one sword' (*una rey y un pastor solo en el suelo . . . un monarca, un imperio y una espada*).[28]

The idea of the golden age was also associated with the Renaissance idea of the Renaissance (for a distinctive feature of this particular cultural movement, in contrast with earlier cultural movements, was the sharpness of its self-definition). Like the discovery of America and the Spanish acquisition of large parts of it, the achievements of the Renaissance were seen as confirming hopes for the return of the golden age. In a famous letter of 1492, the philosopher Ficino wrote that 'If we are to call any age golden, it is beyond doubt that age which brings forth golden talents . . . this century, like a golden age, has restored to light the liberal arts which were almost extinct'.[29] Erasmus wrote to Leo X in 1513 in similar vein: 'I congratulate this our age – which bids fair to be an age of gold – wherein I see, under your happy auspices and by your holy counsels, three of the chief blessings of humanity are about to be restored to her . . . Christian piety . . . learning . . . the concord of Christendom'.[30] It was ironic that he should have written about Christian concord to a pope whose reign coincided with the revolt of Martin Luther. The point that needs emphasis here, however, is that of the religious and even millenarian associations of what we view as a secular movement, the Renaissance.

For Protestants, Luther's reformation of religion was a sign that the golden age was about to return. The Elizabethan poet George Peele, in his pageant *The Descent of Astraea* (1591), written in order to welcome a Lord Mayor of London, associates Elizabeth with the goddess Astraea and her support for the reform of the Church as a sign that the iron age of war was over and that 'Saturn's golden reign' of justice was about to return.[31]

28 H de Acuna, 'Soneto al Rey'.
29 Quoted in J B Ross (ed.), *Renaissance reader* (London 1958), 79.
30 Ross, *Renaissance reader*, 83.
31 Discussed in Yates, *Astraea*, 60 ff.

The religious wars of the second half of the sixteenth century made the triumph of peace and justice seem increasingly remote as well as increasingly desirable. In the early years of the seventeenth century, the imminent return of the golden age was awaited with confidence and enthusiasm in some circles in Italy and Germany.[32] With the deflation of these expectations in the iron age of the Thirty Years' War (1618–48), the concept lost a good deal of its significance. By this time, only the idea of a golden age of culture continued to seem reasonably plausible.

The idea of the golden age did not of course come to an end with the Renaissance, in 1600 or thereabouts, but it continued to change its meaning. As the cyclical view of history was abandoned for a more linear view of the rise of progress and civilisation, the phrase lost much of its significance. It has sometimes been suggested that from the late eighteenth century onwards, the golden age was placed in the future instead of the past. It is true that conceptions such as Marx's classless society have more in common with the traditional age of harmony that Marxists are usually prepared to admit. As for the phrase itself, it came to be employed less and less literally and more and more loosely. When the poet-politician Francisco Martinez de la Rosa wrote (in 1827) of the *siglo de oro* of Spanish literature in the late sixteenth century (a phrase which has stuck like a leech to the period ever since), all he was claiming was the existence of outstanding achievements.[33] In the *siglo de oro* itself, the phrase had generally been associated with a much wider range of much more precise expectations.

The main conclusion of this rapid survey is that European writers traditionally took the idea of a golden age much more seriously than their counterparts in other cultures. Apparent similarities in the style of nostalgia need to be distinguished. For example, Ottoman references to an age of harmony, justice and prosperity under Süleyman or Mehmed II, in memoranda to the sultan in the sixteenth and seventeenth centuries analysing the decline of the empire and proposing measures to arrest this decline, have their parallels in the proposals of the so-called *arbitristas*, proposing the reform of the other great empire, Spain, in the same period. These *arbitristas* generally looked back to the age of the 'reconquest' of Spain from the Muslims as the time when order and harmony prevailed.[34] However, the parallel should not be pushed too far. The idea of a golden age had a much greater range of significance and association in western Europe than it had in the

32 E de Mas, *L'attesa del secolo aureo (1603–25)* (Florence 1982).
33 Quoted in Levin, *Myth of the golden age*, 144.
34 M D Gordon, 'Morality, reform and the empire in seventeenth-century Spain', *Il pensiero politico* 11 (1978), 3–19.

Ottoman empire, or indeed in any other part of the world, from China to Peru. In this respect the golden age differs from the idea of the millennium, which took similar form in western Europe and the Ottoman empire in the sixteenth and seventeenth centuries, the age of Sabbatai Sevi, the Fifth Monarchy men, and of the expectations associated with the Muslim year AH 1000.[35]

---

35 B Capp, *The Fifth Monarchy men* (London 1972); G Scholem, *Sabbatai Sevi: the mystical Messiah* (London 1973).

CHRISTINE WOODHEAD

Perspectives on Süleyman

The tree of the Ottoman state was planted by Osman Şah Gazi [c. 1300–24], and nourished by the endeavours of his successors until it reached the limit of mature perfection in the time of Kanuni Sultan Süleyman Han. Thereafter, it experienced variously both autumnal decay and distress, and spring restoration and rejuvenation, but eventually suffered such misfortunes that it was reduced to a miserable condition. Then by the skill and enterprise of Sultan Mahmud Han II [1808–39] it was restored . . .

Ahmed Cevdet Paşa, c. 1890
Ottoman *vakanüvis* (official historian)[1]

The ideal prince is a timeless necessity.[2]

I

Among Süleyman's first acts as sultan immediately after his accession in October 1520 was to grant freedom of movement to the members of six hundred prominent families whom Selim I had deported from Egypt to Istanbul after his conquest of Cairo in 1517; those who wished to do so could return home. Next, he rescinded Selim's ban on the silk trade with Iran and restored all confiscated goods to the merchants concerned. He then turned his attention to the behaviour of Ottoman government officials. An investigation into complaints of extortion and murder made against the admiral-in-chief Cafer Bey resulted swiftly in the latter's execution. The *bey* (lord) of Prizrin was similarly punished for having captured and sold as slaves a number of *reaya* (peasants) in his province. The *agas* commanding the palace-based *silahdar* (lit. 'sword-bearing') corps were dismissed following attacks upon the houses of

1 Ahmed Cevdet Paşa, *Tarih-i Cevdet* (Istanbul 1309/1891–2), I, 86–7.
2 Bernard Guenée, *States and rulers in late medieval Europe* (Oxford 1985), 69.

government officials in Istanbul, for which five members of the troop were also executed.

Most or all of these 'examples of justice and equity'[3] appear at the beginning of each of the principal sixteenth and seventeenth-century Ottoman histories of Süleyman's reign, immediately after the announcement of his accession. They clearly serve to define the character of his rule, and to place it in sharp contrast to the severity and arbitrariness of the eight years of Selim I's sultanate (1512–20). In the words of Celalzade, Süleyman's long-serving *nişancı* (chancellor) and author of the most substantial and authoritative contemporary history of his reign, written in the sultan's last decade:

> the sweet perfume of his just deeds was spread to the four corners of the earth, people breathed the pleasing fresh scent of his benevolence, talk of his justice was on everyone's tongue; thus was his concern for the care of the *reaya* made manifest.[4]

The same deeds and a similar evaluation of them were noted by Mustafa Ali in his universal history, *Künhü'l-ahbar* (Essence of history), written in the 1590s.[5] Peçevi, writing in the 1630s and 1640s, began his history of the Ottomans in 1520 with a resounding endorsement of Süleyman's character and policies as evidenced by these initial acts, which had presaged a long and successful reign. Further, continued Peçevi:

> in his reign, no holder of a government post, no military or judicial appointee, was dismissed without good cause. In fact, dismissal was extremely rare and those against whom there was any shadow of suspicion would never be reappointed to office. Accordingly, all officials acted with justice and moderation for fear of losing all chance of further employment. In this way blameworthy traits were eliminated.[6]

The *Süleymanname* (History of Süleyman) of Kara Çelebizade, written around the same time as Peçevi's history, opens with an introduction on the virtues of Süleyman's style of government and sets a similar tone for the interpretation of subsequent events.[7]

Whilst it was standard practice to hail the beginning of a new reign

---

3 İbrahim Peçevi, *Tarih-i Peçevi* (Istanbul 1281/1864), I, 5–6.
4 Petra Kappert (ed.), *Geschichte Sultan Süleymān Kānūnīs von 1520 bis 1557, oder Tabakāt ül-memālik ve derecāt ül-mesālik von Celālzāde Muṣṭafā* (Wiesbaden 1981), ff. 27a–8b, esp. 28a.
5 Jan Schmidt (ed.), *Pure water for thirsty Muslims: a study of Muṣṭafā 'Ālī of Gallipoli's Künhü' l-ahbār* (Leiden 1991), 322–23. See also Cornell H Fleischer, *Bureaucrat and intellectual in the Ottoman empire: the historian Mustafa Âli (1541–1600)* (Princeton 1986), *passim*.
6 Peçevi, I, 6–7; see also M Tayyib Gökbilgin, 'Süleyman I', *İslam Ansiklopedisi* 9, 101.
7 Kara celebizade Abdülaziz, *Süleymanname* (publ. Bulak 1248/1832–33), 5 ff., 12, 22.

as the inauguration of an era of order, prosperity, and light, it is clear that, for both contemporary and later historians, Süleyman's era held a special significance in this respect. The concept of *adalet* (justice) dominates the historiography of the reign. With it are associated the qualities of decisiveness, maintenance of order and of moral and cultural standards, personal dignity and moderation, and above all concern for the *reaya*, his subjects. *Adalet* was given particular emphasis by the conscious choice of '*Kanuni*' ('the lawgiver') as Süleyman's regnal name, signifying the priority to be given to the development and enforcement of *kanun* administrative law, and hence to law and order, internal peace and prosperity generally. Whether or not the *kanunname* (collection of *kanun* law) attributed to Süleyman was actually compiled under his auspices is perhaps less significant than the prominence given to attempts to implement it.[8] Süleyman's association with *kanun* was particularly appropriate in view of the need to develop administrative and bureaucratic structures to cope with the increasing size and complexity of the empire consequent upon territorial gains in Syria, Egypt, Iraq and Hungary within the space of a mere twenty-five years (1516–41). It emphasised the practical nature of his rule and his involvement in the kind of everyday detail (tax regulations, markets, etc) which affected the lives of all members of the *reaya*. The epithet '*Kanuni*' also contrasted well with the names adopted by the three preceding sultans: '*Fatih*', 'the conqueror', for Mehmed II (1451–81), a common title for Muslim rulers, but here referring specifically to the prestigious conquest of Constantinople; '*Veli*', 'the saint', for Bayezid II (1481–1512), whose less flamboyant, more cautious reign may offer some of the more instructive parallels with that of Süleyman; and '*Yavuz*', in his own time meaning ruthless but subsequently ameliorated to stern or resolute, for Selim I.

One of the commonplaces adduced by sixteenth-century Ottoman historians for the value of the written word is its role in maintaining the fame and reputation of a ruler. Like his grandfather Bayezid II, Süleyman was especially appreciative of the merits, both political and cultural, immediate and long-term, of historiography. His reign not only offered ample material to record and celebrate; he himself offered ample encouragement and reward to diligent writers. He took an active interest in the production of the written record of his reign, and must

---

8 See Halil İnalcık, 'Süleyman the Lawgiver and Ottoman law', *Archivum Ottomanicum* I (1969), 105–38.

therefore be considered to a significant extent the creator of his own image. Part of the purpose of this essay is to suggest the nature of and the need for this image, within the Ottoman context.

As shown briefly above, an obvious continuity appears between the image of Süleyman presented in accounts written during or shortly after his reign and that found in seventeenth-century works such as Peçevi's history. There can be no doubt of the success of the written word in helping to maintain his prevailing reputation as the *Padişah-i cihan-penah* ('the Padisah who is the refuge of the world') par excellence. However, some aspects of Süleyman's image were clearly seen by seventeenth-century Ottoman writers of history and of political tracts not merely as part of the historical record, but as a means of highlighting their own concerns. A second purpose of this essay is to indicate the nature of such usage, since this – in combination with the inability of subsequent sultans to challenge successfully the record of Süleyman's achievements – played a considerable part in determining his era as an Ottoman golden age.[9]

Although the principal concern of this essay is the image of Süleyman portrayed in Ottoman historiographical sources,[10] account must also be taken of the variety of visual representations of power available during his reign, including those demonstrations of authority and wealth which consisted of acts rather than artefacts and which were therefore visible only to observers at the time. At the most obvious and ubiquitous levels, sultanic authority was evident to the general population through the building and maintenance of mosques and colleges, and of roads, bridges, caravanserais, water courses and fountains essential for the promotion of trade and economic prosperity, and of good administration and military communications;[11] through the Janissary garrisons stationed in strategic towns and cities; through the local *kadi* (Muslim judge) and, in Anatolia and Rumelia, the *timar*-holding *sipahi* (provincial

---

9 N V Riasanovsky, *The image of Peter the Great in Russian history and thought* (New York/Oxford 1985), and Peter Burke, *The fabrication of Louis XIV* (New Haven/London 1992), offer models for the study of both contemporary and subsequent aspects of a ruler's image but are able to draw upon a much larger body of existing research than that available for Süleyman. By comparison, the present study is brief and preparatory.

10 Complementary aspects of Süleyman's image, its historical precedents, and more specifically its legal interpretation, are dealt with by Colin Imber elsewhere in this volume.

11 See e.g. Y Halaçoğlu, 'Osmanlı imparatorluğu'unda menzil teşkilâti hakkında bazı mülâhazalar', *Osmanlı araştırmaları* II (1981), 123–5, for establishment of posting stations during the grand vezirate of Lutfi Paşa, 1539–41.

cavalryman), the daily representatives of central authority;[12] through Süleyman's name on the coinage and, for Muslims, in the Friday prayer. In contrast to most subsequent sultans, who rarely left the confines of Istanbul or Edirne, Süleyman travelled fairly widely in Rumelia and especially in Anatolia. Whilst much of this was in connection with military campaigns, the opportunity was always taken to make the most of the sultan's progress through his empire, with regular halts in the major towns and cities en route, to visit tombs and shrines, receive gifts and petitions, and 'relieve the distress of his people'. On the Iraq campaign of 1534–35, for example, it was the grand vezir and *serdar* (general) İbrahim Paşa who led the army eastwards and conducted military operations. Süleyman followed several months later, in June 1534, via Kütahya, Akşehir, Konya (where he visited the tomb of the Mevlevi *şeyh* Celaleddin Rumi), Kayseri, Sivas and Erzincan to meet the army at Tabriz in late September. He entered Baghdad in state in November, the Safavid governor having abandoned the city in the face of the Ottoman advance. Four winter months were spent setting up a local administration and visiting Kerbela and the other principal Muslim shrines in the area, making repairs and endowments as appropriate. The eventual return was made via Diyarbekir, Aleppo (again, pausing to visit the principal mosques and the castle), Antakya, Adana and Konya, arriving in Istanbul in January 1536.[13] For Süleyman personally the entire journey was less a military campaign than an extremely visible and impressive imperial progress, a consideration which offers a new perspective on the much-vaunted claim that he led the thirteen major campaigns of his reign.[14] The amount of time Süleyman spent away from Istanbul on such occasions was considerable – eighteen months in 1534–36 for the Iraq campaign, eighteen months again in 1548–49 for the Tabriz campaign in support of Elkas Mirza, rebel brother of the

12 See e.g. İ Ortaylı, 'On the role of the kadi in provincial administration', *Turkish public administration annual* 3 (1976), 1–4.

13 Campaign summarised in Gökbilgin, 'Süleyman I', 116–18. Matrakçi Nasuh, *Beyan-ı menazil-i sefer-i Irakeyn-i Sultan Süleyman Han*, ed. H G Yurdaydın (Ankara 1976) is a contemporary description of the stages of the campaign, copiously illustrated with maps and town plans.

14 Indicative of this is the increasing preference in Ottoman chronicles for *sefer* (essentially 'journey') over *gaza* ('military expedition, holy war') to describe the sultan's campaigns.

For a description of Süleyman setting out from Edirne on the 1543 Hungarian campaign, see J M Rogers and R M Ward, *Süleyman the Magnificent* [Catalogue of the 1988 British Museum exhibition] (London 1988), 27–8 (hereafter Rogers and Ward). For the routes of the 1521 and 1526 Hungarian campaigns, see A C Schaendlinger, *Die Feldzugstagebücher des ersten und zweiten ungarischen Feldzugs Süleymans I* (Vienna 1978).

Shah of Iran, and more than two years in 1553–55 during the Iranian campaign leading to the treaty of Amasya. Aleppo, with its congenial climate and status as an old Islamic city, was a favourite choice for winter quarters.[15] Such journeying was due partly to the need for Süleyman's presence as a motivating force for the household troops, when a vezir could not command the full loyalty of the army. It also served partly to demonstrate his own continuing competence in affairs of state, and to maintain his personal authority in the provinces, particularly during the later 1540s and 1550s when his sons provided potential foci for discontent. A progress through Anatolia provided opportunity for the *şehzades* (princes) to be summoned to pay homage to their father.

Istanbul was the principal setting for the most significant public spectacles. These ranged from the sultan's weekly ride to attend Friday prayers at one of the city's imperial mosques, through the festivities marking departure on both military and naval campaigns and on subsequent triumphal re-entry to the city, to the celebration of circumcision or wedding feasts for members of the Ottoman dynasty. The *sünnet düğünü* (circumcision festival) for the three *şehzades*, Mustafa, Mehmed and Selim, in 1530, and that for *şehzades* Bayezid and Cihangir in 1539 – the latter coinciding with the marriage of Süleyman's daughter Mihrimah Sultan with Rüstem Paşa – each lasted two to three weeks. Celalzade's careful description of the 1530 ceremonies emphasised the restful, contemplative elegance of the traditional Persian garden theme adorning the Atmeydanı in which were held entertainments and displays of crafts and military skills from all over the empire. He was particularly concerned to show the richness of the pavilions and their furnishings, and of the gifts exchanged, and the exact order of precedence of military and administrative officials and members of the learned professions at feasts, debates, and in the giving and receiving of presents. His account reflects an essential display of cultural sensibility, of wealth, talent, orderliness and versatility, and above all of confidence in the dynasty, its achievements and its future.[16]

Süleyman's architectural projects and their associated *evkaf* (endowments) were the dominant physical symbols of his status as supreme Muslim ruler and benefactor of his people. His long reign of forty-six years allowed time for mosques, *medreses* (colleges) and other public buildings to be built or restored and tombs to be refurbished in

---

15 Add to this, time spent on expeditions to Rhodes, Belgrade and Hungary, and, according to Ogier Ghiselin de Busbecq, *Turkish letters*, tr. E S Forster (Oxford 1968), 89, virtually annual winter sojourns in Edirne to hunt.

16 Celalzade, 194a–201b; Peçevi I, 153–5; see also Rogers and Ward, 28.

his name in virtually all major cities – Baghdad, Konya, Damascus, Mecca and Medina, Jerusalem, Edirne, Aleppo – and many lesser buildings elsewhere. His legacy to Istanbul included not only the Süleymaniye complex (under construction 1550–57), dominating both the skyline of the city and the judicial-theological curriculum, but six other large mosques, several *medrese*s, and the reconstruction of a vitally important water distribution system.[17] Such works provided significant employment for architects, engineers, masons, labourers, calligraphers, copyists, bookbinders, jewellers, goldsmiths, etc, and encouraged the development of industries such as pottery and tiles, textiles and metalwork.[18] All this ensured a considerable degree of economic activity and well-being, particularly amongst urban populations, which formed part of the general perception of the reign.

Similarly, Süleyman's natural role as patron of literature and learning produced an extended sense of bustling productivity amongst poets, scholars, littérateurs and historians. *Divan* poetry (lyric verse in 'classical' format) was cultivated both as a form of expression in itself and for the sense of communion with the prestigious Perso-Islamic cultural tradition from which it was derived. From the mid-fifteenth century onwards, sultans had actively promoted the development of Ottoman poetry as an essential counterpart to the military and administrative activities of the state, providing deserving poets with posts or pensions and themselves writing poetry under an appropriate *mahlas* (pen name).[19] Süleyman's *mahlas*, '*Muhibbi*' ('lover', 'affectionate friend') denoted a sincere lover of God with the aspect of a dervish, but also reinforced the notion of gentle care for his people.[20] Although the study of Ottoman lyric poetry has centred mainly on that produced by or directed towards members of a relatively small court circle, to be a poet in the *divan* tradition – and certainly to appreciate that poetry – was not necessarily an elite occupation and provided a binding interest through various sections of Ottoman Muslim society, its sufi termin-

---

17 Rogers and Ward, 37–41 on Süleyman as builder and his chief architect Sinan; for details of costs and materials in the building of the Süleymaniye, see Ö L Barkan, *Süleymaniye camii ve imareti inşaatı* (2 vols, Ankara 1972, 1979); on the Istanbul water system, see R Anhegger, 'Istanbul su yllarının inşasına ait bir kaynak: Eyyubi'nin Menâkib-i Sultan Süleyman', *Tarih Dergisi* I/i (1949), 119–38.

18 On the arts and crafts of Süleyman's era, see Rogers and Ward, 46–214.

19 See H Sohrweide, 'Dichter und Gelehrte aus dem Osten im osmanischen Reich (1453–1600)': Ein Beitrag zur türkisch-persischen Kulturgeschichte', *Der Islam* 46 (1970), 263–302.

20 Rogers and Ward, 85–9, on Süleyman as poet and copies of his *divan*. For Süleyman as *derviş–nihad*, see below, p. 176.

ology echoing the religious poetry of the widespread dervish lodges.[21] Süleyman's contemporary reputation as a worthy ruler was greatly enhanced by his status as both practicising poet and patron of poets, and thereby as promoter of a prestigious cultural tradition. The first Ottoman *tezkire* (biographical dictionary of *divan* poets) was compiled by Sehi in the 1530s, followed in subsequent decades by those of Latifi and Aşık Çelebi. Such works – and a similar compendium on the lives of Ottoman scholars by Taşköprüzade (d. 1561) – were inspired by long-established Arabic or Persian models, but their significance here is that they were records of achievement which first appeared in Süleyman's reign, and which gave pride of place in their opening sections to the poets of the dynasty.[22]

It has often been claimed that Ottoman Turkish did not attain the status of a recognised literary language (in prose particularly) until the sixteenth century, having been hampered previously by the lack of an established grammar and by the dominant cultural prestige of Persian, the language of much fifteenth-century court literature. Although the commissioning in parallel by Bayezid II of two major literary histories of the dynasty – Bidlisi's *Heşt bihişt* (Eight paradises) in Persian and Kemalpaşazade's *Tevarih-i al-i Osman* (Annals of the house of Osman) in Ottoman – had helped set Ottoman on a par with the older language,[23] it was again the increased volume of literary activity stimulated by Süleyman's patronage and by the achievements of his reign which allowed Ottoman to become finally established as the principal literary language. Particularly noticeable is the growth in popularity of historical writing, especially histories of the reigns of Selim I and Süleyman (in whole or in part) and *gazaname*s (campaign monographs).[24]

Celalzade's *Tabakatü'l-memalik ve derecatü'l-mesalik* (Levels of the dominions and grades of the professions) is an essential source for the study of Süleyman's desired image, both as a contemporary record

---

21 W G Andrews, *Poetry's voice, society's song: Ottoman lyric poetry* (Seattle 1985), 62–88; J R Walsh, 'Yunus Emre and *divan* poetry', *Journal of Turkish Studies* 7 (1983), 453–64.

22 J Stewart-Robinson, 'The Ottoman biographies of poets', *Journal of Near Eastern Studies* 24 (1965), 57–74.

23 On Bayezid II's use of historiography, see H İnalcık, 'The rise of Ottoman historiography' in B Lewis and P M Holt (eds), *Historians of the Middle East* (London 1962), 163–7.

24 On the various genres of Ottoman literature, see Agâh Sırrı Levend, *Türk edebiyatı tarihi* I (Ankara 1973), 99–121. For a brief survey, see J R Walsh, 'Turkey: bibliographical spectrum', *Review of National Literatures* IV/ (Spring 1973), 115–22. On historical writing, see Abdülkadir Özcan, 'Historiography in the reign of Süleyman the Magnificent' in [Ministry of Tourism and Culture] *The Ottoman empire in the reign of Süleyman the Magnificent*, II (Ankara 1988), 167–222.

by a senior government official and for its considerable influence on later Ottoman historians.[25] Despite its title, it is a prime example of the Ottoman royal biography. The author describes his work as 'this register of exemplary events' which will not only constitute 'a monument in the treasury of time' to the 'distinguishing qualities and admirable attributes' of 'the king of kings (*şehinşah*) skilled in the heroic virtues (*menakıb*) of government', but will also enumerate the types and qualities of the learned, the military, the state servants and the *reaya*, of the towns, the cities, the fortresses and the treasuries of valuables, which together bear witness to 'the miraculous and unique nature of the age'.[26] Süleyman is unequivocally *zübde-i al-i Osman*,[27] 'the quintessence of the Ottoman dynasty'. Of his sultan's innumerable virtues, Celalzade in his introduction emphasises three. First is Süleyman's natural exercise of *adalet*, the 'crown, cloak and seal' of which seemed to have been designed expressly for him. Interestingly, Celalzade makes no reference in this section (in contrast to the main text) to *kanun* or *Kanuni*, preferring to describe Süleyman as *şeriat-ayin* ('distinguished by adherence to the *şeriat*'), in line with his emphasis upon the sultan's worthiness in the eyes of God. Second is the concept of liberality and munificence, *cudi*, here extending beyond the disposal of largesse and the elimination of want, to join with *adalet* in the notion of the sultan as protector, refuge and benefactor of his people. Third is his military prowess as *sahibkıran* ('world-conqueror'), where trust in God brings divine aid and assurance of success in all Süleyman's ventures. For Celalzade, justice, liberality, and military success are the chief characteristics of Süleyman's rule; they are by implication the main themes in his subsequent presentation of events.[28]

The *Tabakatü'l-memalik* was intended – within the understanding of its author – to be a comprehensive history. However, many of the historical works produced during Süleyman's reign tended to focus upon a specific event or series of events, or upon a specific aspect of his rule. The *gazaname* style of campaign monograph quickly established

25 See Kappert's introduction to *Celalzade*, 11–35.
26 *Celalzade*, 7b–9a.
27 *Celalzade*, 6a.
28 On the ideal king in traditional Islamic 'mirrors for princes' inherited by the Ottomans, see Pal Fodor, 'State and society, crisis and reform, in 15th–17th century Ottoman mirrors for princes', *Acta Orientalia Hungarica* XL (1986), (2–3), 217–23. For one of the most influential 'mirrors' translated from Persian into Turkish in the 15th century, see R Levy (tr.), *A mirror for princes: the Qābūs Nāma by Kai Kā'ūs ibn Iskandar, prince of Gurgān* (London 1951); E Birnbaum (ed.), *The book of advice by King Kay Kā'us ibn Iskander: the earliest Old Ottoman Turkish version of his Kabusname* (Harvard 1981).

itself as the most popular form of short account, for obvious reasons.[29] Here Süleyman's role as warrior king, the sultan of the *gazis*, dominates: he surpasses the achievements of his predecessors in extending the territorial bounds of empire and of Islam; he marches with a magnificently arrayed, invincible force, reduces the strongest fortresses, slays the irredeemable infidel, and puts rebels to flight. His inherent leadership qualities are clearly demonstrated, typified perhaps by Celalzade's depiction of the tension in the Ottoman camp on the eve of the battle of Mohaç, 1526, and the sultan's public prayers which inspire his troops to victory.[30]

The proliferation of works of the *gazaname* type implies that the sultan's principal role was as military leader; campaign and conquest become his primary occupation. Even in a more unusual work like Eyyubi's *Menakıb-i Sultan Süleyman* (Exemplary deeds of Sultan Süleyman), written to commemorate Süleyman's rebuilding of the Istanbul water supply system in 1563–64, the author felt it necessary first to list the sequence of campaigns to establish the sultan's stature before proceeding to the real subject of the work. Even here, Süleyman's principal 'exemplary deeds' are those military victories vouchsafed to him by God.[31]

A subtly different image of the sultan begins to appear towards the end of Süleyman's reign in a form of literary historiography consciously developed under his auspices. In origin a celebration of the glories of war, the *şehname* (king's book) evolved into a cross between court history, panegyric, and (occasionally) elegant literature. Its model was the epic of ancient Iranian kings and heroes as told in the prestigious *Şahname* (Book of kings) of the eleventh-century Persian poet Firdevsi. Also composed in Persian, in the *mesnevi* form of rhymed couplets, occasional *şehname* works had been produced by Ottoman writers from the time of Mehmed II. The style was deliberately promoted by Süleyman, to the extent of establishing in the 1550s a regular salaried post as *şehnameci*, 'writer of *şehname*s', a form of court historiographer.[32] By general implication and by specific allusion, such works associated

29 Cf. Imber's discussion of the closely-related *menakıb* genre, above pp. 141–2.
30 Celalzade 1445–45b. For a stylistically simpler but more dramatic rendering of this essential scene, see Solakzade, *Tarih* (Istanbul 1279/1880), 455.
31 Eyyubi, *Menâkıb-i Sultan Süleyman (Risâle-i Padişâh-nâme)*, ed. M Akkuş (Ankara 1991), 64–112 (followed by shorter sections on Süleyman's justice, status as poet, generosity, and architectural patronage, before the second half of the text (pp. 156–266) dealing with the water distribution system).
32 Christine Woodhead, 'An experiment in official historiography: the post of *şehnameci* in the Ottoman empire, c.1555–1605', *Wiener Zeitschrift für die Kunde des Morgenlandes* 75 (1983), 157–82.

Süleyman not only with military success but also with an elevated imperial elegance and style, raising him one step above the practical roles of *gazi* sultan and *kanun* administrator. Such historiography presents a literary parallel to Ebussuûd's attempts to formulate a legal claim to universal sovereignty on Süleyman's behalf.[33]

The *Süleymanname* (Book of Süleyman, completed 1558) of the first *şehnameci* Arif is in essence a chronological account in verse of the principal events of the years 1520 to 1555, with the usual emphasis upon military and political affairs. However, it differs from other accounts in two chief respects. One is that as writing progressed Arif submitted drafts for the sultan's approval – evidence of Süleyman's close interest in the work. The other is that the *Süleymanname* was among the first major Ottoman histories to be illustrated, in this case with sixty-nine miniature paintings executed mainly by palace artists.[34] The choice of topics for illustration, and the reflection of status and significance in the arrangement of each composition, must have been matters of very careful consideration and thus have brought the themes of the work to the attention of a wide range of people within the court circle. It would appear from the works of Lokman, *şehnameci* c. 1562–96, that some later *şehname* works came to be prized as much for their illustrations as for their text, and that they were conceived partly as *objets d'art* for the sultan's private collection.[35] There was no doubt an element of this in the production of Arif's *Süleymanname*, the manuscript of which was deposited in the sultan's private library and was never copied for wider circulation. It was a work commissioned and to some extent controlled by the sultan; the end product seems also to have been largely for his own gratification.

Since the text (as opposed to the miniatures) of the *Süleymanname* remains unpublished and little studied, it is possible to speak only in general terms of the image of Süleyman presented therein. The expected notions all seem to be present: the warrior king, the just ruler, the promoter of Islam, the cultural patron. The narrative is prefaced by twenty-four folios describing the 'laws and ranks' of the various groups in society and the functions of military and naval per-

---

33 See Imber, above pp. 152–3.
　　For an attempt to establish an image of Süleyman's universal status vis-à-vis western Europe, see Gülrû Necipoğlu, 'Süleyman the Magnificent and the representation of power in the context of Ottoman-Habsburg-Papal rivalry', *The art bulletin [of the College Art Association of America] LXXI/3 (1989)*, 401–27, *on the significance of the four-tiered helmet-crown made for Süleyman by Venetian goldsmiths in 1532.*

34 For miniatures and synopsis, see Esin Atil, *Süleymanname: the illustrated history of Süleyman the Magnificent* (Washington/New York 1986).

35 Woodhead, 'Şehnameci', 169.

sonnel and equipment, all suggesting a well-ordered, well-oiled governmental machine.[36] The overall impression is undoubtedly one of luxury, ease, and prestige, conveyed above all by the illustrations. By association with the Persian epic heroes, Süleyman himself becomes an almost legendary figure, both as warrior and as sovereign. The notion of imperial (as opposed to military) grandeur implied by the *şehname* style was further cultivated by Süleyman's immediate successors, Selim II (1566–74) and especially Murad III (1574–95) – neither of whom aspired to the visibly active role of warrior sultan, and in whose reigns it became more usual to think of the sultan presiding in his palace than out amongst his people. Certain aspects of Süleyman's behaviour suggest that he too would have preferred a more remote involvement in day-to-day affairs. Following a precedent set by Mehmed II, he ceased early in his reign to attend meetings of the *divan-i hümayun* (imperial council), the principal administrative and judicial council, thus removing one of the main areas in which the sultan could be seen and evaluated, and in which he could see and evaluate matters for himself. He increased the number of central vezirs from three in 1520 to five in 1565,[37] and for almost two-thirds of his reign (twenty-eight out of forty-six years) was content to rely heavily on the competence and loyalty of the two grand vezirs, İbrahim Paşa (in office 1523–36), and Rüstem Paşa (1544–53, 1555–61). If the general image of Süleyman in a work like the *Süleymanname* implies a more remote, imperial figure, it would be of a piece with the development of the role of the sultan under his successors.

The images of Süleyman presented in the principal historiography of his reign are in one sense just that – images within an exemplary framework, where the ruler is expected to conform to certain conventions of the ideal king. Indeed, until the later sixteenth century, much Ottoman historical writing continued to be of an exemplary and moralistic nature, designed to show the dynasty and its individual members as worthy of their claims to rule. In Süleyman's case, favourable circumstances made it relatively easy for him to live up to the image and to be a just and liberal ruler, a mighty conqueror, and a master of competent servants. The personality behind the image is difficult to assess from such works. An 'official' description of Süleyman by the *şehnameci* Lokman in the 1580s, with its emphasis on sobriety and humility, suggests a character in some ways in conflict with the highly visible, active protagonist of the existing sultanic ideal:

36 Atil, *Süleymanname*, 239.
37 Peçevi, I, 413.

175

from head to foot he was a mine of talent, a quarry of abundance and munificence; he had no equal in grace and charm; he was free from vanity and arrogance and wore no robe of pride; he was known for his humble, dervish-like temperament and distinguished by the purity of his religious beliefs; he trod the path of the *şeyh*s righteously and without ostentation, and at the end of his life, when he was over seventy, he attained the status of spiritual pole.[38]

This portrays a man of great personal merit and diligence, but not necessarily one who relished his imperial role or who was politically adept.[39]

Ottoman historians of Süleyman's era naturally dealt with controversial issues within the same exemplary and moralistic framework as they did achievements. This means, in effect, that much revolves around largely stereotyped personalities and, where appropriate, their seemingly instant fall from grace when they overstep the bounds of their position: when white becomes black it does so with very little grey in between. The principal example of this in Süleyman's reign is the fate of the grand vezir İbrahim Paşa, who is portrayed as falling, literally overnight, from his position as *makbul*, 'the favourite' to *maktul*, 'executed'. Celalzade, who had worked closely with İbrahim for twelve years, implies that until the 1535 Baghdad campaign he had been a model vezir. It was İbrahim's suddenly changed manner in the later stages of that campaign – falling into bad company, acting contrary to the *şeriat* and allowing *zulm-u-delalet*, 'tyranny and error', to take hold, and requesting for himself the title *serasker sultan*, 'sultan-general' – which incurred Süleyman's justified wrath and his own summary execution.[40] To admit that Süleyman could have been aware of such faults prior to 1535 would suggest that he had continued to allow an unworthy person to represent him and that he had thus fallen short of the requirements of the ideal king.

Süleyman's promotion of the relatively young and untried İbrahim

---

38 [Lokman], *Kiyâfetü'l-insâniyye fî şemâili'l-'Osmâniyye* [ed. M Tayşi], (Ministry of Culture and Tourism, Istanbul/Ankara 1987), 48b ('pole' in the sufi sense of a leader among God's saints/holy men on earth). Although Lokman's description is primarily that of Süleyman in old age, when he became notably more devout, there is no reason to doubt that he always exhibited such basic character traits to some degree.

39 For Süleyman characterised in Ottoman *divan* poetry as 'the shy, coquettish, retiring beloved', see Andrews, *Poetry's voice, society's song*, 94.

40 On İbrahim's negligence during the Iraq campaign and his bad advisors, see Celalzade 274b-5a, 277a-8b; Peçevi I, 188–90.

The title *sultan* was regularly used with the given name for sons and daughters of the reigning sultan. However, from İbrahim's use of the term after the perfectly valid one of *serasker* (general/commander-in-chief), contemporaries would have assumed him to be claiming equality with – even membership of? – the dynasty, and thereby posing a potential challenge to Süleyman's authority as ruler.

to the grand vezirate in 1523 over the heads of older, more experienced claimants, and his subsequent, almost complete, reliance upon his powerful protégé can be portrayed in two ways. Commendably, it can show Süleyman as a good judge of men – for İbrahim Paşa appears from various sources to have been an extremely competent and hardworking vezir and general[41] – and as a leader whose trust once placed would not be withdrawn at whim: a worthy king attracts able people to his service and knows how to get the best out of them. Alternatively, it can betray an unbecoming partiality for a personal favourite at the expense of others perhaps equally able, an unacceptable narrowing of channels of communication between the ruler and his subjects, and the danger that the servant will come to rival the master in power and influence. A sultan who allows this casts doubt on his own worthiness. Hence, whatever practical imperatives there may have been for İbrahim's downfall, the theory of good government also demanded it. The severity of the sentence – execution rather than dismissal and exile – presumably reflects not merely the magnitude of İbrahim's perceived presumption, but also fear of his residual influence and the possibility of his becoming a focus of intrigue in future. In terms of Süleyman's positive image, it demonstrates the decisive authority of the powerful ruler determined not to allow evil to infiltrate his realm.[42]

Süleyman's personal feelings on this occasion were not a matter for record. However, from his later reliance on Rüstem Paşa and his devotion to his wife Hurrem Sultan, it may be surmised that Süleyman was trusting by nature and that he was glad to have strong, established figures upon whom he could rely. This would have been particularly so in the case of a grand vezir who relieved him of responsibility not only for the mundane administrative and organisational aspects of sovereignty, but also for much of the conduct of war and of relations with other states.[43]

Rüstem Paşa's career as grand vezir (1544–53 and 1555–61) supports this view to a very large degree. However, although he was husband of Süleyman's daughter Mihrimah, Rüstem never acquired quite the same status as favourite as had İbrahim and was therefore subject to more open criticism. A greater wariness on Süleyman's part may in

---

41 M T Gökbilgin, 'İbrahim Paşa', *İslam Ansiklopedisi* 5, 908–15. See also H D Jenkins, *Ibrahim Pasha* (New York 1911, repr. 1970), an old but still useful account based largely on European sources.

42 For such actions feeding Süleyman's external reputation as a typical oriental despot, see e.g. C D Rouillard, *The Turk in French history, thought and literature* (Paris 1938), 42–66.

43 E.g. Necipoğlu, 'Süleyman the Magnificent and the representation of power', 406, 417–21, on one aspect of İbrahim's propaganda vis-à-vis Habsburg Europe.

some measure account for this. The chief features of Rüstem's grand vezirate generally quoted by later Ottoman historians, and which overshadow his positive achievements, are his involvement in the execution of *şehzade* Mustafa in 1553, and his alleged introduction of bribery and the sale of offices – yet he retained Süleyman's favour, and died a natural death whilst still in office. It is more difficult to represent Rüstem's career in moralistic terms since (aside from two years out of office, 1553–55) he did not pay heavily for his apparent sins.

That the nature of the grand vezirate and the qualities required of its occupants gave cause for concern during Süleyman's reign is seen in the *Asafname* (Book of [Solomon's wise vezir] Asaf) of Lufti Paşa. Grand vezir from July 1539 to April 1541, Lufti Paşa's tenure of that office was the shortest of Süleyman's reign, and ended in abrupt dismissal. The *Asafname*, written in exile during the 1540s, is ostensibly a book of counsel for grand vezirs modelled on traditional advice literature, but has particular contemporary significance. A product partly of personal disillusionment and partly of genuine concern, the principal emphasis of the work is upon the difficulties inherent in the sultan–grand vezir relationship, many of which seem directly related to the style evolving under Süleyman, particularly that set by İbrahim Paşa.[44]

Another area of controversy which could shed light on Süleyman's character is the well-known one of relations with his family. Once again, however, Ottoman historians treat the deaths of *şehzade*s Mustafa and Bayezid largely within the moralistic framework, which must show Süleyman in the right. The role played by Hurrem Sultan, Süleyman's wife and mother of Bayezid and Selim, has no part in this presentation.[45]

In view of the competitive system of dynastic succession and the precedents for fratricidal strife, it was inevitable that, as the sultan aged, his adult sons would jostle for advantage in advance of his death. In the case of the popular and competent *şehzade* Mustafa, Süleyman proved unable to deal with rumours of impending treachery except by the sudden panic measure of his son's summary execution, in October 1553. The resulting outcry was unprecedented and damaging. Several poets were quick to compose *mersiyes* (elegies) and chronograms lamenting Mustafa's death – the first instance of such 'public' criticism of a *şehzade*'s death. The most well-known *mersiye*, that of Dukaginzade Yahya Bey, circulated rapidly and subversively amongst the troops assembled on campaign. Outwardly, blame for Mustafa's death was

---

44 R Tschudi (ed.), *Das Asafname des Lutfi Pascha* (Berlin 1910); see also B Lewis, 'Ottoman observers of Ottoman decline', *Islamic Studies* I (1962), 71–87.

45 On Hurrem's role as *haseki* 'favourite concubine', see Leslie P Peirce, *The imperial harem: women and sovereignty in the Ottoman empire* (Oxford 1993), *passim*.

attributed immediately to Rüstem Paşa, who was quickly dismissed from the grand vezirate to forestall an insurrection, but considerable damage was also done to Süleyman's image as the just sultan and the competent ruler.[46] Celalzade provides more of a defence than a justification of Süleyman's action, indicating that even the sultan's most reliable and experienced supporters had doubts:

> no one had full details of the matter, everyone had his own line in gossip. Those of wisdom and experience put [the execution] down to fate and divine decree. The sultan – pure in thought and belief, obedient to the *şeriat* of God – adhered to the path of correct conduct . . . ; his son was the light of his eye and very dear to him . . . but had there not been some great fault and potentially dangerous crime concealed within his nature he would not have become the victim of such punishment. It is clear . . . that only God can confer sovereignty upon a person . . . and that this is in the interests of continuing justice for the *reaya*.[47]

At the end of his account Celalzade provides flimsy evidence of Mustafa's misdeeds. These amount not to intended usurpation of the sultanate, but to the fact that certain of his *kul* (retainers) had perpetrated various *mazalim*, 'tyrannical crimes', upon the *reaya* within his governorate of Amasya – although Celalzade is careful to state that the *şehzade* himself had always striven to uphold the principles of *adalet*.[48]

Süleyman was noticeably more careful in handling his two remaining sons, Bayezid and Selim. The 'revolt' of Bayezid was channelled into a conflict between brothers rather than between father and son, which kept Süleyman at arm's length (despite his tacit support for Selim) until Bayezid's flight to Iran in 1559 demonstrated the latter's indisputable 'treachery'. Hence, although Süleyman may appear hard-hearted in his famous response in verse to Bayezid's plea for clemency, it is Bayezid's reputation which suffers in the end, not that of Süleyman. Since most accounts of the Bayezid affair were written in the knowledge that his adversary Selim would, or had already, become sultan, it is not surprising that Bayezid appears as a largely worthless and doomed character.[49]

It is significant that the two major histories of Süleyman's reign – Celalzade's *Tabakatü'l-memalik* and Arif's *Süleymanname* – both originated largely in the troubled decade of the 1550s. Both Arif's *şehname* and his role as court historiographer can be seen as conscious attempts

46 For contemporary elegies and their significance, see Mehmed Çavuşoğlu, 'Şehzade Mustafa mersiyeleri', *Tarih enstitüsü dergisi* XII (1981–82), 641–86.

47 Celalzade, 437a–8a.

48 Celalzade, 438a–8b. On the broader context of Mustafa's situation, see Ş Turan, *Kanunî'nin oğlu şehzade Bayezid vak'ası* (Ankara 1961), 15–36.

49 Turan, *Kanunî'nin oğlu şehzade Bayezid vak'ası, passim*; for the famous exchange in verse, see pp. 208–10.

to raise Süleyman's reputation to less assailable heights and to bolster him against his critics: Arif's role was that of imperial spokesman. An Ottoman precedent for the removal of an ageing sultan already existed in the fate of Süleyman's grandfather Bayezid II, deposed and assassinated by Selim I in 1512, during a succession struggle. When similar strife loomed amongst his own sons, and when undisputed military and political successes were fewer and farther between in the 1550s, Süleyman could nevertheless have his earlier achievements displayed to best effect through the written word, not least to boost his own morale. Although Arif's work did not become a major source for later historians, it was the only history of Süleyman's reign which Celalzade professed to admire. This suggests not merely an appreciation of detail and of style but also an alliance of purpose.[50] In Süleyman's case the need to project an appropriate image was, despite his outward successes, at least as important at the end of his reign as it had been at the beginning. In contrast to the career of Saladin, for instance, Süleyman achieved great things relatively early and was consequently under pressure to maintain a comparable reputation for the rest of his reign.[51]

Part of the glory of Süleyman's reign, both at the time and in retrospect, stemmed from his patronage of gifted individuals such as the *müfti*s (Muslim legal experts) Kemalpaşazade and Ebussuûd, the architect Sinan, and the poets Hayali and Baki.[52] Although Baki's long and distinguished career as judge and poet belongs mainly to the later sixteenth century, he is irrevocably associated with Süleyman, who was his first imperial patron and the sultan for whom he wrote one of the most celebrated pieces of Ottoman poetry. Even in the present writer's regrettably unpoetic translation, the following extract from Baki's *mersiye* on the death of Süleyman may still convey the sense of majesty and awe at the heart of Süleyman's later image:

> in truth he was [the epitome of] elegance and beauty, of prosperity and
>   dignity
> the monarch with the crown of Alexander, the army of Darius
> the sphere bowed its head in the dust at his feet
> the earth before his gate served as prayer mat for the world
> his smallest gift would make the poorest beggar rich
> one favour of his was worth all the liberality of many a sovereign

---

50 Celalzade, 10a–10b.
51 Cf. P M Holt's discussion of a contemporary biography of Saladin, above pp. 123–8.
52 On the major poets of Süleyman's reign, see E J W Gibb, *History of Ottoman poetry*, III, (London 1904) *passim*; and A Çelebioğlu, 'Turkish literature in the period of Süleyman the Magnificent', in [Ministry of Tourism and Culture] *The Ottoman empire in the reign of Süleyman the Magnificent*, II, 70–163.

the earth upon which he stood, his threshold of felicity, was source of all
    hope for the learned and the eloquent
he submitted to the decree of fate though he was a king [whose commands
    were] as powerful as fate
do not suppose him wearied by this fickle sphere
in abdicating his sovereign place his purpose was to be nearer God
what matter if our eyes no longer see life and the world?
his shining beauty was sun and moon to all
    when men behold the sun their eyes fill with tears
for then they remember that moon-like beauty[53]

II

'In Süleyman's reign of justice the Ottoman state found its equilibrium
(*mizan*).'[54] By *mizan*, meaning essentially 'a balance, pair of scales', the
historian Solakzade (writing in the 1650s) probably had at least two
notions in mind: Süleyman's pre-eminent reputation as the just sultan,
and also the increasingly popular perception of his reign as the high
point of the development of the Ottoman state. By the mid-seventeenth
century this view had been reinforced by the influence of at least half
a century of criticism and analysis in Ottoman political treatises. These,
combined with a new style of historical writing, contributed to the
notion – later the conviction – that in the simpler days of Süleyman
the sultanate had achieved a more or less ideal state, with the so-called
'classical institutions' of government at their most efficient.

The further Süleyman's reign receded into the past, the more its
difficulties and discrepancies faded, particularly in the wake of the
Ottoman 'time of troubles' between 1617 and c. 1630, when the undermining of sultanic authority was clearly demonstrated.[55] Externally, a
series of long, expensive, and largely unsatisfactory wars from the late
1570s onwards, culminating in stalemate in Hungary and the loss of
territory to the Shah of Iran, induced a natural tendency to dwell upon
Süleyman's military achievements; internally, the *celali* disruptions in
Anatolia during the late 1590s and 1610s emphasised the need for
strong government. The efforts of would-be reforming sultans, princi-

---

53 For an exuberant, late Victorian, rendering of this elegy, see Gibb, *History of Ottoman
    poetry*, III, 151–5 (Ottoman text in v. VI, 157–61, no. 214).
54 Solakzade, 4.
55 Symbolised by, but not restricted to, events concerning the sultanate itself: the first
    deposition of the imbecile Mustafa I (1618), the deposition and assassination of
    Osman II following a Janissary revolt (1622), the second deposition of Mustafa I
    (1623), and the minority of Murad IV (to c. 1630) and the revolt of Abaza Mehmed
    Paşa in Erzurum during the 1620s.

pally Murad IV (1623–40) but also Osman II (1618–22), to recreate the role of warrior sultan – and in Murad IV's case successfully to recapture Baghdad from the Safavids in 1638, practically on the centenary of Süleyman's first entry into the city – reinforced the notion of Süleyman as exemplar.[56] Fortunately for Süleyman's longer-term reputation, neither Murad IV nor any later sultan could offer a comparable record of achievement, militarily, administratively or culturally. Since no successor challenged Süleyman's stature as he had challenged that of Mehmed II, his image as the quintessential Ottoman sultan gained all the more force over time.

Widespread disquiet about the general health and direction of the state led to a growing sense of nostalgia for the past. Aspects of this emerge clearly in Peçevi's history. Although at first glance his work has no obvious political or didactic purpose, it is significant that the narrative commences with Süleyman's accession in 1520. The existence of Hoca Sadeddin's much-admired *Tacü't-tevarih* (Crown of histories) for the period up to the death of Selim I, and Peçevi's desire to include the whole history of Ottoman rule in his native Hungary, were perhaps the principal reasons for his decision to begin the work at that point. However, running through the text is another determinant: a clear vein of nostalgia and admiration for the achievements and qualities of the 'good old days' of Süleyman, which constitutes an important subtheme. Often implicitly and sometimes explicitly, Pecevi laments the loss of personal integrity, reward for merit, order and discipline, and military zeal. A typical example is the passage already quoted, written at a time when competition for posts was heavy, tenure short, and many Ottoman administrators at whatever level were clearly disappointed by the insecurities of their profession.[57]

In general scope and content, as well as its underlying tone, Peçevi's history reflects the altered conditions of Ottoman government service also suggested by other contemporary histories. By 1600 the exemplary royal biography and its cumulative dynastic equivalent the *tevarih* (annals) had been challenged as the major historiographical form by a broader-based, comparatively more mundane type of historical writing, more generally termed simply *tarih*. The calibre of the sultan might remain a principal concern but in a period when sultans were less visibly active

56 Significantly both Osman II and Murad IV attempted to revive the post of *şehnameci* (defunct since c. 1605; Woodhead, 180); Kara Çelebizade's *Süleymanname* was also a product of the reign of Murad IV.

57 See above, p. 165. For a minor but typical example of Peçevi's nostalgia, see Christine Woodhead, 'Kuru kadı hikayesi: Peçevi, Ömer Seyfettin and the headless corpse' (forthcoming).

in all spheres of government the scope of the *tarih* gradually broadens to include several other components of government – on their own merits, and not merely as appendages of the sultan. Two major histories from the 1590s clearly demonstrate this changing focus of interest. The *Tarih* of Mustafa Selaniki, compiled in the then unusual form for Ottoman historians of an almost daily diary of events, has a large and varied cast of characters, many of them quite minor figures.[58] Mustafa Ali's *Künhü'l-ahbar* contains extensive biographical sections commenting on the personalites and careers of vezirs, *beylerbeyi*s, *defterdar*s, *nişancı*s, *emir*s, members of the *ulema*, physicians, *şeyh*s, and poets.[59] The practice of listing such *erkan-i devlet*, 'pillars of state', and major cultural figures at the end of each reign, and the increasingly regular inclusion of obituary notices and of appointments to and dismissals from office all indicate an appreciation of the growing complexity of the state, and also of the potential for its mismanagement.

The *Künhü'l-ahbar* was conceived originally as a universal history having 'as its central concept the ideal state ruled by an ideal king'.[60] However, Ali was convinced that since the mid-sixteenth century – more specifically since Süleyman's execution of Mustafa in 1553 – the Ottoman state had entered a serious decline.[61] His work therefore resulted not in a celebration of the Ottoman state as the ultimate Islamic polity but in a severe critique of contemporary government and society intended to warn against creeping decay. One of Ali's earlier works, *Nushatü's-selatin* (Counsel for sultans), had been even more clearly designed to identify, and urge action to curb, malign influences within the government.[62] Although he may not have been the first, and was certainly not the only, writer of the late-sixteenth century to offer such critical analysis, the broad scope of Ali's work, his vehemence, and his influence on later Ottoman and European historians has marked him as the most perceptive of the early prophets of Ottoman doom.[63]

A series of diagnostically critical works was produced over the following century, principally in the *risale* form of a treatise on administra-

---

58 For a complete edition of Selaniki's history and an assessment of it, see Selaniki Mustafa Efendi, *Tarih-i Selânikî*, 2 vols., ed. Mehmed Ipşirli (Istanbul 1989).

59 Cf. Schmidt, *Pure water for thirsty Muslims*, Appendix I, 348–62.

60 Schmidt, *Pure water for thirsty Muslims*, 279.

61 Schmidt, *Pure water for thirsty Muslims*, 153; Cornell H Fleischer, 'Royal authority, dynastic cyclism and "Ibn Khaldunism" in sixteenth-century Ottoman letters', *Journal of Asian and African studies* XVIII, 3–4 (1983), 212–13.

62 Andreas Tietze (ed.) *Mustafa ʿĀlī's Counsel for sultans of 1581*, 2 vols, (Vienna 1979, 1983).

63 For a study of Ali and his works see Fleischer, *Bureaucrat and intellectual*. For his later influence, see also Schmidt, *Pure water for thirsty Muslims*, 4–18.

tive and political reform, a development of the traditional 'mirrors for princes' style of *nasihat* or advice literature. These include Hasan Kafi el-Akhisari's *Usulü'l-hikem* (1596); the anonymous *Kitab-i müstetab* (1620); the *Risale* of Koçu Bey presented to Murad IV in 1630/31, and re-presented to sultan İbrahim in 1640; Katib Çelebi's *Düsturü'l-amel*, compiled in 1653 for Mehmed IV; and the *Nasa'ihü'l-vüzera* of 1703 by the *defterdar* (director of finance) Sarı Mehmed Paşa.[64] Each such work presents its own picture of contemporary corruption, irregularity, disorder and insecurity, and offers suggestions for their remedy, within its particular sphere or spheres of interest.[65] Although the need to make a valid point and to justify writing such treatises encouraged a disproportionate emphasis upon problems, there was genuine, apparently well-founded, concern on principal themes:

(i) the *timar* system is breaking down; the calibre and dedication of sections of the military are in decline

(ii) state expenditure regularly outpaces income; money and wages in cash are losing their value

(iii) there is little respect for learning; members of the judiciary – like many other holders of government office – resort to bribery and embezzlement

(iv) law and order are everywhere in retreat; insecurity causes the *reaya* to flee to the towns and cities; large tracts of abandoned land are becoming prey to bandits and rebels

(v) ill-educated people of dubious moral standards bribe their way into government office, and into the *timar* system; they catch the attention of those who ought to know better

(vi) above all, there is no strong leadership in the state, neither from the sultan nor from the man to whom he delegates his authority, the grand vezir.

The natural remedy proposed for all this was to restore firm leadership and the rule of law. State and society would thus be put to rights and

---

64 M İpşirli, 'Hasan Kâfî el-Akhisarî ve devlet düzenine ait eseri *Usûlü' l-hikem fî nizâmi'l-âlem'*, *Tarih enstitüsü dergisi* 10–11 (1979–80), 239–78; Y Yücel (ed.), *Kitâb-i müstetâb*, Ankara 1974; A K Aksut (ed.), *Koçu Bey Risalesi*, Istanbul 1939; text of Katib Çelebi's *Düsturü' l-amel li-islahü' l-halel* included in M T Gökbilgin (ed.) [Aynî 'Ali] *Kavanin-i Al-i Osman* (Istanbul 1979), 119–40; W L Wright (ed.), *Ottoman statecraft* [Sarı Mehmed Pasha's Book of counsel for viziers and governors], Princeton 1935. For surveys of these and similar Ottoman works, see Lewis, 'Ottoman observers of Ottoman decline', and Fodor, 'State and society', 224–40.'

65 Katib Çelebi's work differs in solution, his *Düsturü' l-amel* being more a philosophical tract on the rise and fall of states; see Fodor, 'State and society', 233–5.

as an automatic consequence the campaigns of conquest, and thereby the empire's general momentum, would be resumed.[66]

The crucial word here is 'restore': to bring back something which had previously existed, rather than to create something new for the future. The Ottoman utopia lay definitely in the past – though as befitted the general pragmatic nature of the Ottoman outlook, this was a relatively recent and potentially recoverable past, not a remote, idealised one which had little practical relevance. Whereas the older Islamic tradition of advice literature in the 'mirrors for princes' style frequently resorted to models of exemplary behaviour in the very distant or semi-legendary past – amongst the pre-Islamic kings of Iran, the early caliphs, dominant personalities like Harun-i Raşid or Mahmud of Ghazna – seventeenth-century Ottoman commentators looked preferably to the nearest example of good practice, and elevated it into their model. The consequence of this apparently universal view for Ottoman attempts at reform, revival or rejuvenation seem obvious: a natural tendency to look back to a 'system' which was tried and tested and had produced results, rather than to seek new measures to cope with changing circumstances. All writers stress again and again the need to observe the old law, *kanun-i kadim*. An increasingly close association with Kanuni Sultan Süleyman would seem unavoidable.

It has too often been taken for granted that the writers of these treatises did indeed have an ideal vision of Ottoman government clearly in their minds as a basis for comparison, and that that vision was the era of Süleyman. However, looking more closely at just how far they actually took Süleyman's reign as an explicit comparison, clear references within a text are surprisingly moderate in number. Most writers devote the greater part of their work to detailed indictments of current failings and to specific proposals for their remedy. References to the past may substantiate either part of the argument, but are an essential part of neither in terms of factual detail.[67] Süleyman and his era emerge as the major focus for comparison only gradually, through several works and over a long period of time. This culminated eventually in the entrenched notions of ideal sultan and ideal state found in the schematic shorthand of the 'rise, decline, and fall' paradigm of nineteenth- and twentieth-century historiography, both Western and Turkish.

Take the example of Mustafa Ali. In 'Counsel for sultans' his greatest

---

66 Cf. Peter Burke's reference to the Spanish *arbitristas*, p. 162 above.
67 On the dangers of incautious reading of such reform tracts, see Rifa'at 'Ali Abou-El-Haj, *Formation of the modern state: the Ottoman empire sixteenth to eighteenth centuries* (New York 1991), *passim* (and review by Linda Darling, *International Journal of Middle East Studies* 25/1, 1993, 118–20).

admiration was reserved for the fifteenth-century courts of Mehmed II and of the Central Asian Timurid sultan Hüseyn Baykara. Writing in 1581, Ali was perhaps too close to the end of Süleyman's era to eulogise it. However, in his later works of the 1590s, Süleyman begins to emerge as a principal standard of comparison, above all when the issue of *kanun* observance came to dominate Ali's thoughts. An ageing official in a rapidly expanding, increasingly complex bureaucracy, Ali yearned for simpler, more orderly times, which he too located in the early years of Süleyman's reign. Then, he thought, education had been given its due respect and men of clear ability – like himself – were assured of a regular path to high office. In appointments to the scribal service, he presented what he understood to be older, Süleymanic practice as *kanun*, and interpreted more recent usage as harmful innovation – whereas in fact specific legislation had probably never existed, and any earlier practice may have been custom only.[68]

Then again, the anonymous author of the *Kitab-i müstetab* of 1620, while citing Süleyman favourably on some topics, treats others in much more general terms. He places the onset of visible decline, disorder and corruption in 1595 after the death of Murad III, obviously equating it with the sudden increase in *celali* activity in Anatolia.[69] Koçu Bey also uses the 1595/96 date as the time when the *timar* and financial systems began to be corrupted, and when real confusion began to spread into the ranks of the *ulema* – both the seeking of *mülazemet*s (licences/certificates) at one end of the scale, and unwarranted dismissals of the *şeyhülislam* (head of the learned hierarchy) at the other. The fact that this timing approximates to the end of the first *hicri* millenium (AH 100 = 1591/92 AD) has an additional significance.[70] However, for a number of other comparisons, Koçu Bey cites so-called irregularities at various stages during the reign of Murad III, and by giving comparative figures of the 'unacceptable' growth in central administrative personnel from Murad III's accession in 1574 to the time of writing, c. 1630, clearly places the onset of 'decline' early in Murad's reign. His attitude to Süleyman is not entirely favourable, presenting a far from ideal picture. A brief section on the *kemal*, 'perfection', of Süleyman's reign highlights the geographical extent of the latter's empire, his wealth, and his *şevket*, 'dignity, majesty', but also criticises Süleyman for not

---

68 Fleischer, *Bureaucrat and intellectual*, 226–7, esp. n.23.
69 Mustafa Akdağ, *Türk halkının dirlik ve düzenlik kavgası: Celali isyanları* (Ankara 1975) is the most thorough account of provincial unrest in Anatolia throughout the sixteenth century; specifically on the later period, see W J Griswold, *The great Anatolian rebellion 1000–1020/1591–1611* (Berlin 1983).
70 On Ali's millennial awareness, see Fleischer, *Bureaucrat and intellectual*, 244–5.

attending meetings of the *divan*. This section is followed by one on the *ihtilal*, 'disorder', evident in Süleyman's reign: the uncertainty caused by these absences from the *divan*; the sultan's 'unprecedented' promotion of İbrahim Paşa and his favouritism towards Rüstem Paşa; alienation of state land into private property, and then into *vakf* (charitable endowment); and the striking increase in numbers of the sultan's household and the central administration, which was not merely a drain on the treasury, but to Koçu Bey was also symptomatic of unnecessary display and ostentation. He presents these developments as instances of Süleyman circumventing whatever law there might have been, of his disregarding *kanun*.[71]

No doubt many *kanun* laws existing in Süleyman's era were often flouted; merely to pass a law did not ensure that it could be carried out. Probably more important, however, is the '*kanun* consciousness' of later writers which led them to attribute to Süleyman later or sometimes non-existent *kanun*s which they would have liked to see implemented in their own time. Many a seventeenth-century suggestion for reform (in a more modern sense) would have been couched in terms of a return to some often unspecified *kanun-i kadim* in an attempt to legitimise it, to make it seem less of an innovation and consequently more acceptable. Pure innovation was considered inherently harmful. Thus it proves difficult to separate the practices which Ottoman writers knew or believed to have existed in the past from those proposals which, although put forward as 're-form' on the lines of the past, were in effect new formulations with a definite view to the present and future. It is also worth considering how far Ottoman writers were themselves aware of a distinction between the two.[72]

The juxtaposition of old and new both under the sanction of *kanun-i* kadim, and the presumed association with Süleyman gives an overall impression of conservative, if not reactionary views. When taken at face value, and in the apparent context of the repeated failure of largely superficial reforms throughout the century, such political tracts indeed suggest that seventeenth-century analysts and reformers had utterly failed to move with the times and that the Ottoman mind, unable to escape the trammels of a 'classical' system, could find no alternative direction.

71 See Abou-El-Haj, *Formation of the modern state*, Appendix B, pp. 79–89, for detailed summary of Koçu Bey's *risale*.
72 For an individual example of 17th-century reformulation of 'classical' political views, cf. İ M Kunt, 'Derviş Mehmed Paşa, *vezir* and entrepreneur: a study in Ottoman political-economic theory and practice', *Turcica* 9 (1977), 205–14.

III

From the above discussion, it can be seen how the once almost uni-
versally-held notion among historians that from the late sixteenth to the
late eighteenth century the Ottoman mind suffered from an increasing
bankruptcy of ideas and the Ottoman body politic from a consequent
paralysis of infirmity was rooted in a persuasive combination of circumstances, propaganda, and rhetorical form. Political, military, and socio-
economic difficulties from the 1580s onwards induced pessimism among
Ottomans and elements of relief and wishful thinking in the Christian
West. From either point of view, the end of the sixteenth century or
of the *hicri* millennium became a convenient symbol also for the beginning of the end of Ottoman power, for the onset of decline. Thus the
images of order, justice, and perfection in the historiography of
the 'classical age' culminating in Süleyman's reign both contributed to
and were emphasised by the concerns of the seventeenth-century treatise writers, and came eventually to dominate the study of Ottoman
history.

More recently, however, research on Ottoman archival sources has
demonstrated the dangers of over-reliance on such literary material.
Histories and political tracts (also, in this case, derived from a literary
form) can be extremely successful in conveying a desired image or
point of view; they do not necessarily reflect 'reality'. Seventeenth-
century registers indicate, for example, that the Ottoman government
remained perfectly capable of adjusting its financial and administrative
practices to changing methods of taxation and altered provincial power
structures.[73] Such changes were obviously known to the treatise writers,
most of whom were serving government officials. However, the tax
farmer and the provincial grandee – whatever their achievement in
practical terms – were inimical to the classical theories of strong central
government and could be seen only as undermining existing practices
rather than as contributing to a potentially positive evolution. Similarly,
the concentration of the Ottoman family in Istanbul, the development
of the imperial household, and the increasing involvement of Ottoman
women in political life was generally seen at the time as detrimental to
the sultanate. One recent study suggests, however, that it was only

---

73 E.g. H İnalcık, 'Military and fiscal transformation in the Ottoman empire,
1600–1700', *Archivum Ottomanicum* VI (1980), 283–338; I Metin Kunt, *The sultan's
servants: the transformation of Ottoman provincial government 1550–1650* (New York
1983), 88–93, and more generally, 95–9.

through such means that the dynasty – and therefore the state – was preserved during the crucial first half of the seventeenth century.[74]

Ottoman commentators of that century and later almost invariably describe the period from c. 1595 onwards as *zaman-i ihtilal*, meaning 'a time of disorder' in the specific sense of disturbance of a system. This is regularly contrasted with such terms as *zaman-i nizam-u-intizam* (or simply *zaman-i intizam*), 'a time of good [i.e. proper] order and regularity, of systematic arrangement', and more loosely with *zaman-i kemal*, 'a time of maturity and perfection'. There is no specific Ottoman equivalent to the Western term 'golden age', either linguistically (except perhaps occasionally in literary rhetoric) or semantically in the sense of an imaginary utopian ideal.[75]

The notion of *zaman-i kemal* obscures the fact that, rather than being the culmination of two centuries of directed development which would provide a permanent model for the future, Süleyman's long reign marked a period of accelerated transition between two styles of Ottoman sultanate. The older style of personal leadership 'from the front' favoured particularly by Mehmed II and Selim I required the sultan's active military and political involvement on behalf of a dynastic patrimony comparatively small territorially; here the sultan occupied the pinnacle of a triangular representation of hierarchical authority and was the essential kingpin keeping the edifice intact. The second, newer style of sultanate more appropriate to the extended empire of the later sixteenth and subsequent centuries conformed increasingly to the ancient model of the 'circle of equity', whereby the sultan's role as guarantor of justice and prosperity remained crucial, but now as one of the regulatory cogs in a wheel of balancing forces, rather than at the apex of a pyramidal structure.[76] This second model, recognising the complexities of large-scale imperial administration, allowed for the sultan to become a more symbolic figurehead, less personally involved or responsible.

Many aspects of Süleyman's reign suggest that he should be regarded not as the last of an old order of sultans so much as the first in a new order, instigator rather than exemplar. The increasingly powerful role of the grand vezir coupled with Süleyman's non-attendance at the *divan*,

74 Peirce, *The imperial harem*, 153 ff.
75 A possible exception is the era of the Prophet Muhammed, although by Süleyman's time this was primarily a social and personal exemplar and had little political significance.
76 See Fleischer, 'Royal authority', 201. For a complementary development of the Ottoman self-image on a more personal level, see İ Metin Kunt, 'Ottoman names and Ottoman ages', *Journal of Turkish studies* 10 (1986), 233.

the issue of dynastic succession, the gradual strengthening of Istanbul as a settled capital at the expense of peripatetic journeyings, personal preference for a quieter existence, the gradual withdrawal from personal military leadership – such developments cannot be ascribed simply to Süleyman's advancing age, but also to *raison d'état*. They are complemented by other aspects of a more formal empire, begun under Süleyman and developed under his successors: a palace-based sultanate with an expanded household; a stricter religious orthodoxy; greater regulation of the teaching and judicial careers and expansion of the standing army. Later came an increasing emphasis upon rank, position and qualification, entailing queueing for posts, short tenure, the dominance of political factions, and an increasing sense for individuals of distance and difficulty.

Ottoman sultans to mid-seventeenth century

[Ertuğrul	d.c. 1280	father of Osman]
Osman	d.c. 1324	Osman's emirate emerging c. 1300
Orhan	1324–1362	
Murad I	1362–1389	
Bayezid I	1389–1402	Yıldırım, 'the thunderbolt'
–	1402–1413	reunification of sultanate by Bayezid's sons following its dispersal by Timur
Mehmed I	1413–1421	
Murad II	1421–1451	
Mehmed II	1451–1481	Fatih, 'the Conqueror' [of Constantinople]
Bayezid II	1481–1512	Veli, 'the saint'
Selim I	1512–1520	Yavuz, 'the grim', or 'the resolute'
Süleyman	1520–1566	Kanuni, 'the law-abiding', 'the law-giver'
Selim II	1566–1574	Sarı, 'the sallow'
Murad III	1574–1595	
Mehmed III	1595–1603	
Ahmed I	1603–1617	
Mustafa I	1617–1618	deposed as mentally unfit to rule
Osman II	1618–1622	deposed and assassinated in Janissary revolt

Mustafa I	1622–1623	deposed a second time
Murad IV	1623–1640	
İbrahim	1640–1648	Deli, 'the mad'; deposed as insane
Mehmed IV	1648–1687	

Glossary of Ottoman Turkish terms

The following glossary includes those Ottoman Turkish terms which occur in several places in the essays in this volume. It does not include the more specific terms (e.g. on the Ottoman navy or on taxes in Ottoman Europe) which occur only once or twice in a particular essay and which are fully explained in their context.

Arabic terms used in Peter Holt's essay, 'The sultan as ideal ruler', are transcribed according to the system used for Arabic in the *Encyclopaedia of Islam*, and are glossed in the text as they occur.

adalet	the quality of justice, equity
ağa	commander of a military unit
ahi	member of urban organisation/brotherhood with social and economic functions
ahkam-i maliye	financial decrees
akçe	asper; basic Ottoman silver coin valued at 60 to the gold coin in mid-16th century
akın	raid
akıncı	one of a band of armed raiders, sometimes preceding main Ottoman army; frontiersman
alaybeyi	commander of a unit of provincial cavalry under the authority of a *sancakbeyi*
askeri	general term for Ottoman officials, remunerated and tax-exempt; lit. 'military', but use not confined to the army; counterpart to *reaya* in traditional descriptions of Ottoman polity
azeb	(pl. *azeban*) marines

bey	lord, commander; early title of Ottoman rulers
beylerbeyi	governor-general of a province (lit. *bey* of *beys*)
beylerbeyilik	province governed by a *beylerbeyi*
celali	general term for Anatolian provincial rebel
cihad	holy war; jihad
cizye	poll tax on non-Muslims
defter	administrative register
defterdar	finance officer
devşirme	(i) periodic 'collection' or levy of male children for sultan's household from Christian communities within Ottoman empire to be trained as military and administrative personnel, many to the highest levels (ii) also a person so recruited
dirlik	lit. 'living'; i.e. general term for tax revenue assignments; cf. *timar, zeamet, hass*
divan	or *divan-ı hümayun*: imperial council presided over by the grand vezir in lieu of the sultan
emir	leader, commander
erkan-ı devlet	'pillars of state', i.e. leading vezirs and other judicial-military men
ferman	imperial edict
gaza	holy war; military campaign, battle or frontier raid, especially for the glory of Islam; cf; *gazi, gazaname*
gazaname	narrative account of a military campaign or series of related campaigns
gazi	warrior for the faith
hass	(pl. *havass*) highest category of revenue grant, min. 100,000 *akçe*
hicri	(or *hijri*) dates according to Muslim lunar calendar
iskele	(pl. *iskeleha*) port, harbour
kadı/kadi	judge of Islamic *şeriat* law, with responsibility under Ottomans also for local administration of *kanun* (dynastic) law
kadı sicilleri	records of *kadı* courts
kadıasker	see *kazasker*
kadılık	geographical area of *kadı*'s jurisdiction
kanun	dynastic administrative law, as opposed to Islamic *şeriat* law
kanunname	collection (lit. 'book') of *kanun* regulations for a specific area or subject
kapudan paşa	admiral in chief/grand admiral
kazasker	(or *kadıasker*, lit. 'judge of the military') title of state

	judges of Anatolia and Rumeli, in Süleyman's time responsible for all appointments to judicial and *medrese* teaching posts in the two principal divisions of the empire
kul	specifically
	(i) 'slave' (whether captured, bought, or in the sultan's case, recruited through the *devşirme*), esp. those used for military purposes
	more generally
	(ii) any servant of the dynasty, not necessarily slave or former slave
liva	provincial district (synonymous with *sancak*)
maliye	financial
medrese	college teaching Islamic religious sciences and law
memluk	(also *mamluk*) personal slave
menakıb	heroic deeds of saints/popular stories of same
mersiye	elegy in verse
mirliva	military governor of province (*liva*) (synonymous with *sancakbeyi*)
mücahid	(also *mujahid*) 'one who strives'/fighter
müfti	jurisconsult, interpreter of Islamic law
mühimme	as in *mühimme defterleri*: 'registers of important events' (summaries of imperial council decisions)
mukataat	revenue from designated items/areas farmed out for specific period
mülazemet	certificate/licence
nahiye	subdivision of *kaza* or *kadılık*
nişancı	keeper of the seal (*nişan*); hence, head of the Ottoman chancery
para	Ottoman coin, esp. in Egypt and Arab lands, worth 3 *akçe*
paşa	title added to personal names of *beylerbeyis* and vezirs
reaya	non-*askeri*, tax-paying subjects of Ottoman sultan, Muslim and non-Muslim, urban and rural, but often used to refer specifically to agricultural peasantry
reis	(i) (pl. *rüesa*) [sea] captain
	(ii) also head, e.g. *reisülküttab*, head of the scribal service
risale	treatise on ethical or political matters
Rumeli	lit. 'Roman [i.e. east Roman/Byzantine] lands'; official Ottoman term for the south-east European provinces of their empire

rüus	(pl. of res) 'heads'; rüus defteri, register of individual appointments
saliyane	annual payment; e.g. saliyaneli, having/being entitled to an annual payment
sancak	flag, banner; division within a beylerbeyilik (i.e. containing those who march under the same banner)
sancakbeyi	governor/commander of a sancak
şehname	'king's book'/panegyric (generally) account of reign/exploits of a particular ruler
şehzade	(lit. 'son of the shah/king') title of Ottoman princes from mid-15th century onwards
serdar	(i) general-in-chief
	(ii) also commander of a detachment
şeriat	(also sharī'at) Islamic law
şeyh	spiritual leader; head of dervish group
şeyhülislam	müfti of Istanbul and chief Ottoman jurisconsult; from mid-16th century head of Ottoman learned hierarchy
sikke-i hasene	gold coin worth 60 akçe in mid-16th century
silahdar	(i) swordsman, esp. the sultan's swordbearer
	(ii) also one of the six household cavalry regiments
sipahi	provincial cavalryman sustained by revenue grant; cf. dirlik, timar
sultani	Egyptian gold coin
sünnet	(i) 'tradition', i.e. of the Prophet Muhammed
	(ii) circumcision; sünnet düğünü, circumcision festival
tahrir	provincial census of land and populace upon which certain taxes and timar assignments were based
tarih	(lit. 'date') general term for narrative history
tevarih	(pl. of tarih) annals
timar	grant of revenue from designated area(s) of (usually) agricultural land made to a sipahi in return for military and local policing services; annual value between 3000 and 20,000 akçe
ulema	'learned men': i.e. judges, teachers, müftis
ümera	(pl. of emir) senior Ottoman military/administrative officers
vakıf	(pl. evkaf) charitable endowment for benefit of mosque, medrese, or other public works
vilayet	province (usually synonymous with beylerbeyilik)
yeniçeri	(lit. 'new troop', probably est. late 14th cent.) Janissary; sultan's elite household infantry
zeamet	as timar, but for grants worth 20,000–100,000 akçe.

Bibliographical guide

REFERENCE WORKS

Alderson, A D, *The structure of the Ottoman dynasty* (Oxford 1956). Detailed survey of dynastic issues.

Encyclopaedia of Islam, second edition (Leiden and Paris, in progress – to letter S in 1995). Expert source on persons, places, institutions.

İslam Ansiklopedisi (Istanbul, 1940–1988). Translation of the original *Encyclopaedia of Islam*, considerably expanded on Turkish-Ottoman themes.

Pitcher, D E, *An Historical Geography of the Ottoman Empire* (Leiden 1972). An annotated atlas.

Türkologischer Anzeiger/Turcology Annual, published by the Institut für Orientalistik, University of Vienna, is a comprehensive guide to current publications.

GENERAL WORKS

Akşin, Sina, ed., *Türkiye Tarihi, Vol. II: 1300–1600* (Istanbul 1987).

Cook, M A, ed., *A History of the Ottoman Empire to 1730* (Cambridge 1976). Chapters from the *The Cambridge History of Islam* and *The New Cambridge Modern History*, with a concise Introduction by the editor.

İnalcık, Halil, *The Ottoman Empire: the classical age, 1300–1600* (London 1973; reprinted Phoenix 1994). Excellent general introduction, covering all aspects of Ottoman history of the period.

Itzkowitz, Norman, *Ottoman Empire and Islamic Tradition* (New York

1972; reprinted Chicago 1991). Concise, very readable sketch to 1700.

Karpat, Kemal, ed., *The Ottoman state and its place in world history* (Leiden 1974). Articles by leading world historians.

Lewis, B, and P M Holt, eds, *Historians of the Middle East* (London 1962). Important articles by V L Ménage, H İnalcık, and J R Walsh on Ottoman historiography.

Mantran, Robert, ed., *Histoire de l'empire ottoman* (Paris 1989). Comprehensive history by leading French scholars.

EARLY OTTOMAN HISTORY

Babinger, Franz, *Mehmed the Conqueror and his time*, English trans. R Manheim, ed., W Hickman (Princeton 1978). The only comprehensive biography of a sultan.

Beldiceanu-Steinherr, Irène, *Recherches sur les actes des règnes des Sultans Osman, Orhan et Murad I* (Munich 1967). Analysis of early Ottoman documents.

Cahen, Claude, *Pre-Ottoman Turkey* (London 1968); expanded French version, *La Turquie pré-ottomane* (Istanbul–Paris 1988).

Imber, Colin, *The Ottoman Empire, 1300–1481* (Istanbul 1990).

Köprülü, M Fuad, *The origins of the Ottoman empire*, Gary Leiser, trans. and ed., (Albany 1992) from the 1935 French original and the 1959 expanded Turkish version.

Lindner, Rudi Paul, *Nomads and Ottomans in medieval Anatolia* (Bloomington 1983). A fresh look at the field dominated by Köprülü and Wittek for half a century.

Vryonis, Speros, *The decline of medieval Hellenism in Asia Minor and the process of Islamisation from the eleventh through the fifteenth century* (Berkeley 1971).

Wittek, Paul, *The rise of the Ottoman empire* (London 1938).

Zachariadou, Elizabeth, ed., *The Ottoman emirate (1300–1389)* (Rethymnon, Crete, 1993). Articles by leading scholars on the first Ottoman century.

ASPECTS OF THE SIXTEENTH CENTURY

Allouche, Adel, *The origins and development of the Ottoman–Safavid conflict (906–962/1500–1555)* (Berlin 1983).

Busbecq, *The Turkish letters of Ogier Ghiselin de Busbecq* trans., E S

Forster, (reprint Oxford 1968). Famous letters of the Habsburg ambassador.

Cook, M A, *Population pressure in rural Anatolia, 1450–1600* (London 1972).

Faroqhi, Suraiya, *Towns and townsmen of Ottoman Anatolia: trade, crafts, and food production in an urban setting, 1520–1650* (Cambridge 1984).

Fleischer, Cornell H, *Bureaucrat and intellectual in the Ottoman empire: the historian Mustafa Ali (1541–1600)* (Princeton 1986).

Guilmartin, John Jr, *Gunpowder and galleys: changing technology and Mediterranean warfare at sea in the sixteenth century* (Cambridge 1974).

Heyd, Uriel, *Studies in old Ottoman criminal law*, ed. V L Ménage (Oxford 1973).

Kortepeter, C M, *Ottoman imperialism during the Reformation*, New York, 1972.

Kunt, İ Metin, *The Sultan's servants: the transformation of Ottoman provincial government, 1550–1650* (New York 1983).

Kuran, Aptullah, *Sinan the grand old master of Ottoman architecture* (Washington, DC and Istanbul 1987).

Lybyer, Albert H, *The government of the Ottoman empire in the time of Suleiman the Magnificent* (Cambridge, Mass 1913). A classic study.

Peirce, Leslie P, *The Imperial Harem* (Oxford 1993). Political impact of the institution in the 16th and 17th centuries.

Repp, Richard, *Mufti of Istanbul* (Oxford 1986).

THE AGE OF SÜLEYMAN

Atıl, Esin, *Süleymanname: the illustrated history of Süleyman the Magnificent* (Washington-New York 1986).

İnalcık, Halil and Cemal Kafadar, eds, *Süleyman the second and his time* (Istanbul 1993).

Ministry of Tourism and Culture, Turkey, *The Ottoman empire in the reign of Süleyman the Magnificent* 2 vols (Ankara 1988).

Rogers, J M and R M Ward, *Süleyman the Magnificent* [*Catalogue of the 1988 British Museum Exhibition*] (London 1988).

Veinstein, Gilles, ed, *Soliman le magnifique et son temps* (Paris 1993).

HISTORICAL FICTION

Andrič, Ivo, *The Bridge on the Drina* (first published in Belgrade, 1945; English trans. first published in 1959). An Ottoman bridge in Bosnia over four centuries, by the Bosnian Serb author, a Nobel Prize · winner.

Morris, Roderick Conway, *Jem: memoirs of an Ottoman secret agent* (London 1988). Authentic and imaginative novel on Prince Cem in European exile.

Savage, Alan, *Ottoman* (London 1990). An English family in Ottoman service, 1453 to 1571.

Waltari, Mika, *The Wanderer* (English trans. New York 1951). A Finnish adventurer at Sultan Süleyman's court.

Maps

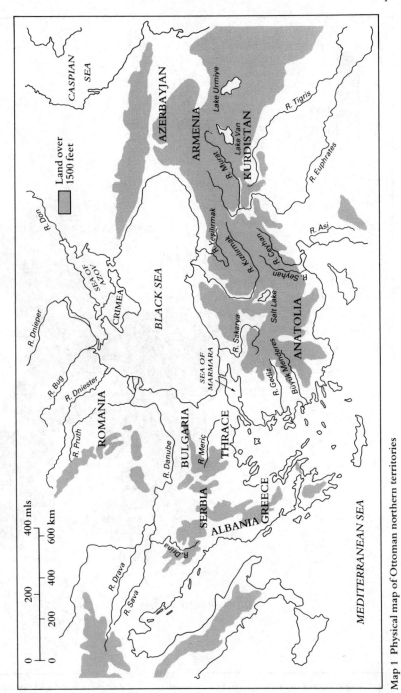

Map 1 Physical map of Ottoman northern territories

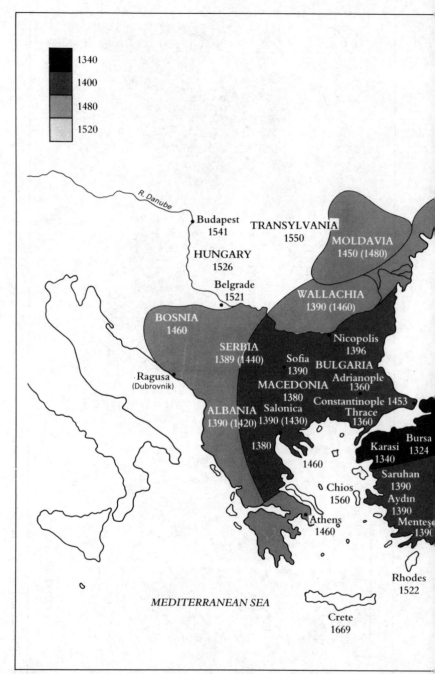

Map 2 Expansion of the Ottoman state with approximate dates of conquest and (definitive

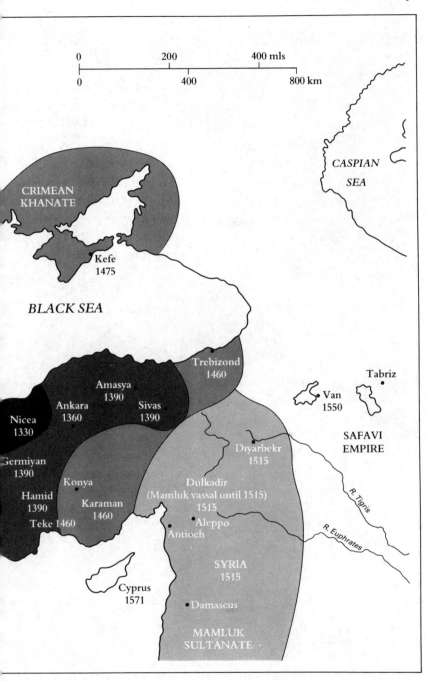

CRIMEAN
KHANATE

Kefe
1475

BLACK SEA

Trebizond
1460

*CASPIAN
SEA*

Tabriz

Amasya
1390

Van
1550

Ankara
1360

Sivas
1390

Nicea
1330

Diyarbekr
1515

*SAFAVI
EMPIRE*

Germiyan
1390

Konya

Dulkadir
(Mamluk vassal until 1515)
1515

Hamid
1390

Karaman
1460

R. Tigris

Teke 1460

Aleppo

Antioch

R. Euphrates

Cyprus
1571

*SYRIA
1515*

Damascus

*MAMLUK
SULTANATE*

conquest)

Map 3 The Ottoman empire and its neighbours c1550

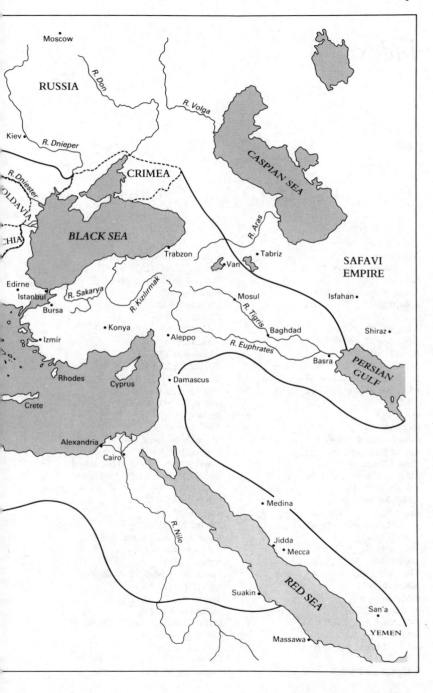

Index

Index

Index

Index

Index